A Short History of Structural Linguistics

Andrew Linn
Cambridge 2001

This book is a concise history of structural linguistics, charting its development from the 1870s to the present day. It explains what structuralism was and why its ideas are still central today. For structuralists a language is a self-contained and tightly organised system whose history is of changes from one state of the system to another. This idea has its origin in the nineteenth century and was developed in the twentieth by Saussure and his followers, including the school of Bloomfield in the United States. Through the work of Chomsky, especially, it is still very influential. Peter Matthews examines the beginnings of structuralism and analyses the vital role played in it by the study of sound systems and the problems of how systems change. He discusses theories of the overall structure of a language, the 'Chomskyan revolution' in the 1950s, and the structuralist theories of meaning.

PETER MATTHEWS is Professor of Linguistics at the University of Cambridge. He is the author of *Syntax* (1981), *Morphology* (2nd edn, 1991) and *Grammatical Theory in the United States: From Bloomfield to Chomsky* (1993), also published by Cambridge University Press.

A Short History of
Structural Linguistics

Peter Matthews

Professor of Linguistics, University of Cambridge

CAMBRIDGE
UNIVERSITY PRESS

PUBLISHED BY THE PRESS SYNDICATE OF THE UNIVERSITY OF CAMBRIDGE
The Pitt Building, Trumpington Street, Cambridge, United Kingdom

CAMBRIDGE UNIVERSITY PRESS
The Edinburgh Building, Cambridge CB2 2RU, UK
40 West 20th Street, New York NY 10011–4211, USA
10 Stamford Road, Oakleigh, VIC 3166, Australia
Ruiz de Alarcón 13, 28014 Madrid, Spain
Dock House, The Waterfront, Cape Town 8001, South Africa

http://www.cambridge.org

First published 2001

Printed in the United Kingdom at the University Press, Cambridge

Typeface 10/12pt Times   [GC]

A catalogue record for this book is available from the British Library

Library of Congress Cataloguing in Publication data

Matthews, P. H. (Peter Hugoe)
    A short history of structural linguistics / P. H. Matthews
       p.   cm.
    Includes bibliographical references and index.
    ISBN 0 521 62367 7 (hardback) – ISBN 0 521 62568 8 (paperback)
    1. Structural linguistics – History.   I. Title.

    P146.M36 2001
    410′.1′8–dc21   00–045524

ISBN 0 521 62367 7 hardback
ISBN 0 521 62568 8 paperback

In memoriam
R. H. R.
1921–2000

Contents

Preface

The last chapter of this book was finished on the day when Bobby Robins, whose *A Short History of Linguistics* has been admired for more than thirty years, was found dead. It is with sadness and affection that I dedicate it, with its presumptuously similar title, to his memory.

I was initially not at all sure how this history should be written: in particular, how selective and, in consequence, how long it should be. For advice at that stage I am especially grateful to Jeremy Mynott and, in a sense that they will understand, to my fellow editors of the Cambridge Textbooks in Linguistics. Conversations with Kasia Jaszczolt have since helped, at various times, to clarify my thinking.

I am also grateful to Andrew Winnard for waiting patiently for the book to be written.

1 Introduction

What is 'structural linguistics'? Do most linguists still accept its principles? Or are they now believed in only by old men, clinging to the ideas
that were exciting in their youth? Who, among the scholars who have
written on language in the twentieth century, was or is a structuralist?
Who, by implication, would that exclude?

It may seem, at the outset, that the first of these questions should be
fundamental. We must begin by asking what, in general, we mean by
'structuralism'. There are or have been 'structuralists' in, for example,
anthropology; also in other disciplines besides linguistics, such as literary criticism and psychology. What unites them, and distinguishes them
from other theorists or practitioners in their fields? In answering this
question we will identify a set of general principles that structuralists
subscribe to; and, when we have done that, we will be able to ask how
they apply to the study of language. From that we will deduce the tenets
that a 'structural linguist' should hold; we can then see who does or, once
upon a time, did hold them. But an inquiry in this form will lead us only
into doubt and confusion. For different authorities have defined 'structuralism', both in general and in specific application to linguistics, in what are
at first sight very different ways. There are also linguists who are structuralists by many of the definitions that have been proposed, but who
would themselves most vigorously deny that they are anything of the kind.

Let us look, for a start, at the definitions to be found in general dictionaries. For 'structuralism' in general they will often distinguish at least
two different senses. Thus, in the one-volume *Collins* (1994 edn; originally
Hanks, 1979), 'an approach to linguistics' (sense 2) has one definition and
'an approach to anthropology and to other social sciences and to literature' (sense 1) has another; and, for a reader who does not know the
problems with which the editor had to deal, it is not obvious how they
are connected. In anthropology or literature, structuralism is an approach
that 'interprets and analyses its material in terms of oppositions, contrasts, and hierarchical structures', especially 'as they might reflect universal mental characteristics or organising principles'. 'Compare', we are

told, 'functionalism'. In linguistics, it is an approach that 'analyses and describes the structure of language, as distinguished from its comparative and historical aspects'. The next entry defines 'structural linguistics' in terms that are in part different and in part supply more detail. It is, first of all, 'a descriptive approach to a synchronic or diachronic analysis of language'. But a 'diachronic' analysis is precisely one that deals with 'historical' and, where they are a source for our knowledge of the history, 'comparative' aspects. This analysis, to continue, is 'on the basis of its structure as reflected by irreducible units of phonological, morphological, and semantic features'. This seems to imply that the units that structural linguists establish are necessarily of these three kinds.

The *New Shorter Oxford English Dictionary* (Brown, 1993) distinguishes two main senses of 'structuralism', one in early twentieth-century psychology (compare *Collins* under 'structural psychology'), the other covering all other disciplines, but with specific subsenses (2 *(a)*, 2 *(b)* and 2 *(c)*) in linguistics, in anthropology and sociology, and as 'a method of critical textual analysis'. In sense 2 in general, structuralism is 'any theory or method which deals with the structures of and interrelations among the elements of a system, regarding these as more significant than the elements themselves'. It is also, by a second or subsidiary definition, 'any theory concerned with analysing the surface structures of a system in terms of its underlying structure'. So, specifically in linguistics (sense 2 *(a)*), it is 'any theory in which language is viewed as a system of inter-related units at various levels'; especially, the definition adds, 'after the work of Ferdinand de Saussure'. There is nothing in this entry about synchrony or diachrony. But under 'structural' (*special collocations*), 'structural linguistics' is defined, in terms which recall the *Collins* definition under 'structuralism', as 'the branch of linguistics that deals with language as a system of interrelated elements without reference to their historical development'. Thus, by implication, structuralism in linguistics is again not diachronic. One is also left wondering about the reference to surface and underlying structure. The term 'underlying' is picked up, in the subdefinition for anthropology, with reference to the theories of Claude Lévi-Strauss ('concerned with the network of communication and thought underlying all human social behaviour'); but not specifically for linguistics. However, in the *Supplement* to the main *Oxford English Dictionary*, which is the immediate source of these definitions, the term 'structural' is also said to mean, under sense 5a, 'relating to or connected with the "deep" structures that are considered to generate "surface" structures'.

These are good dictionaries, and I am not out to criticise them. I can hardly claim that the entry in my own concise dictionary of linguistics (Matthews, 1997: 356f.) is more definitive. For the root of our difficulty is that linguists themselves do not apply these terms consistently. In a leading survey of the subject, Giulio Lepschy suggests that 'structural linguistics' has at least three possible senses (Lepschy, 1982 [1970]: 35f.). But of these one, as he in effect remarks, is vacuous. Another applies so narrowly that most of what has generally been perceived as structuralism does not fall within it. The third remains, as a definition, tantalisingly general.

'In the widest sense', with which Lepschy begins, 'every reflection on language has always been structural'. In any grammar, for example, units are identified; units of any one kind are related to others of their own or of another kind; and through these relations, which will be in part hierarchical, successively larger 'structures' are quite clearly formed. In that sense, any 'synchronic or diachronic analysis of language' (*Collins*) cannot but be 'structural'. Hence, for Lepschy's and our purposes, this first use of the term 'is scarcely revealing' (1982: 36).

Lepschy's narrowest sense dates from the 1960s, when the American linguist Noam Chomsky was attacking what he called the 'taxonomic' methods of his predecessors. The charge was levelled against a specific school in the United States, who were also accused at the time, in apparent variance with a hint in one of our dictionaries, of a concern with no more than the 'surface structures' of language, to the exclusion of its 'deep structures'. For Chomsky and his followers, 'structuralists' were above all members of that school. Hence, in some accounts, like that of David Crystal in *The Cambridge Encyclopaedia of Language*, the term 'structuralist' is used only of them and 'structural(ist) linguistics' only of a limitation of the subject in a way that they alone proposed (Crystal, 1997 [1987]: 412; glossary, 438).

The middle sense refers, in Lepschy's words, to 'those trends of linguistic thought in this [the twentieth] century which deliberately tried to gain an insight into the systematic and structural character of language'. This is indeed 'more widely accepted' (36) than the largest sense with which he began. But Lepschy's wording again leaves one wondering whether structuralism can be defined precisely. For no one will deny that language has a 'systematic and structural character'; and, as we move into a new century, many scholars are still seeking to understand it. Yet Lepschy refers to trends that 'tried', in the past tense, to do so. What is it that those trends specifically, which are by implication characteristic of the twentieth century, had in common? What were the particular insights, or the particular ways of trying to gain an insight, that lead us to distinguish them from other trends that are not 'structural'?

Lepschy's *Survey of Structural Linguistics* is the best book of its kind, and I am not seeking to pick holes in it. For what this makes clear is that structuralism has to be defined, in part, historically. The term 'structural linguistics' dates, as we will see, from the late 1930s, and referred to an intellectual movement that was by then well established. But it had no single leader, and no wholly uniform set of principles. In the view of most continental Europeans, it had been founded by Ferdinand de Saussure, whose lectures on general linguistics (*Cours de linguistique générale*) had been reconstructed and published after his death in 1913. Hence the specific reference to him in *The New Shorter Oxford English Dictionary*. But 'structural' and 'structuralisme' were not terms that Saussure had used. Therefore he had not laid down the principles, by name, 'of structuralism', and the ideas that he had expounded were already being developed, by different scholars, all of whom could reasonably claim to be his followers, in varying directions. In the United States, by contrast, linguists who were young at the end of the 1930s were influenced above all by the American scholar Leonard Bloomfield, whose great book *Language* had appeared in the first half of the decade. But he did not talk of 'structuralism' either. Nor did the theory that he propounded agree entirely with Saussure's. By the time the movement had a name the 'trends' (plural) to which Lepschy refers could already be distinguished.

But, as a broad movement, it quite clearly existed. 'Structuralists' in general, of whatever more precise persuasion, came to be lumped together by their critics; and, among the structuralists themselves, there was a sense of unity. A political party, if we may take one obvious parallel, includes many shades of opinion. It would again be hard to say exactly what set of beliefs its members all have in common, from one time to another or even at any one time. But the trends within it form a network of shared interests and shared inspirations, in which all who belong to it have some place. With intellectual movements, such as structuralism, it is often much the same.

Or should we say, in this case, that it 'was' the same? Lepschy used, once more, the past tense; and it is now more than thirty years since he was writing. But on the next page he speaks of Chomsky's theories, which had by then come to dominate the subject, as from his perspective 'an heir to . . . structural linguistics' and 'one of its most interesting developments'. There is no doubt that, by the end of the 1960s, the sense of party unity had been lost, at least between Chomsky and the older generation in the United States. But the implication is that structuralism, in a broad sense, passed into a new phase. Has there, since then, been a real break? Or is the thinking of most scholars now, about what Lepschy called 'the systematic and structural character of language', still continuous with the tradition that was dominant earlier?

I will return to these questions in the final chapter. But first we have more than a hundred years of history, and the thought of some of the best minds that have studied language, to work through.

2   Languages

Linguistics is said in dictionaries to be 'the branch of knowledge that deals with language' (*New Shorter Oxford English Dictionary*) or 'the scientific study of language' (*Collins*). But for structuralists it has been much more the study of, in the plural, languages. This was true at the outset, for Saussure, and is still true for many as we enter the twenty-first century. What then constitutes 'a language'? It is easy to give examples: English is one, Japanese another, and so on. But what, in general, are they?

Let us look again at dictionaries. For the first editor of *The Oxford English Dictionary* (Murray *et al.*, 1933 [1884–1928]), the earliest sense of 'language' (§1) was that of 'the whole body of words and of methods of combination of words used by a nation, people, or race'; alternatively, 'a tongue'. The dictionary itself was thus an account of the 'whole body' of words that constitute the lexicon of English. The second definition (§2) adds a 'generalized sense': 'words and the methods of combining them for the expression of thought'. But where Murray saw a 'body', *The New Shorter Oxford Dictionary* speaks of a 'system'. Language is 'a system of human communication using words ... and particular ways of combining them'; it is 'any such system', the definition adds, 'employed by a community, a nation, etc.' (§1a). In the *Collins* dictionary, it is 'a system for the expression of thoughts, feelings, etc. by the use of spoken sounds or conventional symbols' (§1); also in general (§2) 'the faculty for the use of such systems'. These accounts have much in common. In particular, a specific language is related, either by definition or by historical association, to a 'nation' or other 'community'. But a 'system' is potentially more than a 'body'. A 'body', in the sense that Murray must have had in mind, can be described by an inventory. A dictionary is thus an inventory of words, arranged for convenience in alphabetic order. A grammar is in turn an inventory of 'methods of combining' words, arranged perhaps by classes to which combinations can be assigned. But a 'system' is not simply a collection of individual components. Suppose that, from an inventory, we omit one item: say, from the inventory of words in English, we omit the word *we*. The remainder of the inventory is unchanged. But if a language is a system then, as part of that system, *we* is related to other words: most obviously to *I, you, us* and others that are traditionally called pronouns. If *we* is omitted, the relations that the other pronouns enter into must in turn change.

It is with this basic insight that, in the closing decades of the nineteenth century, structuralism began. It did not develop fully until later, according to most commentators with the publication of Saussure's *Course in General Linguistics*. But by then this insight had already informed the study of sound systems, as we will see in the next chapter (3.1). We can also find at least one earlier and independent programmatic statement, in an introduction to linguistics of the early 1890s by the German Orientalist Georg von der Gabelentz. 'Every language', he writes, 'is a system all of whose parts interrelate and interact organically' ('Jede Sprache ist ein System, dessen sämmtliche Theile organisch zusammenhängen und zusammenwirken'). Thus, in our example, *we* relates to and interacts not just with *I* and *you* but, directly or indirectly, with all other elements of the wider system of which pronouns are part. 'One has the impression', Gabelentz continues, 'that none of these parts could be missing or be different, without alteration to the whole' ('Man ahnt, keiner dieser Theile dürfte fehlen oder anders sein, ohne dass das Ganze verändert würde') (Gabelentz, 1901 [1891]: 481). Thus, if there were no pronoun *we*, the repercussions would extend throughout English generally. In a famous Saussurean formula, a language is 'a system in which everything holds together' ('un système où tout se tient'). Change again one element, and the system is different.

The origins of this formula have been explored by Konrad Koerner, in an essay dealing with the connections between Saussure and the French Indo-Europeanist Antoine Meillet. It is not, on paper at least, Saussure's own. But Meillet was a young man in the 1880s; he had heard lectures by Saussure in Paris; and by 1893 he was saying already that the units of sound in each form of speech ('les divers éléments phonétiques de chaque idiome') form such a system. The point can be appreciated, he remarks, by anyone who has tried to learn the pronunciation of another language. But it must also apply to children learning their first language: 'A child, in learning to speak, assimilates not an isolated articulation, but the whole of the system' ('Or l'enfant, en apprenant à parler, s'assimile non une articulation isolée, mais l'ensemble du système'). The passage is cited by Koerner (1989 [1987]: 405), and Saussure was not mentioned. But the formula fits so beautifully with the ideas developed in Saussure's *Cours de linguistique générale* that, as Koerner points out, it was later cited as if it were his. For the Russian linguist N. S. Trubetzkoy, writing in the early 1930s, this conception of a language was one of the basic principles that Saussure had proclaimed (Trubetzkoy, 1933: 241; also 243, with the formula cited as if it were a quotation).

Like Meillet, Saussure was a student of Indo-European, the vast family that links most languages in Europe with most of those from Persia to Southern India. It was established early in the nineteenth century that these had developed from a common prehistoric language; but it was not until the 1870s, when Saussure was a student in Leipzig, that, in Leipzig especially, the structure of that language was first satisfactorily reconstructed. It was not that of any ancient language historically attested: not that of Latin, nor of Greek, nor even, as had still been assumed in some important respects in the 1860s, of the ancient Indian language Sanskrit. Nor was its reconstruction simply a matter of comparing individual units. It was precisely the structure that was recovered. Saussure's first book was written in Leipzig, and was itself a striking contribution to this enterprise. It is therefore worth our while to glance at some of the details.

Let us begin with a specific problem that Saussure could take as solved. In Ancient Greek, for example, the accusative singular usually ends in -*n*: *hodó-n* 'road' or *oikíā-n* 'house'. Compare -*m* in Latin (*dominu-m* 'master' or *puella-m* 'girl') or in Sanskrit (*devá-m* 'god'). But in Greek it could also be -*a*: thus in the words for 'mother' and 'father' (*mētér-a, patér-a*). Is this simply an irregularity, by which some nouns in Greek decline aberrantly? At first sight it is: in Latin, for example, the corresponding forms again end in -*m* (*matre-m, patre-m*). But let us suppose, as a hypothesis, that in the prehistoric language the ending was throughout *-*m*. It is marked with an asterisk, to show that this is a reconstruction and not, for instance, the historical -*m* of Latin. But phonetically the consonant had, we can assume, a nasal articulation, which is preserved in both the -*m* of Latin *dominu-m* and the -*n* of Greek *hodó-n*. Let us also suppose, as a further hypothesis, that the phonetic element *m* was neither simply a consonant nor simply a vowel. Instead it was one that could, in general, either accompany a vowel to form a syllable (consonant + vowel + *m*, *m* + vowel, and so on) or, itself, have the position of a vowel within one (consonant + *m*, or consonant + *m* + consonant). In that respect it is like, for example, the 'n' in spoken English, which forms a syllable with 't', again with no vowel sound, in a word like, in phonetic spelling, [bʌtn̩] (*button*) or [bʌtn̩həʊl] (*buttonhole*). The apparent irregularity will then make perfect sense. In the form that prehistorically underlay, for example, *hodón* the ending *-*m* came after a vowel and developed in Greek into -*n*. In the form that underlay, for example, *mētéra* it came after a consonant (consonant + *m*). In that context it became, instead, -*a*.

For an account of this period I must defer to the masterly history of nineteenth-century linguistics by Anna Morpurgo Davies (1998 [1994]:

Ch. 9): the solution outlined is one facet of a wider hypothesis developed by Karl Brugmann and Hermann Osthoff (Morpurgo Davies, 1998: 242f.). But it is plain already that the argument does not affect a single unit. That the prehistoric language had a sound *m was not new: it was obvious enough, at the beginning of a syllable, from sets of words like those for 'mother', 'honey' (Greek méli, Latin mel), and so on. What matters are the relations in which it is claimed to have stood to other units. They are wider than those borne by any unit, such as m in Latin, that has hypothetically developed from it. But, given its role as reconstructed, it was possible to explain, by different historical developments in different languages and in different positions in the syllable, what would otherwise remain puzzling.

The next step, or what with hindsight seems most logically to have been the next step, was to posit units in the prehistoric language that are not directly attested. In Greek, by the hypothesis we have outlined, *m changed, in the position of a vowel, to a. To be precise, it merged with it; so that, from the direct evidence of mētéra and other such forms, we cannot know that anything other than an a had ever been there. But if a unit can lose its identity in one position, it can lose it in all. This can happen in just one member of the family; and, in that case, evidence for it will emerge when forms in which it had been present are compared with corresponding forms in other languages. But it could also happen, by a series of connected or independent changes, in all members known to us. Is it possible, in that case, that it might still be reconstructed?

It was Saussure who first showed how it might. In the case of *m the evidence we cited is of an irregularity: between, in Greek itself, the -a of accusative singulars such as mētér-a and the -n of, for example, hodón; and, across languages, between the -a of mētéra and the -m of, for example, Latin matrem. But by essentially similar reasoning it is possible to explain a whole sheaf of irregularities, many at first sight unconnected, by positing what specialists in Indo-European call 'laryngal' elements. In Greek, for example, the verb for 'to put' has a long ē in some forms and a short e in others. Compare tí-thē-mi 'I put' (thē-) with adjectival the-tós 'placed' (the-). The historical explanation rests in part on the hypothesis that, in the prehistoric language, there were other elements that could appear in either position in a syllable. Some, like *m, were directly attested: for example, in Greek leíp-ō 'I leave behind' the i derives hypothetically from a *y which follows a vowel (*leyp-), while in é-lip-on 'I left behind' it derives from the same unit *y, but in the position of a vowel (*lyp-). Of others there was, in the Indo-European languages as they were known in the 1870s, no direct trace. But suppose that, in the prehistoric language, the form for 'to put' had such an element. We have no evidence of its phonetic character; all we are saying is that it fitted into a certain system of relations. So, in the form underlying Greek *thē*- this element (call it, for the sake of a symbol, *H*) came after a vowel: *theH*-. By a subsequent sound change, *eH* became, in Greek, *ē*. In the case of *the*-, the underlying form was hypothetically *thH*-; then, in the position of a vowel, *H* became *e*. The variation between *theH*-, changing to *thē*-, and *thH*-, changing to *the*-, is thus, so far as its form is concerned, precisely like that of, for example, *leyp*-, changing to *leip*-, and *lyp*-, changing to *lip*-.

Decades later, remains of the Hittite language were discovered at an archaeological site in Turkey; it was shown to be Indo-European, and in it, for the first time, there was direct evidence that 'laryngals' such as *H* had existed. But the seeds of most of what we have said in the last paragraph were sown by Saussure at the end of the 1870s, when such elements could be established only as terms in a prehistoric system. They could not, like *m*, be given a phonetic value. The hypothesis was simply that each was a unit and bore certain relations, in the structure of a syllable, to other units.

Saussure was twenty-one when this work appeared (Saussure, 1879). Unfortunately, he published very little after it, and from the 1890s, when he returned from Paris to a chair in his native Geneva, almost nothing. It is therefore unsafe to speculate too much about the route that might have led him from this early work on Indo-European to the ideas for which he is later famous. But what was reconstructed was a system of relations among units. Each of the historical languages had a different system. Therefore what changed, in the development of Greek, etc., from the prehistoric language, was in each case more than just an inventory of units. Now the historical languages were known to us through texts associated with specific communities. They thus had an identity in time and place, independent of the system that their units formed. Of the prehistoric language we otherwise know nothing. It is constituted solely by the system that we are able to reconstruct.

It is unsafe, I repeat, to speculate about a train of thought that we cannot document. But the view that Saussure in the end reached was not simply that a language has, or that its units form, a system. As in the passage cited earlier from Georg von der Gabelentz, it quite literally 'is' a system: 'Jede Sprache ist ein System'. Hence, at a long remove, the dictionary definitions cited at the beginning of this chapter. Hence also two immediate conclusions, both of which Saussure, in particular, drew.

First, if languages are systems they are, from an external viewpoint, closed. Each will have a determinate set of basic units, and a determinate set of relations among them, and will be distinguished sharply both from other languages and from anything that lies outside such systems. Therefore the study of each individual language is separate from that of any other individual language; and within linguistics, if conceived more widely as the investigation of all aspects of human speech, that of individual languages must form a distinct science. In Saussure's terms this is a 'linguistique de la langue' (a 'linguistics of languages'), which is autonomous and whose object is limited to what we may call 'language systems'.

Secondly, if 'everything' in a system 'holds together', any change which affects it will result in a new and different system. In the prehistoric Indo-European language *m entered, hypothetically, into one set of relations. In the development of Greek it changed, in one position in the structure of the syllable, to a. This may not have affected the inventory of elements; but, in consequence of this one change, m in Greek now entered into a new set of relations, the roles that a had in the structure of the language were different, the accusatives of distinct declensions of noun diverged, and so on. The study of systems must, accordingly, be separated strictly from that of historical relations between systems. As historians, we can describe the changes that relate, for example, the Indo-European system to the Greek, or, in historical times, the Greek system as it was in fifth-century Athens to that of Modern Greek as it is spoken now. In Saussure's terms, that is to practise 'diachronic linguistics', the study of languages on the time dimension. But, to be able to carry out such studies, we must first have established the systems that we are relating. Each system, as we have said, is different. Therefore, in investigating, for example, the system of Modern Greek, we are not concerned in any way with that of Greek in ancient Athens, or of Greek in any intervening period. We are concerned just with the system that exists now. We are thus practising what Saussure called 'synchronic linguistics': a pure linguistics of the language system, to which the dimension of time and history is irrelevant.

It is now time to look in greater detail at what Saussure's *Cours* said.

2.1   Linguistics as the study of language systems

It must be stressed at once that the book is not, in any strict sense, by him. He gave three series of lectures on general linguistics between 1906 and 1911; but, as his literary executors were to discover, he did not keep notes (Saussure, 1972 [1916]: 7). What we have is therefore a 'recréation' or reconstitution (9) using all the materials available, but, in particular, the notes of students who had followed the third course. At some points it is based on no tangible source.

If one thing ought to drive the perfectionists among us into publication, it is the thought that when we die our lectures might be immortalised, however objectively and conscientiously, in this way. In Saussure's case, it has given work to a small army of interpreters. Anyone who tries to set out his ideas is faced with a text compiled and in part composed by others, with skeletal references to the tradition in which his thought was formed, and understood since the 1920s in every possible way. The earliest interpretations are those of Bloomfield, Trubetzkoy, and other structuralists in the years between the two World Wars. These are important as they are themselves part of our history. But note 'interpretations' (plural): there was no single reading even at that stage. Since 1960 potted accounts have passed into textbooks, often reflecting in part the work of later followers. But new exegesis still appears, challenging what Paul Thibault has recently called the 'conventional wisdom' (Thibault, 1997: xvii). In the interval, the notes on which the *Cours* is based have also been published. These were not, of course, available when it had its greatest influence.

It is hard to read the text without this overlay of commentaries in mind. But in the context I have outlined three notions stand out.

The first is that of linguistics as a science of language systems. If we try to study all the phenomena of language ('langage'), we will open the door to other sciences ('psychology, [physical] anthropology, normative grammar, philology, etc.') that could claim it for their domain (Saussure, 1972 [1916]: 24f.). There was as Saussure saw it only one solution. We must engage in the first instance with the individual language ('la langue') and take that as the point of reference for all other relevant phenomena ('il faut se placer de prime abord sur le terrain de la langue et la prendre pour norme de toutes les autres manifestations du langage'). Here and elsewhere, there is an important distinction between 'la langue' ('the language' or 'the language system') and 'langage' (in English, 'language' with no article) as the wider phenomenon to which 'la langue' is central. 'Langage' remains, by implication, the concern of various disciplines. But 'the integral and concrete object of study in linguistics' ('l'objet à la fois intégral et concret de la linguistique', 23) will be 'la langue'.

A distinction is then drawn, within 'langage', between 'la langue' and 'parole' ('speech') as the individual act of communication. When people talk to one another a circuit is established in which their brains are linked. Part of the link is physical (movement of sound waves); other parts are physiological (activation of the vocal organs and the organs of hearing); still others are mental ('psychique') and involve a coupling of 'acoustic images' and 'concepts'. Thus in the mind of a speaker a given concept 'triggers' ('déclanche') an acoustic image, and in the mind of a hearer the acoustic image of what is heard is associated, in its turn, with a concept (28). But, for these concepts to match, the speaker and hearer must have something in common. This is of its nature a social phenomenon ('fait social'). The physical and physiological parts of the circuit are irrelevant. Even the mental part is not entirely relevant, since its executive aspect (glossed 'parole') remains individual and not social. But if we could encompass 'the totality of the verbal images stored up in all individuals' ('la somme des images verbales emmagasinées chez tous les individus'), we would arrive at 'the social bond that forms the language' ('le lien social qui constitue la langue', 30). This is a stock or store ('trésor') that is built up by the experience of speech ('parole') in people who belong to the same community. It is a 'grammatical system' that exists potentially in each brain, or more precisely, since it is not complete in any individual person, in the brains of the entire group.

For a psychologist of Saussure's day, let alone ours, this might not bear too close an examination. But what matters is the distinction, within the phenomena of 'langage', between the language system as a 'social fact' ('fait social'), or 'social product' ('produit social') of the functioning of our intellectual faculties (30), and speech ('parole') as an act that is individual and contingent. The term 'fait social' had been used, in Saussure's formative period, by the French sociologist Émile Durkheim, again in identifying an objective reality whose study was specific to sociology as opposed to other sciences. Take, for a simple illustration, what we might call a system of table manners. In any society one learns how to eat as that society expects: in Europe to hold knives, forks and spoons in certain ways, to put them on the plate in a certain way when one has finished, to keep one's hands at other times above or beneath the table, and so on. The system is not that of one individual only: its existence is in the society, in the community of people who, when on any particular occasion they are sitting at table, conform to it. But, to the point at which their behaviour will be accepted in the society, all individuals must individually learn it. Although this is not Saussure's analogy, what he was teaching was that, though a language is enormously more complex, its nature is essentially like that. Each member of a community has learned it, again to the point at which they communicate as other members. But it exists over and above the individual act of communication and the individual communicator.

Since 'la langue' is our first object of study, Saussure distinguished a linguistics 'of the language system' ('une linguistique de la langue') from a linguistics 'of speech' ('de la parole') which is secondary to it. The latter has both a mental and a physical (that is, physiological and acoustic) side. But the former is exclusively mental ('uniquement psychique', 37).

Its object of study exists in the community as a whole, in the form of a 'totality of imprints registered in each brain' ('La langue existe dans la collectivité sous la forme d'une somme d'empreintes déposées dans chaque cerveau', 38). The study of this is 'linguistics in the strict sense' ('la linguistique proprement dite', 38f.).

Our second notion concerns the division between 'synchronic linguistics' and 'diachronic linguistics'. Both belong to Saussure's 'linguistics of the language system'. But the former is abstracted, as we have seen, from history. It is therefore a study of the relations among elements that form a system ('des rapports . . . reliants des termes coexistants et formant système') 'as they are perceived by a single collective consciousness' ('tels qu'ils sont aperçus par la même conscience collective', 140). So, to resume our analogy, a synchronic study of table manners would deal with those that are general in a specific community, within a period in which they can be treated as unchanging. A diachronic study might instead compare, for example, the handling of knives at table in early mediaeval Europe with their handling in later periods. It would thus deal with 'the relations among successive elements that are not perceived by the same collective consciousness' ('les rapports reliant des termes successifs non aperçus par une même conscience collective'). Such elements 'replace one another without themselves forming a system' ('se substituent les uns aux autres sans former système entre eux', 140).

The terms 'synchronic' and 'diachronic' are Saussure's; otherwise this may not seem a striking insight. But for Saussure these were wholly separate approaches ('deux routes absolument divergentes'), in a way that 'very few linguists' seemed to him to realise (114). Accordingly great care is taken to explain the differences between them: in the abstract, through a glance at the history of linguistics, through examples, and through his own analogies. Let us start with one of Saussure's illustrations (120f.). It was and is a stock example, and what the *Cours* says is, at a certain level, what any lecturer on the history of language might have been expected to say. But, in granting that, we can appreciate the shift of emphasis that his followers were to seize on.

In English, then, a plural noun is generally formed by adding -*(e)s*: *trees* from *tree*, *grasses* from *grass*, and so on. But in just a few the vowel of the singular is changed: *feet* from *foot*, *teeth* from *tooth*, *geese* from *goose*. For a historian this cries out for explanation: why are the forms these and not *foots* and *tooths* and *gooses*? The answer, which was again well known in Saussure's day, is that, in an earlier period which is not recorded, these nouns must have had a plural in -*i*. Such forms are attested in the earliest records of German, with which English shares a common ancestor: Old High German *gast* 'guest', plural *gasti*, or *hant* 'hand', plural *hanti*. So, alongside the ancestral singulars *fōt*, *tōþ* and *gōs*, which are attested in Old English, we reconstruct, for a prehistoric period, the unattested plurals **fōt + i*, **tōþ + i*, **gōs + i*. The forms we actually have can then be explained by intervening changes. First the *ō*, in which the body of the tongue is raised towards the back of the mouth, changes to *ē*, in which it is raised towards the front. That is plausibly due to the influence of the *-i*, in whose articulation the tongue is raised still more towards the front. So, hypothetical **fōt + i*, **tōþ + i*, **gōs + i* become, still hypothetically, **fēt + i*, **tēþ + i*, **gēs + i*. Then, still hypothetically, the *-i* is weakened to the point at which, in the end, it disappears; this gives us the forms attested in Old English: *fēt*, *tēþ*, *gēs*. Finally, from the later middle ages, the *ē* or (in modern spelling) *ee* changed to, in phonetic notation, [iː].

This was and is, to repeat, a stock example; and it illustrates perfectly how, from a historical linguist's viewpoint, something that in the modern language is a pure irregularity can be shown to make sense on the basis of a reconstructed pattern. That is the insight, as we have seen, that Saussure himself learned when he was young. But at any period in the history of English what exists is a specific system, and such systems ('langues') are formed by the collective knowledge of their speakers. What then is known to speakers of the present day? They know, of course, the forms *feet*, *teeth* and *geese*; they know their meanings in relation to those of *foot*, *tooth* and *goose*. Likewise, for example, speakers of Old English knew the forms *fōt*, *tōþ* and *gōs*, and their relation in meaning to *fēt*, *tēþ* and *gēs*. In either period, both the forms as they are then and the relations in which they then stand constitute the language ('la langue') that exists at that time. The same is true of any period intervening between Old English and the present; also of any earlier period in which, hypothetically, a set of speakers knew forms such as *fōt* and *fōti* or *fōt* and *fēti*. But in no such stage do speakers know the forms that have been current in earlier periods, or the relations of meaning that they entered into, or the changes that have led from those forms to their own. Therefore these are not part of their 'langue', and a linguist's description of the 'langue' of any body of speakers, at any stage in this history, deals in irrelevancies if it says anything about them. For a 'langue' is formed, once more, by the collective knowledge of its speakers and these are things that speakers do not know.

Linguists in general are therefore dealing with relations of two kinds. There are relations, on the one hand, between forms belonging to 'la langue' as it is known in different periods: between earlier *fōti* and later *fēti*, *fēt* or *feet*; or, for that matter, between *fōt* as reconstructed and Old English *fōt*, or *feet* as known to speakers in the sixteenth century and present-day *feet*. These belong to the time dimension or, in Saussure's terms, to the axis 'of succession'. His treatment of them was again within the tradition in which he stood.

On the other hand, there are relations between forms that belong to the same period: between present-day *foot* and present-day *feet*, between Old English *fōt* and Old English *fēt*, and so on. These belong to the axis not of time but, in Saussure's terms, 'of simultaneity'. Now for historical linguists they are as they are because of changes that have given rise to them. 'Synchrony', in Saussure's terminology, is in that sense the product of 'diachrony'. But in a synchronic view 'English' exists only in the collective knowledge of particular bodies of speakers. To say, for instance, that *fēt* changes to *feet*, or that, by a sound law, *ē* in general changes to [iː], is to presuppose 'langues' that exist for different bodies of speakers in different periods. To study 'diachrony' is to establish relations between successive 'synchronies'.

A diagram in which these axes are contrasted (115) has often been reproduced. But their 'absolute divergence' is best illustrated by a comparison, which in the *Cours* itself is claimed to be more revealing than any other, between the history of a language and a chess game. Between moves chessmen form a specific pattern on the board, in which the relation of each piece to the whole depends on its position and the positions of the others. This corresponds to a specific 'state of the language' ('un état de la langue', 125): that is, to a state of synchrony. But each such state is strictly temporary. In the game a player moves just one piece at a time, but that one change results in a new 'equilibrium', or new 'synchrony'. It has 'a repercussion on the entire system' ('un retentissement sur tout le système'), and it is impossible for the player to foresee all its effects (126). Likewise, in the language, each change affects only isolated elements; but again a new synchrony, as a whole, replaces the old synchrony. The movement of a piece is, finally, 'a fact entirely distinct' from the states of equilibrium that precede and follow it ('un fait absolument distinct de l'équilibre précédent et de l'équilibre subséquent'). Nor, in considering a particular state of the board, does an observer need in general to know the sequence of moves that have led to it. 'All this', we are told, 'applies equally to the language, and confirms the radical distinction of what is diachronic and what is synchronic' ('Tout ceci s'applique également à la langue et consacre la distinction radicale du diachronique et du synchronique', 128). The only difference is that changes in a language are not intentional, while moves in the game are. In other respects, a game of chess 'is like an artificial realisation of what the language presents in a natural form' ('est comme une réalisation artificielle de ce que la langue nous présente sous une forme naturelle', 125).

First, then, the study of language in general ('langage') is divided into those of languages ('langues') and of speech ('parole'). The former is 'linguistics in the strict sense'. Secondly, the linguistics 'of languages' is in turn divided into diachronic linguistics and synchronic linguistics. These are equally valid but diverge 'absolutely'. Our third point then concerns the notion of a language as a system of 'values'. In economics, for example, there are systems of values that relate work to the wages that are paid for doing it. Likewise (for Saussure) the values of words are their meanings. In each case we are concerned with 'a system of equivalences between things of different orders' ('il s'agit d'un *système d'équivalences entre des choses d'ordres différents*', 115). In one it is between work and wages. In the other it is between a 'signifiant', or something that 'means', and a 'signifié', or something that 'is meant'.

To understand the relation between these it may help if we begin with another analogy. In the system of coinage that is in use in Britain as I write, a piece of metal of a certain alloy, size and design has, for example, the value of ten pence. It is one of a determinate set of coins with different values, and these values are interrelated. For example, ten coins with the value of ten pence are equivalent to one with the value of one pound. The system holds only for a specific society at a specific time. There is no independent reason why this particular piece of metal should have that particular value, or why this particular set of values should be involved. There was a period in which a larger coin, which had among other things the words 'two shillings' on it, also had the value of ten pence. There was a period in which a coin with 'sixpence' on it had the value of two and a half pence; now no coin has that value. Earlier still there was a period in which the values were in shillings and pence, with twelve pence to the shilling and twenty shillings to the pound, whereas now they are decimal, with a hundred pence to the pound. Coins are coins, moreover, solely in that they have values. A piece of metal which in many respects resembles a coin is no more than a piece of metal if it has no value in the system. Thus an object that was once a sixpence is, in the present system, a coin no longer. Equally, two bits of metal that are partly different may, in a specific system, be the same coin. Thus a one-pound coin may have a thistle on the back and, round the side, the Latin inscription 'nemo me impune lacessit'. Alternatively, it may have the royal arms and the inscription 'decus et tutamen'. Alternatively, it may have a leek and the Welsh inscription 'pleidiol wyf i'm gwlad'. But each of these is equally a one-pound coin. In all these ways the system is a matter of convention, again in a specific society at a specific time.

The example of coins is used only briefly in the *Cours* (160), and not for this purpose. But it is easy to see how the analogy would apply. A language is a system of 'signs' relating 'signifiers' and things 'signified'; and, just as a coin has its value only in a specific system of coinage, a signifier has its value only in a specific language system. Outside the system of coinage a coin is a mere piece of metal. Outside the language system a word would likewise be nothing. It is a word precisely because it has a value; and, just as the value of coins is in relation to those of other coins, so the value of words is in relation to those of other words.

This is a bold conception, and its full originality may not at once be clear. The notion that words are 'signs' was not, of course, new. Derivatives of the Greek word for 'sign' (*sēmeîon*) were part of the terminology of the Stoic philosophers in the third century BC; terms like 'signify' and 'signification' are from the Latin word corresponding to it; and among Saussure's more immediate predecessors, the American linguist William Dwight Whitney writes straightforwardly of a language as an 'aggregate of articulated signs for thought' (1867: 22), or a 'system of signs' (1971 [1875]: 115). Nor was it new to insist that signs in language were matters of convention. In Saussure's terms they are 'arbitrary'; and, as Eugenio Coseriu has shown, this term derives ultimately, through various changes of formula, from a concept of convention in Plato and Aristotle (Coseriu, 1967). The *Cours* contains few acknowledgments of Saussure's predecessors. Again we must remind ourselves that it was in origin a course of lectures, in days long before handouts. But for this point Saussure specifically referred to Whitney (*Cours*, 110). In the second of the passages I have cited Whitney made clear that the relation between the sign and what it signifies is 'one of mental association only'. Each individual 'form of human speech' is 'a body of arbitrary and conventional signs for thought' (1867: 32). For any individual who learns to use it, every 'vocable' is first 'arbitrary, because any one of a thousand other vocables could have been just as easily learned . . . and associated with the same idea'; secondly, it is conventional, because it 'ha[s] its sole ground and sanction in the consenting usage of the community of which it formed a part' (14).

In part, then, what the *Cours* says was familiar and ancient. But other things were not, and the notion of 'values' is central to them. The most obvious, which I have consciously glossed over, is the way in which 'signs' are defined. For Whitney, for example, the sign was the word or 'vocable' itself. Each word is a 'sign for thought' and, as such, stands in a relation to an idea or concept. For the *Cours*, the signifier is an 'acoustic image' in the minds of speakers; what it signifies is a 'concept' that, as we saw earlier in this section, is triggered by it. But the 'linguistic sign' as such encompasses both. It is 'a mental entity with two sides' ('une entité psychique à deux faces'): one a 'signifiant' or 'signifier', and the other a 'signifié' or what is 'signified' (99).

This may at first sight seem perverse. When we say, for instance, that a black cloud is a sign of rain what we are calling a sign is precisely the black cloud. In the same way, if we are told that the word *tree*, or an 'acoustic image' corresponding to *tree*, is a sign in our minds of the concept 'tree', we might normally take the sign to be the word or 'acoustic image' itself. It is perhaps not surprising, therefore, that many writers who talk of 'signifiants' and 'signifiés' in fields other than that of language, while appealing ostensibly to Saussure's theory of 'l'arbitraire du signe', in reality revert to ordinary usage. But the reason for defining the sign in the way he did is that neither side of it exists independently. The cloud is one thing, the rain another: we can identify each as a separate entity. But in the case of language we cannot point to a 'signifiant' independently of its 'signifié', or to a 'signifié' independently of its 'signifiant'. A 'linguistic entity' exists 'only through the association' of one with the other ('L'entité linguistique n'existe que par l'association du signifiant et du signifié', 144). Thus, on the one hand, an acoustic image '*tree*' is identified solely by its relation to the concept 'tree'; and, on the other hand, a concept 'tree' is identified solely by its relation to the acoustic image '*tree*'. The sign as a whole, moreover, is identifiable solely by its relation to other signs, within the system of values of which it is one term.

Let us begin with the 'signifié'. An ancient view, which was still current enough in Saussure's day, is that words are names for 'things'. Trees are things of one kind, stones things of another kind, and in each language there are names, like *tree* and *stone*, for each of them. The *Cours* dismisses this view from the outset: a language is not a 'nomenclature' (97). Various reasons are given, but the point that most concerns us is that there is no preexisting set of 'meanings'. From a psychological viewpoint, 'taken in abstraction from its expression by words, our thought is simply a shapeless and undifferentiated whole' ('Psychologiquement, abstraction faite de son expression par les mots, notre pensée n'est qu'une masse amorphe et indistincte', 155). Until the language system comes into play ('avant l'apparition de la langue'), nothing is distinct.

It is no better with the 'signifiant'. Traditionally, what 'signifies' is part of a physical signal, and the *Cours* speaks similarly of a 'slice of sound' ('une tranche de sonorité', 146). But how do we identify recurring 'slices'? They are not physically marked off: in a signal part of which we can represent in writing as *cut trees*, the *t* of *cut* and the *t* of *trees* will run into one another, and the *s* of *trees*, which in a plural like this has a meaning of its own, would be no more a distinct 'slice' than the '*ze*' of *seize*, which does not. A 'slice', in short, is a slice only by virtue of its relation to what it 'signifies'. Nor are recurrences of 'the same slice' physically constant. The *Cours* gives the example of a lecture in which the word *Messieurs!*

'Gentlemen!' is repeated several times. As we perceive it, it is always the same expression: but the speaker's delivery and intonation will vary so much that the physical differences between one instance and another will be as great as those between words that we perceive as different, such as *paume* 'palm of hand' and *pomme* 'apple' (150f.). It is not, then, as a physical entity that *Messieurs* remains the same word.

To make this point, the *Cours* gives among others a famous analogy between the 'sameness' of a word and the 'sameness' of a train in a railway system. The 8.45 p.m. express from Geneva to Paris leaves one day, and the 'same train' leaves again twenty-four hours later. But, physically, it too is not the same: it probably has a different locomotive, different carriages, a different driver, and so on. What makes it that particular train is its time of departure, its route 'and in general all the circumstances that distinguish it from all other express trains' ('et en général toutes les circonstances qui le distinguent des autres express', 151). The identity of words is said to be like that. What makes each instance of 'Messieurs!' the same word *Messieurs* is its place within a system in which, just as one train is distinguished from another within the railway timetable, the 'sign' that it represents, which is again formed by the association of a 'signifiant' with a 'signifié', is distinguished from other signs.

We have now reached the conclusion to which Saussure's thought had been tending. In the beginning, I equated 'meaning' and 'value'; and, when the *Cours* first talks of linguistics as a science that deals with values, it too does so (115). But, as a later section makes clear (158ff.), 'value' is a matter of difference. The value of a ten pence coin lies in its relation to the values of others within a decimal system. What makes the train the 8.45 express is the distinction or opposition between it and other trains in the timetable: its time of departure as distinct from that of other trains from Geneva to Paris, its status as an express in opposition to that of a stopping train, and so on. Likewise a linguistic sign exists by virtue of its opposition to other signs; and, just as coins have values only within a particular system of coinage, and the identity of trains is only in terms of a particular railway system, so the links established between 'signifiants' and 'signifiés' exist only through the system of oppositions by which, literally, that particular language is formed. The conclusion is stark and radical. For what we have said amounts to the statement that 'in the language system there are only differences' ('Tout ce qui précède revient à dire que *dans la langue il n'y a que des différences*'). No unit has an existence independent of the relations between it and other units. 'In the language system there are only differences, with no positive terms' ('dans la langue il n'y a que des différences *sans termes positifs*', 166).

We now have one structuralist answer to the question with which we began this chapter. 'A language', such as English, is a 'social phenomenon' ('fait social') whose existence is solely as a system of values holding in a specific society. Its manifestations through speech ('parole') are individual and fleeting. Therefore, in the first instance, it is the system ('langue') that we must study. When languages change, one system is replaced by another. Therefore the study of changes must be distinguished rigorously from the study of a system in abstraction from time. Each language, as the *Cours* insists at this point, is 'a system of pure values' ('un système de pures valeurs'), 'determined by nothing other than the momentary state of its terms' ('que rien ne détermine en dehors de l'état momentané de ses termes', 117).

How far was this account accepted? The second of our three points has been widely taken for granted. By the middle of the twentieth century many linguists were to deal with synchrony exclusively. But not everyone has followed Saussure's theory of 'la langue'. Languages may be the primary or a primary object of study. But their relation to speech is not as the *Cours* said it is.

2.2   Languages as sets of utterances

Let us begin with one explicit critic. The British linguist J. R. Firth was a structuralist in many ways. From the 1940s, when he founded the first department of linguistics in the University of London, he was certainly a leading member of the group that those who were not structuralists opposed. He also agreed with Saussure's *Cours* on some points. In a famous passage, Saussure had envisaged a new science of 'semiology' ('sémiologie') that would study 'the life of signs in the context of social life' ('la vie des signes au sein de la vie sociale') (*Cours*, 33). Its name is again from Greek *sēmeîon* 'sign'; it would be part of social psychology and would have linguistics, in turn, as one subdiscipline. To Firth, writing in the 1930s, this was 'perhaps the most striking thing in the whole of de Saussure's great work': that 'linguistics can only find a place among the sciences if it is brought into relation' with semiology (Firth, 1957 [1935]: 17).

But for Firth the study of language was that of concrete instances of speech. Such instances are social events, and the reality of language lies in the social behaviour of speakers. Hence he rejected Saussure's concepts of 'langage', 'langue' and 'parole'. For Saussure, in Firth's words, languages were social facts conceived as '*sui generis* and external to and on a different plane from individual phenomena' (Firth, 1957 [1950]: 179). '[T]rue Saussureans, like true Durkheimians, regard the structures formulated by linguistics or sociology as *in rebus*' (181). 'The structure is existent and is treated as a thing.' For Firth this made the individual speaker, in his terms, an 'underdog . . . whose speech was not the "integral and concrete object of linguistics"' (183, translating *Cours*, 23). He thus rejected what he calls, in the same sentence, 'de Saussure's mechanistic structuralism'. The 'systematics' of specific aspects of linguistics, of the study of sounds, of grammar, and so on, do not describe an underlying reality, 'stored in the collective conscience'. They are 'ordered schematic constructs, frames of reference, a sort of scaffolding for the handling of events' (181). Firth does not refer at this point to Saussure's grand vision of semiology. But the reality of language is precisely in 'la vie sociale', 'the social life', of a community of speakers.

This does not tell us what we might mean by 'a language', and perhaps, if we take Firth's view, that issue is not central. But one answer, not his but one that has been very influential, is that it is the sum of the speech that is possible in a community. Anything said by a speaker is, in linguists' terminology, an 'utterance'. A 'language', therefore, is a body of utterances.

This was the answer given, in 1926, in a remarkable article by Leonard Bloomfield. He was then in his late thirties, and had already published a general introduction to linguistics (1914) influenced especially by ideas in Germany at the turn of the century. But by the early 1920s he had read Saussure's *Cours*, whose second edition he reviewed in 1924. At the same time he was converted to what he later calls a 'physicalist' philosophy, in which all statements in science are seen as ultimately about physical events. Its immediate inspiration lay in the new school of behaviourist psychology: in particular, in the ideas of Albert P. Weiss, who was a colleague in the 1920s at Ohio State University. But such a philosophy was also developed independently, in this period, by the logical positivists in Vienna. The Vienna school had 'found', as Bloomfield put it later, 'that all scientifically meaningful statements are translatable into physical terms – that is, into statements about movements which can be observed and described in coordinates of space and time' (Bloomfield, 1970 [1936]: 325). 'Statements which cannot be made in these terms are either scientifically meaningless or else make sense only if they are translated into statements about language.' By the 1930s, one could 'not read modern writings' without meeting such ideas 'again and again' (323); and, in the future testing of this 'hypothesis of *physicalism*', 'linguists will have to perform an important part of the work'.

It is in this philosophical setting that we have to read both Bloomfield's *Language* (1933) and his important article in 1926, which is in part a precursor. Its title is modelled on an essay by Weiss, which had sought to make explicit basic 'postulates' that underlay behaviourism in psychology (Weiss, 1925). In a far more detailed study Bloomfield tried to formulate, as rigorously as possible, a 'set of postulates for the science of language'. A 'postulate' is an axiom or assumption that we have to take as given. For example, by Bloomfield's Assumption H1, with which he begins a section on historical linguistics, we take it as an axiom that 'every language changes at a rate which leaves contemporary persons free to communicate without disturbance'. Such postulates rest, in part, on terms which are defined within our science: thus Assumption H1 rests, crucially, on the prior definition of 'a language'. Then, given the postulate, further terms can be defined. Thus the case in which communication is disturbed but not destroyed by change defines a 'dialect' (Bloomfield, 1970 [1926]: 136). The advantage of the 'postulational method' is that it 'forces us to state explicitly' what factual assumptions we are making, to define our terms precisely and show what depends on what (126).

What do we have to assume in order to talk of languages? Clearly, a language is that of a community, whose members communicate with one another by it. Our starting point might be that there are such systems of communication, 'langues' as Saussure conceived them. But Bloomfield's strategy is more subtle, and begins with the insight that, in such communities, there must be similarities between different acts of speech. They are similar because, in ordinary terms, the members of the community are speaking the same language. So, it is through such similarities that languages are established.

By Bloomfield's first definition, 'an act of speech is an *utterance*'. Our crucial assumption, therefore, is that 'within certain communities successive utterances are alike or partly alike'. Suppose, to follow Bloomfield's illustrations, that a stranger comes to the door and says 'I'm hungry.' Then suppose that, on another occasion, a child who has eaten but does not want to go to bed says 'I'm hungry.' We will take it, as linguists, that these two acts are alike: that the sounds the speakers utter are the same, with the same meaning. There can also be likenesses at individual points. If someone said 'The book is interesting' that would be one utterance; 'Put the book away' would be another. But for a linguist they are partly alike, since both include 'the book'. Any community in which there are such resemblances is by definition 'a *speech-community*'; and, in such a community, a certain range of utterances will be possible. Thus, in the community in which one can say 'The book is interesting', one can also say 'I'm hungry' but not, for example, what would in another speech-community be the utterance (in French) 'J'ai faim.' The '*language* of [a] speech-community' is accordingly 'the totality of utterances that can be made' in it (Bloomfield, 1970 [1926]: 129–30).

This rests, to repeat, on an assumption, which is axiomatic for a particular science. What the stranger at the door says is objectively very different from what the child says. Their voices are pitched differently, one may speak softly and the other loudly, and so on. The actions that accompany their speech will also differ. The stranger stands still on the doorstep; the child might be vigorously resisting a parent who is trying to carry it upstairs. One may indeed be hungry, and their purpose is to ask for food. The other is not hungry at all. 'Outside our science', as Bloomfield says, the similarities 'are only relative'. Only within it are they 'absolute' (again 129f.).

But without this 'fiction', as Bloomfield also calls it, linguistics would be without foundation. We say, for example, that both speakers utter a word *hungry*, and that this word has, in each case, the same meaning. That the child is lying and the stranger telling the truth is not, for us as linguists, relevant. But how can we justify this? The Saussurean answer is that *hungry* is a sign uniting an acoustic image '*hungry*' with a concept ('hungry'); but, unless we can identify these physically, that answer is now closed to us. We simply have to assume that such relations exist. In Bloomfield's *Language* this is 'the *fundamental assumption of linguistics*'. In principle, our statements could be founded on the discoveries of other sciences, regarding physical states of the brain or other parts of a speaker's body. But, failing that, we have to assume that, '*in certain communities (speech-communities) some speech-utterances are alike as to form and meaning*' (Bloomfield, 1935 [1933]: 144). The point is italicised twice (see also 78). Only on this basis can we say that, in the specific case of *hungry*, the 'form' that is phonetically [hʌŋgri] has, in both 'speech-utterances', the same meaning 'hungry'.

Bloomfield did not, in 1933, repeat his earlier definition of a language. But let us take 'English', for example, to be the totality of utterances possible 'in English'. To describe 'English' is thus to describe these utterances, and the structure 'of English' will accordingly be the structure that, taken as a whole, they have. What exactly, then, is an 'utterance'?

For Bloomfield, it was an 'act of speech'. This is again from 1926; in *Language* 'utterance' is not treated or indexed as a technical term. But, as Bloomfield makes plain, the 'act' is that of emitting the sounds that constitute 'speech'. A 'speech event' is described in strictly physical terms: the movements of a speaker's vocal cords and other organs; the resulting sound-waves; their action on a hearer's ear-drums (Bloomfield, 1935 [1933]: 25). An act of speech is therefore distinguished carefully from whatever surrounds it, in the state of the world or in a speaker or hearer's other behaviour (23). An instance of speech is also referred to, in passing (23), as a 'speech-utterance'. The utterances that we describe are thus specifically the sounds that speakers emit. The totality of utterances that 'can be made' in a community is the totality of sounds that, in speaking their language, members of that community may emit. To describe the language is, accordingly, to describe the structure of such sounds.

This leads directly to the programme developed, largely after Bloomfield's incapacity and death in the 1940s, by his follower Zellig S. Harris. In one of his earliest writings as a structural linguist, Harris rejected the notion that a 'language structure', conceived as we will see in the Saussurean tradition, can be studied independently of the 'speech act'. The former, he says, is 'merely the scientific arrangement' of the latter (Z. S. Harris, 1941: 345). With this remark Firth, who we cited at the beginning of this section, might well have agreed. But for Harris what we were studying was not, in the first instance, the entire event of which speech is a part; it was again the sounds uttered. In describing English we establish that, for example, the sounds represented by *I'm hungry* constitute a possible utterance. We analyse them into recurring units: for example, a unit *I* recurs in other utterances such as *I must eat* or *You know I won't*. We establish relations among units: for example, in each of these utterances, *I* bears the same relation (traditionally as subject) to what follows; in *I'm hungry* and *She's clever*, *[a]m* and *hungry* are related to each other in the same construction (as it is traditionally called) as *[i]s* and *clever*. We group units into classes: thus, by virtue of such relations, *hungry* and *clever* are both (again as they are traditionally called) adjectives. In this way we assign a structure to each utterance, by which it is again classed with others. Thus *I'm hungry* has a structure partly shared with *I must eat*, in which a subject is related (still in traditional terminology) to a predicate (*[a]m hungry*, *must eat*). The predicate has a structure in which a certain class of verb (*[a]m*) is related to an adjective (*hungry*); that is also the structure of *[i]s clever*, and so on.

The method is explored in Harris's first book as a general linguist (1951). A 'language or dialect' is, in general, 'the talk which takes place in a language community' (13). Thus, in a particular case, it is 'the speech of the community' (9) selected for study. Our data are instances of such talk, and any particular body or 'corpus' of data is a sample of the talk that is possible. The 'description of the language structure', as Harris calls it in his final chapter (372f.), is an account precisely of the structure that, when we apply this method, talk is found to have.

One further insight remains, whose most important consequence we will reserve for a later chapter (6.1). Briefly, however, a language is in this view a set. Its members are 'utterances'; and, at the level of abstraction at which we are now talking, each utterance is characterised by the relations established over a set of smaller units. Although we are talking, in principle, of sounds that speakers may emit, we have in effect abstracted something very like a set of written sentences, in which determinate words stand in determinate orders. The set as a whole is also, by implication, determinate. We have talked of utterances that 'can be made' in a community; so, at this level of abstraction, certain combinations of smaller units are members of our set. Others, we imply, are not members. What then are the properties of the sets that we call 'languages', that distinguish them, in general, from other sets? In abstraction from reality, sets are mathematical objects. Our question, therefore, is about the properties of 'languages' as mathematical systems.

This insight did not occur to Bloomfield in the 1930s, and he might well have recoiled from it. But it was to inspire Harris for the remainder of his life, which ended in his eighties, a year after his last book (Z. S. Harris, 1991). Meanwhile it had led directly, in the 1950s, to the pivotal concept of a 'generative grammar'. A set is 'generated' if, by following a series of rules or instructions, its membership is specified. For example, the instruction 'multiply x by 2, where x is a whole number' generates the set of even numbers. A language is, in this view, a set; its members are 'utterances' or, equivalently for Harris, 'sentences'. A grammar is traditionally a description of 'a language', and could therefore be 'viewed', as Harris puts it in one paper, 'as a set of instructions which generates the sentences of the language' (1954: 260).

This idea was in the event developed not by Harris himself, but by his pupil Chomsky. It is indeed a pivot on which what is often called the Chomskyan revolution turned. But we will need to remind ourselves again of its Bloomfieldian ancestry.

2.3   The autonomy of linguistics

For the moment, we must return to Bloomfield. We have seen that his technical concept of a language differed from Saussure's. But on what were then essentials they more often agree. In a letter written in the 1940s Bloomfield said that his *Language* reflected Saussure's *Cours* 'on every page' (see Cowan, 1987: 29). To understand the significance of either, we must try to grasp what he meant. In the early 1920s Bloomfield wrote already of a 'newer trend of linguistic study', to which the *Cours* gave a 'theoretic foundation' (Bloomfield, 1970 [1922]: 92). It 'affects', he said, 'two critical points'. The first concerns the status of historical linguistics. 'We are coming to believe', as Bloomfield put it, 'that restriction to historical work is unreasonable and, in the long run, methodically impossible'. Synchronic study, in Saussurean terms, is prior to diachronic. I am citing from his review of another general introduction to language, published in

1921, by his American contemporary Edward Sapir (Sapir, n.d.). Bloomfield is 'glad to see' that Sapir 'deals with synchronic matters . . . before he deals with diachronic'. The same concern was to dictate the structure of his own book, which has a clear division between chapters on the nature of language, roughly its first half, and those on the history of languages. There was at least one earlier precedent, in the work by Von der Gabelentz cited at the beginning of this chapter (Gabelentz, 1901 [1891]). But Saussure's analysis was from now on seen as seminal.

The second 'critical point' concerns the relation of linguistics to psychology. Bloomfield's first book (1914) had been founded in the psychology of Wilhelm Wundt, who had himself published two thick volumes on language at the turn of the century (Wundt, 1911–12 [1900]). Two decades earlier, Hermann Paul's great work on the principles of language history had relied in part on an earlier psychological system (Paul, 1920 [1880]). At the time it was hard to write on the theory of language without reference to either. A monograph by the Indo-Europeanist Berthold Delbrück is in substance an extended review of Wundt's work, in relation, in particular, to Paul's (Delbrück, 1901). But its first chapter is devoted to the underlying psychological systems, on the grounds that, only if they were first understood, could either view of language be assessed (iii).

Delbrück acknowledged that, for practical purposes, it does not matter what view of psychology a linguist holds ('für den Praktiker läßt sich mit beiden Theorieen leben', 44). But in Bloomfield's 'newer trend' it did not matter for any purpose. '[W]e are casting off', in his words, 'our dependence on psychology, realizing that linguistics, like every science, must study its subject-matter in and for itself, working on fundamental assumptions of its own' (again Bloomfield, 1970 [1922]: 92). Bloomfield's *Language* was conceived as a revision of his first book. But in the interim, as he explains, 'we have learned . . . what one of our masters suspected thirty years ago, namely, that we can pursue the study of languages without reference to any one psychological doctrine'. To do so 'safeguards our results and makes them more significant' to, among others, psychologists themselves (Bloomfield, 1935 [1933]: vii). In psychology, Bloomfield was by then a behaviourist, in keeping with his view of science generally. But, as a linguist, he was practising another discipline. It rested on an assumption, as we have seen; but once this was made it would be autonomous.

It will help at this point if we look, in particular, at the problem of defining sentences. Suppose a speaker says 'I'm hungry. Can't we have lunch?' For grammarians two sentences are uttered: first 'I'm hungry'; then 'Can't we have lunch?' But what distinguishes them, and what is the nature of this unit?

In the traditional definitions, speakers 'express thoughts'. They do so by combining words; so, in one of the formulae inherited from late antiquity, a sentence or 'utterance' (Latin 'oratio') is a 'coherent ordering of words' ('ordinatio dictionum congrua') 'expressing a complete judgment' ('sententiam perfectam demonstrans') (Priscian in Keil, 1855–9, I: 53). Definitions like this had been accepted as they stood for centuries. But thoughts or judgments are formed in the mind, and psychology is the science of the mind; therefore psychologists were bound to speculate about the process. Does the thought arise first as an unanalysed whole? If so, it must be subject to a process of analysis; in this way it is divided into logically articulated parts; the sentence as spoken is an expression of that. That was, simply and perhaps crudely, the account proposed by Wundt (II: 242ff.). Alternatively, the thought arises not as a whole, but from the linking of concepts that are initially separate. That was the basis, though I have once more simplified it, of the definition by Paul (121). Throughout this period theories of the sentence multiplied. Although the traditional account raised other problems, it was hard to see how the formation of thoughts in the minds of speakers, and their corresponding perception in the minds of hearers, were not central.

The treatment in Saussure's *Cours* is notoriously inexplicit. But if sentences express thoughts, and thoughts arise in individual minds on individual occasions, the sentence cannot be a unit of the 'social fact' that constitutes 'a language'. That indeed is what, at one point, the *Cours* says: '[la phrase] appartient à la parole, non à la langue' (172). Otherwise it says almost nothing; unusually, for a book of its date. But, if this interpretation is right, the 'linguistique de la langue' had no concern with it.

What did concern it were the relations in which, within Bloomfield's utterances, successive words stood. Suppose again that a speaker says 'I'm hungry.' This act of speech arises, in part, from a free choice of words: the speaker could alternatively have said 'I'm starving', or, in different circumstances, 'We're sorry' or 'How disgusting!' In Saussure's terms, such acts of speech again belong to 'parole'. But the way in which words are combined is, in part, regular: *[a]m* regularly agrees with *I* as *[a]re* agrees with *we*, both regularly precede words such as *hungry* or *sorry*, and so on. Such relations must belong to the language system. They are part of what is shared by members of a community speaking English, just as, to return to the analogy of 2.1, the way that knives are held in one hand and forks in the other, again on individual occasions when people are eating, belongs to a shared system of table manners.

Relations like these are of a kind that the *Cours* describes as 'syntagmatic' (172f.). Unfortunately it says very little about them, and any interpretation beyond this point is pure extrapolation. But if such regularities exist, there must, in any utterance, be combinations of words that conform to them. If someone simply says 'I'm hungry', this combination is by implication the whole sequence *I* + *am* + *hungry*. But suppose again that they say, first, 'I'm hungry' and then, without pause, 'Can't we have lunch?' This too is a single act of speech; in Saussurean terms a single instance of 'parole'. Now there are further regularities that constrain the combination *can* + *not* + *we* + *have* + *lunch*, which is our grammarian's second sentence. But nothing in the language system will constrain the link between it and the first. A speaker could equally well say 'Can't we have lunch? I'm hungry', or, in the same or other circumstances, 'I'm hungry. Stop the car', 'I'm hungry. Why can't we find a restaurant?', and so on. Within sentences relations are part of the language system. Across sentences they are not.

This was effectively Meillet's definition, in a manual of Indo-European that preceded the *Cours* by four years. It is formulated purely 'from the linguistic viewpoint' ('au point de vue linguistique') 'in abstraction from anything to do with logic or psychology' ('et abstraction faite de toute considération de logique ou de psychologie'). The sentence is therefore no more than 'a complex of articulations bound together by grammatical relations' ('un ensemble d'articulations liées entre elles par des rapports gramaticaux') 'which are self-sufficient in that they do not depend grammatically on any other complex' ('et qui, ne dépendant grammaticalement d'aucun autre ensemble, se suffisent à elles-mêmes') (Meillet, 1937 [1912]: 355). If we think back, that was all that Delbrück's practising linguist needed. But by the 1920s it had a clear theoretical foundation, in a linguistics that does not rely on either of the psychological theories with which, at the turn of the century, Delbrück had been obliged to grapple.

The final, classic formulation was Bloomfield's. In his first book he had followed Wundt's definition (Bloomfield, 1914: 60). But in the 1920s he accepted Meillet's, contrasting its 'simplicity and usefulness' (Bloomfield, 1970 [1926]: 129, n. 6). All that remained was to ground it directly in his 'fundamental assumption'. As we have seen, 'I'm hungry' is partly alike in form and meaning, under that assumption, to, for example, 'I must eat' or 'You know I won't.' But utterances are not merely 'alike' to others with which they share words. Under the same assumption, 'I'm hungry' is also alike to other utterances with which it shares its construction. Thus, though the words are different, their arrangement and the meaning associated with it are like those in, for example, 'Mary was furious' or 'We're sorry.' *I'm hungry* is accordingly, by definition, a 'linguistic form': a form that, as a whole, 'has a meaning' (Bloomfield, 1935 [1933]: 138). So too, by a similar analysis, is *Can't we have lunch?* Sentences can then be defined quite simply as linguistic forms that are not included in any larger linguistic form (170). In our speaker's utterance, no specific meaning is associated with the way in which these are in turn arranged. Therefore there is no larger 'linguistic form' *I'm hungry. Can't we have lunch?* Therefore this utterance includes two sentences, not one.

'The trouble over the nature of the sentence' had been 'largely nonlinguistic' (again Bloomfield, 1970 [1926]: 129, n. 6). If linguists simply study their own subject matter, 'in and for itself', such problems are solved. The 'in and for itself' is Bloomfield's (again 1970 [1922]: 92). But it could just as well be from the famous final sentence of Saussure's *Cours*. It is one that, as it happens, was not in his students' notes. But even if it is the editors' own, it makes clear what Saussure could well have called his 'fundamental idea', that 'the only true object of study in linguistics is the language system, considered in and for itself' ('l'idée fondamentale de ce cours: *la linguistique a pour unique et véritable objet la langue envisagée en elle-même et pour elle-même*') (Saussure, 1972 [1916]: 317).

It is in this sense that Saussure's influence is 'on every page' of Bloomfield's own book. But the autonomy of linguistics had clearly been achieved at some cost. In particular, we have to assume, as Bloomfield makes clear, that relations between forms and meanings, both in vocabulary and grammar, are constant. Only on that basis could we speak of 'langues' or 'languages', and only then could a 'linguistics of the language system', to translate once more the formula of the *Cours*, be founded.

The problem Bloomfield and Saussure both faced is that, when people talk, no utterance is exactly like any other. Someone says 'I'm hungry'; the next day, as we will describe it, they say again 'I'm hungry.' But each event is transient, and the sounds emitted will not be the same, in minute or even gross respects. A woman with a bad cold asks 'How should I know?' A tenor sings (from Britten's 'Curlew River') 'How should I know?' The sounds emitted are in that case very different. Nevertheless, we will describe these as the same words. On what basis can we do so?

The answer for Saussure lay in the system of 'values' that constitutes a language system. In it, for example, an 'acoustic image', such as '*know*', is linked indissolubly, as the 'signifiant' that forms one aspect of a linguistic sign, to a 'concept' ('know'), as the 'signifié' corresponding to it. But Bloomfield's answer is in essentials the same. For 'acoustic image' read 'form', which is defined, in his set of postulates, as a recurring 'vocal feature' (Bloomfield, 1970 [1926]: 130). For 'concept' read 'meaning'. But, by his fundamental assumption, forms and meanings are again indissolubly linked. For it is only through the recurrence in tandem of both vocal features and features of meaning, of a distinctive vocal feature that is present whenever someone says 'know' and a distinctive meaning feature that is present whenever someone does so, that a permanent linguistic unit exists.

For Bloomfield meanings were, quite literally, 'present'. As objects of scientific study they had, in principle, to have a physical identity. The meaning of an utterance was accordingly defined by the external circumstances, each describable in space and time, in which the act of speech takes place (Bloomfield, 1935 [1933]: 27). This view was at the time so radical, and differed so clearly from that of anyone who took thoughts or concepts in the mind for granted, that it is on Bloomfield's general philosophy of meaning, often linked specifically to behaviourist psychology, that most commentators dwell. But the point that now concerns us is the link between a 'meaning', however described, and the 'form' associated with it. Under Bloomfield's fundamental assumption, each term in this relation again presupposes the other. For the recurrence of one is only by virtue of the parallel recurrence of the other; and, in Bloomfield's treatment, which is thought through more than that of Saussure's *Cours*, this is true of the arrangements in which recurring parts of utterances stand, and the constant meanings which they, in their turn, must be assumed to have, not just of the parts themselves. We will see later how this view could be developed.

3   Sound systems

The chief, if not the only, interest of the *Cours de linguistique générale* was as an account of the foundations of linguistics. Of its five numbered parts, the last three deal conventionally with sound change and changes in grammar, the distribution in space of languages and dialects, the reconstruction of prehistoric languages, and other topics natural in a manual of its day. These together form more than a third of the whole (193–317). The chapters everyone now cites are part of the introduction, most of Part 1 ('General Principles') and most again of Part 2 ('Synchronic linguistics'), a third again. But the earliest reviewers, as Keith Percival has shown, did not see in these the revolution that was later proclaimed. The book was seen more as old-fashioned (Percival, 1981).

That is perhaps not so surprising. For work on the foundations of a discipline need not have immediate repercussions on the way it is practised. When the *Cours* appeared, most linguists worked on Indo-European or some other family, on the history or grammar of particular languages, in dialectology, and generally in fields to which it offered nothing new. Even a 'synchronic' linguist could learn little. The treatment of speech-sounds, for example, was based on lectures given in 1897 (editors' note, 63) which were already dated. For the rest, we might be tempted to recall a remark by Delbrück cited in an earlier section (2.3). Provided that their methods are not disturbed, practising linguists can live happily with whatever any theorist says about the philosophical principles that underlie what they are doing. Only other theorists, of whom there are at any time few, need respond.

For whatever reason it was not until the 1930s that Saussurean structuralism took off. To understand both why and how it did we have to look especially at the emergence of the basic unit called the 'phoneme'. The term itself (originally French 'phonème') had been coined innocuously in the early 1870s for a single speech-sound (German 'Sprachlaut'). At the time it was a new term and no more. But by the 1930s it was the centre of a new and well-developed theory. Even historians of languages could not ignore it: for sound change, as Bloomfield among others made clear, was change in phonemes (Bloomfield, 1935 [1933]: 351). By the end of the decade there were techniques by which, in any language, phonemes could be identified. Ten years later, as we will see in a later chapter, methods modelled on them were affecting the description of a language generally. Finally, the theory fitted beautifully with what the *Cours* had said about the object of the discipline.

3.1   The prehistory of the phoneme

The strands that led to it are complex, and we cannot survey every contribution. For those I will omit see especially the penetrating history of this field by Stephen Anderson (Anderson, 1985). From the beginning, however, we can distinguish two main ideas.

The first is that of distinctive differences among sounds. English *blather*, for example, has a consonant distinct from that of *bladder*. The sound written '*dd*' is produced by a temporary blocking of the outgoing airstream. In phonetic terminology, it is a stop or plosive (in notation [d]). The one written '*th*' is a fricative, produced with a turbulent airstream but without blocking it (in notation, [ð]). The words are different; and, in general, any word with [ð] or [d] in this position (*feather*, say, or *body*) would be altered if the other were to replace it ('*fedder*', '*bothy*'). The classic theory dates again from the 1930s. But in its terms [ð] and [d] are different phonemes, characterised by 'distinctive features' which in one case might include a feature 'fricative' and in the other an opposing feature 'plosive'. In Saussurean terms, distinctiveness is one of the relations that define a language system. So, in the system we call 'English', fricative and plosive are two elements.

The second idea is that units of sound 'alternate'. In English, for example, the diphthong [ʌɪ] in *drive* ([drʌɪv]) is said to alternate with [əʊ] in *drove* ([drəʊv]) or [ɪ] in *driven* ([drɪvən]). These are forms of the same verb ('to drive'); but, while the *dr . . . v* is constant, the vowels intervening vary. For historical linguists this is an irregularity which has to be explained by older stages of the language and the changes that have ensued; and, for such alternations in English, their account is varied and complicated. But the pattern that has resulted is in part systematic. As *drive* is to *drove* so *strive* is to *strove* and *ride* is to *rode*; and, for some speakers, *dive* is to *dove*. As *sing* ([sɪŋ]) is to *sang* ([saŋ]) and *sung* ([sʌŋ]) so *ring*, for example, is to *rang* and *rung* or *drink* (with final *-nk*) to *drank* and *drunk*. As present tense *read* ([riːd]) is to past tense *read* ([rɛd]) so *lead* is to *led*, *meet* (though its vowel was in an earlier period different) to *met*, and so on. To describe such patterns is, in Saussurean terms, to describe synchronically.

The first idea is in part far older than structuralism. The distinctiveness of consonants, especially, was the principle behind the invention of the alphabet; and in at least one other system of writing, devised for Korean in the fifteenth century, features were represented too. But its current formulation can again be traced back to the 1870s. The study of speech-sounds was by then a separate discipline, called (in English since the 1840s) 'phonetics'. Our story in this section is accordingly of one aspect of that discipline.

Let us begin in Britain, with the work of the Anglicist and phonetician Henry Sweet. Sweet was among other things an acute observer of phonetic detail, immortalised outside the history of linguistics in the character of Henry Higgins in George Bernard Shaw's 'Pygmalion'. But the more exactly we discriminate between the sounds that speakers produce, the more we tend to obscure the differences that matter to them. The *ee* of *heel*, for example, is physically longer than the *i* of *hill*: that they are different, certainly, any speaker will appreciate. But in compensation, as Sweet noted at one point, the *l(l)* of *hill* is also longer. An *l* is also long before a consonant such as *d* in *build*, but shorter before its counterpart in *built* (Sweet, 1971 [1877]: 138). The duration of sounds is relative; and for vowels, in particular, Sweet distinguished in principle five degrees of quantity, though, 'for practical purposes', three were 'generally enough' (1971 [1877, 1890]: 137f.).

Such detail is compounded when we look at other languages. The *l* of *heel* is, in modern terminology, 'alveolar': produced, that is, with the tongue touching the flat ridge behind the upper teeth. But in French *fil* the tip of the tongue is further forward, reaching the teeth themselves. The *l* in French may also be 'regarded as front-modified', in comparison with the 'deeper-sounding' *l* in English: 'the tongue', as Sweet describes it, 'is more convex than in English, its upper surface being arched up towards the front position of', for example, *y* in *yet* (1971 [1908]: 113). Much more could be said about the multiplicity of *l*'s in either language. But for speakers of each they represent a single consonant. They are written alike (either *l* or, for quite unconnected reasons, *ll*); and that causes no confusion. Even when the *l* of French *fil* is pronounced with an English accent, or the *l* of *heel* by a speaker whose accent is different from the hearer's, what will be heard is still the same *l*. The *ee* of *heel* also varies, for example, between a Scottish and a Southern British accent. But replace it with the vowel of *hill* and speakers will be aware that the word is different.

The term 'speech-sound' was, in effect, ambiguous. In one sense it meant what, despite the numerous inherited deficiencies of writing systems, the term 'letter' had meant since antiquity. It was a unit distinguishing one word or syllable from another, and a characteristic of each letter was a sound value distinct from that of other letters. As David Abercrombie showed many years ago, that sense of 'letter' was in Sweet's time not long obsolete (Abercrombie, 1949).

But in another sense a speech-sound was, quite literally, a sound; and the variety of sounds that could be differentiated was far greater than the 'letters' of any language. How then, in particular, were the 'sounds' of speech to be represented in writing? With all the nuances that a phonetician can hear, or just those aspects to which speakers are sensitive? The answer depends, as Sweet saw, on our aims. One aim might be to record on paper a specific accent, or the dialect of a small area. We must therefore note down everything that might be relevant in the fullest scientific detail. Thus, in recording my accent, we must note not just that the vowel in *hill* is shorter than in *heel*, but also that its quality is different: in the notation now used, [hɪl] not [hil]. But the quality of the *l* must also be noted: it is what phoneticians call a 'dark' *l*, articulated with the body of the tongue raised towards the back of the mouth, as distinct from a 'clear *l*' in, for example, *silly*. Thus, again in later notation, [hɪɫ]. But that is still not all the detail we may need. We have not yet shown that the *l* is longer; in other accents [ɪ] may have a slightly different quality, and so on. Such 'scientific' representation was in Sweet's terms 'Narrow'; and, following his usage, phoneticians now talk of a 'narrow transcription'.

Another aim might be to develop a system of spelling. This could be for a language not yet written; but, even for English, the dream of Spelling Reform was not to fade until years later. For that, however, we need to represent 'sounds' in the other sense. We need to show that *hill* and *heel* are not the same word; therefore, at some point, they must be written differently. For example, if *hill* were written 'hil', *heel* might instead be written 'hiːl', with 'ː' showing that its vowel is longer. Alternatively, *hill* could be written 'hɪl' and *heel* 'hil', showing that the vowels have different qualities. But in neither case would there be any need to show more. Our aim is practical, to show as efficiently as possible which word is which. We would defeat it if we were to try to represent the sounds in scientific detail.

In Sweet's terminology, such a system is 'Broad', 'indicating only *broad* distinctions of sound' (1971 [1877]: 231). A 'broad notation' is 'one which makes only the practically necessary distinctions of sound in each language and makes them in the simplest manner possible, omitting all that is superfluous' (1971 [1908]: 242). But what is 'practically necessary' must be what is distinctive; and that varies from one language to another. In the term that Sweet used it is what is 'significant'. Thus, in the earliest of these references, he distinguishes the role in various languages of a difference between 'narrow' vowels (articulated with the tongue tense and convex in cross-section) and 'wide' vowels (with the tongue relaxed and flattened). In French, the sounds in question are always narrow; hence the distinction 'does not exist at all'. In Danish or in Icelandic, it not only exists but often makes the only difference between words. The distinction is thus 'a *significant* one': 'that is, one that corresponds to real distinctions in the languages themselves'. Therefore, in writing them, we have to represent it. In Southern British English, the vowels of *heel* or *pool* are narrow, those of *hill* or *pull* wide. But these are for Sweet distinguished by their length; thus, though the distinction exists, 'it is not an *independent* one, being associated with quantity'. Therefore, in writing English, its representation 'would be superfluous'. In this way, 'we may lay down as a general rule that only those distinctions of sounds require to be symbolized in any one language which are *independently significant*' ([1877]: 230f.).

Sweet's examples are from European languages, whose broad structure was familiar. But suppose that we are investigating one that is entirely unknown to us. We 'hear', for example, an *l*: to be precise, we hear a sound that we perceive as *l* in our own language. So, in our notes, we write '*l*'. At other times we 'hear', in the same sense, a *d*. Therefore we write '*d*'. But, on reviewing our notes, we find that what is evidently the same word has been written differently on varying occasions. Naturally we check. We ask the speakers of the language to repeat what they have said; and, yet again, we sometimes 'hear' *l* and we sometimes 'hear' *d*. Sometimes, when we 'heard' *l* the first time we will now 'hear' *d*, and sometimes the opposite. What has gone wrong?

Such difficulties were not new; but at the end of the nineteenth century they were particularly serious in North America. The Amerindian languages were numerous and contact with them was in many cases recent. They were, to put it Eurocentrically, 'exotic'; still worse, they were very different among themselves. The achievements of field linguists tend to be unsung. But two, in particular, live in the folk memory of linguists. One was Edward Sapir, who worked widely on a multitude of native American languages from 1910 onwards. The other was the anthropologist Franz Boas, who had taught him. In 1900 Boas was already in his forties, and saw clearly how our problem arises. As speakers of one language we will 'hear' sounds in another as we 'hear' those of our own. Thus, as speakers of English, we perceive an *l* when we hear a sound that is like an English *l*, and so on. But our task as linguists is to work out what, in Sweet's term, is 'significant' in the language we are studying. We must instead 'hear' what its own speakers 'hear'.

One naive reaction had been to give up. The language was 'primitive', and those who spoke it sloppy. 'Examples of American languages', Boas said, 'have been brought forward to show that the accuracy of their pronunciation is much less than that found in the languages of the civilized world' (Boas, n.d. [1911]: 11). But that was not true. Every language, of whatever kind of society, has 'its own characteristic phonetic system', distinguishing a 'definite and limited group of sounds' (10f.). Our problem is that the distinctions drawn by one are not those drawn by others. Boas discusses, in particular, a sound in Pawnee (historically of the Great Plains). It 'may be heard', he says, 'more or less distinctly sometimes as an *l*, sometimes an *r*, sometimes as *n*, and again as *d*'; but in the phonetic system of Pawnee it, 'without any doubt, is throughout the same sound'. As Boas describes it, it is 'an exceedingly weak *r*, made by trilling with the tip of the tongue a little behind the roots of the incisors'; so, 'as soon as the trill is heard more strongly', as it might be in the context of some neighbouring sound, 'we receive the impression of an *r*'. But it is a trill produced 'by the lateral part of the tongue adjoining the tip', so that the centre of the tongue 'hardly leaves the palate': this makes it at once potentially *l*-like, since in an *l* like that of English the side of the tongue is distinctively lowered; but also, since its articulation is weak, *d*-like. In addition, it is 'often accompanied by an audible breathing through the nose'; hence the further impression of an *n*, since that is distinctive for English *n* (11f.). Differences in sound that are significant in our language are matters of mere detail in Pawnee; as, of course, vice versa.

Boas did not talk of phonemes; nor Sapir before the 1930s. But the term 'sound' was again potentially ambiguous. The 'sound' in Pawnee is described by Boas as 'throughout the same'. In that respect it is like the *l* of *heel*, *hill*, and so on. But at another level it is not the same: for example, it is 'often' partly *n*-like but, by implication, sometimes not. In that respect it is like the 'dark' *l* of *hill* and the 'clear' *l* of, again in my accent, *silly*. Now in the first sense we are clearly talking of abstractions: *l* in English, for example, is an abstraction which subsumes the range of [ɫ]s and [l]s and so on that, in a literal sense, one hears. What is the nature of such abstractions?

The answer eventually given owes much to a theoretical analysis of alternations, by the Polish linguist Jan Baudouin de Courtenay. In English, the *ee* of *meet* is one 'sound' (in phonetic notation [iː]); the *e* of *met* ([ɛ]) is another. But they are related in that, here and elsewhere, they distinguish words whose meanings systematically contrast. Thus, in meaning as in sound, *meet* is to *met* as *lead* is to *led*, as *sleep* is to *slep-* in *slept*, and so on. We also find an [iː] in adjectives like *obscene* and *serene*, alternating with [ɛ] in the nouns *obscenity*, *serenity*. Such alternations cannot be explained by simple similarities among sounds. As mere sounds, [iː] and [ɛ] are less alike than, for example, [iː] and [ɪ]. So too are, for example, [ʌɪ] (as in *drive*) and [ɪ] (as in *driven*). These too alternate: as *drive* is to *driven* so *ride* is to *ridden*, as *div*[ʌɪ]*ne* is to *div*[ɪ]*nity* so *sal*[ʌɪ]*ne* is to *sal*[ɪ]*nity*, and so on. But in no such pairs are [iː] and [ɪ] related similarly.

Baudouin dealt with alternations in his own and other Slavic languages, and in a monograph in the 1890s he developed his theory in remarkable formal detail. It was a theory of speech-sounds: again, in the term then current, of 'phonetics'. But phonetics, for Baudouin, had two separate branches. In the first branch, sounds were studied simply as sounds. As such they were physical events, distinguished auditorily by a hearer and produced by the vocal organs of the speaker. In Baudouin's term, their study formed the 'anthropophonic' branch of phonetics, or 'anthropophonetics'.

But sounds as such are transitory. In Saussurean terms – and Saussure knew of Baudouin's ideas – they belonged to what the *Cours* calls 'parole'. Therefore there had to be another branch of 'phonetics', to deal with units in a speaker's mind that correspond to them. It was these that entered into alternations: thus, in the minds of speakers of English, the [ʌɪ] of *drive* or *divine* is related to the [ɪ] of *driven* or *divinity*, the [iː] of *meet* to the [ɛ] of *met*, and so on. Their study formed a separate branch, which Baudouin called 'psychophonetics'. What were these units? In Baudouin's terminology, they were specifically the 'phonemes' of the language. Thus the diphthong of *drive* was one phoneme ('Phonem'), the [ɪ] of *driven* another. But a unit at the psychological level was no longer strictly a sound; it was a mental unit corresponding to sounds. The phoneme, as Baudouin defined it, was 'a unitary representation in the phonetic domain' ('eine einheitliche, der phonetischen Welt angehörende Vorstellung'), 'which arises in the mind through the mental amalgamation of the impressions received from the pronunciation of one and the same sound' ('welche mittlelst psychischer Verschmelzung der durch die Aussprache eines und desselben Lautes erhaltenen Eindrücke in der Seele entsteht'). It was 'the mental equivalent' of the physical speech-sound ('= psychischer Aequivalent des Sprachlautes') (Baudouin de Courtenay, 1895: 9).

As such, the phoneme is associated with 'a certain set of individual anthropophonic representations' ('eine gewisse Summe einzelner anthropophonischer Vorstellungen'), either 'articulatory representations', of physiological tasks that can be executed, or the 'acoustic representations' corresponding to them. Thus, to take an earlier example, if *l* is a 'phoneme' in English, the 'dark *l*' of *hill* and 'clear *l*' of *silly* might be said to represent two different 'anthropophonic representations' corresponding to a single '*l*' in 'psychophonetics'.

Baudouin's theory was originally developed in Kazan', at the eastern edge of our academic world, and it is not until the 1920s that, in work by Sapir at its opposite extremity, we find hints that the abstraction might be taken further. There is no evidence that Sapir had read Baudouin: nor, in the beginning at least, Saussure. But in his introduction to language he talks briefly of a system that lies behind the 'purely objective system of sounds'. The latter is already 'peculiar to a language', and corresponds perhaps to Sweet's 'broad' representation. But 'back of' this 'there is a more restricted "inner" or "ideal" system', in which 'phonetic elements' are related in part independently of their objective character. This inner system may indeed persist historically 'as a pattern . . . long after its phonetic content has changed'. 'Every language', Sapir says, 'is characterized as much by its ideal system of sounds and by the underlying phonetic pattern' as by its grammatical structure (Sapir, n.d. [1921]: 55f.).

These remarks were developed further in an article published four years later. Sapir begins by comparing two sounds: one, not a speech-sound, which would be made by someone blowing out a candle; the other a sound objectively similar, made by many speakers of English (though fewer now than when he was writing) in words such as *when* or *wheel*. The 'most essential point of difference', he says, lies in the relation of *wh* to other speech sounds. It is 'one of a definitely limited number of sounds' which 'belong together in a definite system of symbolically utilizable counters'. Each is characterised by 'a distinctive and slightly variable articulation' and by the corresponding 'acoustic image'. But it is also characterised '– *and this is crucial* – by a psychological aloofness from all the other members of the system. The relational gaps between the sounds of a language are just as necessary to the psychological definition of these sounds as the articulation and acoustic images which are customarily used to define them.' By contrast, 'the candle-blowing sound forms no part' of such a system (Sapir, 1949 [1925]: 35).

From this beginning, Sapir leaps to a conclusion that is potentially far more radical. Within such a system, as can be seen already, each sound is 'unconsciously felt as "placed" with reference to other sounds'; if it were not so, it would be 'no more a true element of speech' than, for example, 'a lifting of the foot is a dance step' if it cannot 'be "placed" with reference to other movements that help to define the dance'. But in a footnote to the first use of 'placed' Sapir explains that this 'has, of course, nothing to do here with "place of articulation"'. 'One may feel, for instance, that sound A is to sound B as sound X is to sound Y without having the remotest idea how and where any of them is produced.' It is therefore 'not enough' simply to 'pattern off all speech sounds as such against other sounds produced by the "organs of speech"'. There is, in addition, a 'second phase' of patterning which is 'more elusive and of correspondingly greater significance for the linguist'. This is the 'inner configuration of the sound system of a language, the intuitive "placing" of the sounds with reference to one another' (35f.). In the remainder of the paper Sapir shows by degrees how abstract he conceives it to be. The place that sounds have in it is not affected by the different ways in which two different speakers may produce them (36f.); nor by variations in the way they are produced in contexts formed by other sounds (37f.). With these 'cleared out of the way, we arrive at the genuine pattern of speech sounds'. But in the light of what he has said 'it almost goes without saying that two languages, A and B, may have identical sounds but utterly distinct phonetic patterns', or that languages with 'mutually incompatible phonetic systems, from the articulatory and acoustic standpoint', may nevertheless have 'identical or similar patterns' (38).

The evidence which reveals the 'place' of elements is partly that of alternations. Thus, in English, the *f* of *wife* is related to the *v* of *wives* just as, for example, the [s] of *house*, which like *wife* is singular, is related to the [z] of plural *hou*[z]*es*. But we must also consider how units are related in sequence. Thus, in English, *p* can be preceded by *s*: at the beginning, for example, of a word like *spoon* or at the end in words like *cusp*. So too can *t* and *k*: thus *star* and *scum* ([skʌm]) or *hoist* and *ask*. On that and other evidence these 'belong together in a coherent set' (42). Sounds that are physically alike may then, on similar evidence, not belong together. In sound alone, the *ng* of *sing* ([ŋ]) stands to a *g* ([g]) as an *m* to a *b* or an *n* to a *d*: in phonetic terms *g*, *b* and *d* are plosive; *ng*, *m* and *n* are 'nasal'. But 'in spite of what the phoneticians tell us . . . no naïve English-speaking person can be made to feel in his bones' that the nasals belong together. In particular, both *m* and *n* can come at the beginning of a word. An *ng* cannot, and in this respect it patterns as if it were two elements, first a nasal and then a plosive, not one (43). 'The whole aim and spirit of this paper', Sapir tells us in his final paragraph, has been to 'show that phonetic phenomena are not physical phenomena *per se*' (45).

Let us try to sum up. We have seen that every language has its own sound system, often, as in those that Boas and Sapir had studied, very different from our own. Within it, a determinate set of speech-sounds are distinguished by specific features, those that Sweet had called 'significant'. What is significant in one language may, again, not be significant in another. But such a 'sound' may vary: sometimes longer, sometimes shorter; sometimes with a range of qualities that, to phoneticians or to speakers of another language, seem quite different. Hence the need, in Sweet's terms, for both 'broad' and 'narrow' representations.

Within the system, each sound is related to other sounds. It is related, first, to those from which it is distinguished by 'significant' features: English [iː] from English [ɪ]; English [g] (plosive) from English [ŋ] (nasal). Such relations might be said to define what Sapir called 'the objective system of sounds'. But they are also related by their patterning: in the way they alternate or in the sequences they form. Such relations define what Sapir called an 'inner' system.

By the 1920s all this was, with hindsight, clear. But it is also clear how such ideas connect with those of Saussure. For the 'sounds' we are describing have their existence only in the system of each language. The Pawnee 'weak r' is identified by the distinctions between it and other 'sounds' of Pawnee; the *l* in English by the distinctions between it and other sounds of English. As mere sounds they are nothing, since their physical properties are not constant. In a system of 'speech-sounds', as in the Saussurean system of linguistic signs, there are no positive terms. Readers may have wondered why I have devoted a whole section to ideas that were initially so scattered. But it was in them that Saussurean theory found a concrete application; and from their synthesis the movement that we now call structuralism was born.

3.2   Phonology

The synthesis was above all that of N. S. Trubetzkoy. Trubetzkoy was thirty in 1920, and had escaped from Russia to, eventually, a chair in Vienna. Hence, among other things, the customary German spelling of his name. With Roman Jakobson, who was another Russian émigré eventually in Brno in Czechoslovakia, he became a leading member of what became known as the 'Prague School'. He died in 1938, soon after Austria was incorporated into another tyranny, with his great work on 'The Principles of Phonology' largely but not wholly finished. It was published in the *Travaux* of the Prague Linguistic Circle, whose first volume (1929) had included his first major contribution.

Let us begin with the term 'phonology'. It had in origin a sense like that of 'phonetics': thus, for Saussure, 'phonologie' had been the study of the physiology of speech-sounds, to be distinguished (in a usage subsequently peculiar to French-speaking linguists) from 'phonétique' as the study of sound change (Saussure, 1972 [1916]: 55f.). But by the 1920s a new distinction was needed. For by then, as we have seen, the properties of speech-sounds as sounds were one thing; their place in the system another. In Baudouin's terminology, the first was the domain of 'anthropophonics'; for Trubetzkoy and his associates, and in their wake all later structuralists, the term 'phonetics' was now restricted to it. The change was made by, among others, Baudouin himself (Baudouin de Courtenay, 1972 [1927]: 280). 'Phonology' was then the nearest equivalent to his 'psychophonetics'.

Shifts in terminology are not in themselves interesting. But phonetics and phonology could no longer be said to form a single science of speech sounds (what had earlier been called 'phonetics'). Phonology was concerned with specific languages. It was therefore part of what Saussure had called the 'linguistics of language systems' ('la linguistique de la langue'), or linguistics 'in the strict sense'. Phonetics was a discipline that strictly lay outside linguistics, and had clear links with the wider study of physiology or acoustics. From a linguist's viewpoint – from the viewpoint of a practitioner of 'la linguistique de la langue' – it became ancillary.

In his 'Principles of Phonology', Trubetzkoy began by drawing a distinction like that in Saussure's *Cours* (27ff.) between an act of speech ('Sprechakt') and the 'language or language structure' ('die Sprache oder das *Sprachgebilde*') that a speaker and person spoken to must share. Each has two sides which are related reciprocally: one 'signifying' ('die *bezeichnende*') and the other 'signified' ('die *bezeichnete*'). So, there must first be a signifier in each individual act of speech. This lies in the audible flow of sound, which will naturally include all manner of features with which linguists, in the Saussurean sense, are not concerned. Thus, to recall an illustration from the *Cours*, the form *Messieurs!* may be uttered physically in grossly different ways; but in the structure of French it remains, for any linguist, the same word. In each act of speech there is also something signified, and that too will include much that is peculiar to the individual context. But, in abstraction from each individual concrete message, we must then distinguish what is 'signified' in the language structure. This is not concrete, but is formed by rules which, in a specific language, differentiate and order units of meaning. As elements of the language structure these are finite in number. In parallel there must likewise, in the structure of the language, be a 'signifier'. This is in turn formed by the rules which, again in a specific language, differentiate and order units of sound. In individual acts of speech, signifiers are formed from an infinite variety of physical sounds. But, in the language structure, differences must again be finite (Trubetzkoy, 1939: 5–6).

Trubetzkoy's account is clearly inspired by Saussure, and the overall symmetry of his scheme is characteristic, as we will see in later chapters, of this period. But in the case of 'signifiers', we must now distinguish rigorously between two disciplines. One is concerned directly with the physical sounds that form the signifying side of acts of speech. This was henceforth what most linguists called 'phonetics', and is a natural science dealing with the 'material aspect' of speech-sounds ('die *Wissenschaft von der materiellen Seite der (Laute der) menschlichen Rede'*, 14). It is precisely, as a definition at the beginning of the decade had made clear, an auxiliary discipline ('discipline auxiliaire de la linguistique') 'whose subject matter is the sounds of speech in general, in abstraction from their functions in the language' ('traitant des phénomènes phoniques du langage, abstraction faite de leurs fonctions dans', if we may substitute the Saussurean term, '[la langue]') (Prague Linguistic Circle, 1931: 309).

Phonology, in contrast, is a discipline concerned with 'signifiers' in the language structure. It is the 'part of linguistics', therefore, 'dealing with the phenomena of sound from the viewpoint of their functions in the language' ('partie de la linguistique traitant des phénomènes phoniques au point de vue de leurs fonctions dans la langue'). This is again from 1931; and, as the 'Principles' make clear, a phonologist considers as a 'sound' nothing that does not have such a function. 'Der Phonologe hat *am Laut* nur dasjenige ins Auge zu fassen, *was eine bestimmte Funktion im Sprachgebilde erfüllt*' (Trubetzkoy, 1939: 14).

The basic unit of this discipline is then, as for Baudouin, the 'phoneme'. But for its new definition it will help if we look back to Sweet. For what has a 'function' in the language structure is whatever, in Sweet's term, is 'significant'. Thus, in English, the 'l' of *hill* is 'significantly' different from, for example, the 't' of *hit* or the 'd' of *hid*. It has a function in English, in distinguishing one word from another; therefore it belongs to an account of the phonology of English. But the 'l' of *hill* is not 'significantly' different from the 'l' of *heel*. What is 'significant' in these words was, in Sweet's analysis, the difference between a relatively short and a relatively long vowel: in 'broad' notation, [hil] versus [hiːl]. Therefore that alone has a 'function', and that alone has 'relevance', as Trubetzkoy now put it, to the 'phonological system' of the language.

The phoneme is then defined precisely by what is 'significant'. In Trubetzkoy's terms, the 'dark l' of *hill* would as a whole have one phonetic shape or 'sound form' ('Lautgebilde'). The 't' of *hit* would have another; so would, for example, the 'clear l' of *silly*. As 'sounds', all three are different. But a clear 'l' and a dark 'l' never distinguish one word from another. Therefore the phonetic feature that differentiates their sound forms is not 'relevant', in his term, to the phonological system. The features shared by both a dark 'l' and a clear 'l' do, however, distinguish words with, in a broad notation, [l] from words with [t] or, for example, [d]. Compare *hill*, *hit* and *hid*; *silly* and *city* (in a standard notation [sɪli] and [sɪti]); *Billy* and *Biddy*. Therefore these features, and these alone, do have 'relevance' to the system. The [d]s of *hid* or *dip*, for example, are distinguished by one 'relevant' feature from the [t]s of *hit* and *tip*; by another from the [l]s of *hill* or *lip*; by another from the [m]s of *him* or *mill*; by yet another from the [b]s of *fib* or *bill*. A phoneme, such as 'd', can accordingly be defined by just the features that distinguish it, as one unit, from all others. In Trubetzkoy's own formulation, it 'can be said', in general, to be 'the sum of all the features that are phonologically relevant' ('*die Gesamtheit der phonologisch relevanten Eigenschaften*') in a sound form (Trubetzkoy, 1939: 35).

There were other definitions of the phoneme, as we will see in a moment. But none shows more clearly how Sweet's insights, as a practical phonetician, could be elucidated by Saussurean theory. Each phoneme is an element of a system in the Saussurean sense, defined by intersecting 'differences' between it and other elements. Each 'difference' was in Trubetzkoy's account an 'opposition', and each opposition ('Gegensatz') involves one or more phonetic features. For example, 'd' in English is distinguished from 't' by the role of 'voice' (= vibration of the vocal cords) in its articulation; from 'b' by its articulation with the tongue against the ridge behind the upper teeth ('alveolar'), and so on. The phoneme itself is not a sound, identifiable independently. It is an abstraction, constituted solely by the set of 'relevant' or distinctive features, such as 'voiced' or 'alveolar', by which it is opposed to other similar abstractions.

The rest follows straightforwardly. As abstractions, phonemes enter into other relations: in their role, as we have seen from earlier studies, both in alternations and in forming sequences within words. Thus, among the rules that form 'signifers' in the structure of English is one by which, in initial position, 's' may precede, for example, 'k' (*s*[k]*um, skill,* and so on), but not follow it. For Sapir such relations had established an 'inner' system, implicitly distinguished from the 'objective system of sounds'. For Trubetzkoy, they were similarly different from the oppositions by which phonemes were themselves defined. The term 'morphology' had been used since the nineteenth century to refer to inflections and other aspects of the shape (Greek 'morphḗ') of words. In studying such relations we accordingly investigate the use, in morphology, of the phonological units of a language. In the morphology of English there are also alternations linking 'signifiers' like *drive, drove* and *driven*. Such relations had been central, as we have seen, to Baudouin's 'psychophonetics'. In Trubetzkoy's account, both alternations and relations of sequence within 'signifiers' were a part of 'morphonology' or, more fully, 'morphophonology' (Trubetzkoy, 1931: 160).

If morphonology was concerned with Sapir's 'inner' system, the 'objective system of sounds', as he described it, was the topic of phonology itself. But, in the light of what we have said, this wording is no longer as appropriate as it may at first have seemed. For, crucially, a phoneme is not simply a 'sound'. It is instead an abstraction from a multitude of sounds, and is characterised solely by particular features that are constant. We must therefore envisage a further relation by which, in the terminology of Trubetzkoy and of most other structuralists, it is 'realised by' or 'manifested by' the sounds from which it is abstracted. A speaker of English who utters, on a particular occasion, the word 'hill' can be expected to produce at the end a sound, [ɫ], which we can identify as a typical realisation, in that position, of the 'l' phoneme. But this sound that we identify is not itself that phoneme. A speaker who utters the word 'leave' will normally produce at the beginning a clear [l] which we will identify as a different realisation of 'l'. But 'l' itself is no more an [l]-sound than an [ɫ]-sound. It is no more than the set of features by which one 'symbolically utilizable counter', again in Sapir's words, is distinguished in the structure of the language from all other 'counters'. The sounds by which it is realised are describable only as the concrete 'variants', as Trubetzkoy defines them, of a unit of the language structure that is itself invariant (Trubetzkoy, 1939: 36).

These points are dealt with rather briefly. But their importance in the Saussurean tradition will at once be obvious. In the analogy that has caught the imagination of so many readers of Saussure's *Cours*, the express train from Geneva to Paris is an abstraction realised, on differing occasions, by a different engine, driver, set of carriages, and so on. Despite this it is on each occasion the 'same' train, by virtue simply of the differences between it and all others in the timetable. But analogies, however seductive, cannot be entirely convincing. The development of phonology showed for the first time, through the analysis of language itself, how a deliberate abstraction from the physical reality of speech can advance our understanding in a way that is impossible if the physical phenomena are studied directly. To describe 'sounds' as mere sounds was to embark on a sea of infinite detail. To describe them as the realisations of phonemes was to reveal a finite underlying order that, to those who discovered it, was exactly of the kind that Saussure had foreshadowed.

A final problem was that of method. The origins of phonology had lain, in part, in practical linguistics: in studies of languages or dialects in the field, and in applied phonetics. Both traditions continued, the latter in the work, especially, of the English phonetician Daniel Jones. The theory offered a foundation, therefore, for techniques that were tried and useful. Could these now be codified?

How, in particular, was a linguist to work out what the phonemes of a language are? Let us imagine, for the sake of argument, that the structure of English is unknown. We encounter people who speak it, and our first task is to discover which distinctions of sound are significant. The way we will do so followed naturally from the theory that has been explained.

We will begin by looking for word-like units that have different meanings. For example, we find that *hill* is different from *hit*, *full* from *foot*, and so on. Let us say that such words 'contrast'. We then look for minimal contrasts, between units with the shortest time span. For example, we find that *foot* contrasts with *feet*; *feet* in turn with *leat*; *feet* with *feel*. Failing evidence of still shorter time spans, we thus form the hypotheses that [f] at the beginning of a word contrasts minimally with [l], [t] at the end of a word with [ɬ], and, between them, [ʊ] with [iː]. In this way, we establish contrasts of sound in specific positions. Then, as a final step, we relate sounds that are found in different positions. Thus, at the beginning of words, we have distinguished an [l] and, at the end, an [ɬ]. We also find sounds that resemble both in medial position: for example, in *silly* and *fuller*. But nowhere will we find words in which one 'l' is in minimal contrast with another 'l'. Therefore we conclude that they are variants of a single phoneme, which we distinguish in all positions from all other phonemes.

The method was developed in elaborate and rigorous detail in the 1940s, in an early paper by the American Charles F. Hockett (Hockett, 1942). But the basic rules had been set out by Trubetzkoy (1958 [1935]: 10ff.; 1939: 41ff.) and have been taught in practice to most apprentice linguists, in one version or another, ever since. They have thus become banal; and it is hard for any writer of a later generation to recapture the enthusiasm that this unity of theory and method once inspired. Decades later, one American linguist who was young in the 1930s was to describe the phoneme, not entirely in jest, as his 'darling' (Hill, 1980: 75). Its attraction was, in large part, that the theory and method were so closely linked, each new and each informing the other.

But the link was so close that, in America in particular, the method came to dominate. In particular, the definition of the phoneme, which in Trubetzkoy's account had flowed from basic principles or assumptions, came to rest instead on codified procedures by which, in an ideal application, phonemes could be induced from data.

Let us return once more to the 'l' in English. From a phonetician's viewpoint, it is effectively a range of variant sounds: those that, in Trubetzkoy's term, 'realise' it. Thus, for Jones, a phoneme was 'a family of sounds'. It was a family 'in a given language', of sounds 'related in character' and 'used in such a way that no one member occurs in a word in the same phonetic context as any other member'. Thus a dark [ɬ] is related in its phonetic character to a clear [l], and there is no phonetic context, as defined by a position in the word or by specific sounds preceding or following, in which both are found. I have cited the definition from a book first published in 1950 (Jones, 1962 [1950]: 10). But Jones was then nearing seventy, and such definitions had been in use 'since about 1916' in 'practical language teaching' (vii). A formulation similar in essentials had been given earlier in his practical account of English phonetics (Jones, 1975 [1918]: 49).

'Definitions of the phoneme' have been a topos for commentators. For many phonologists it was in the beginning still a unit of what Baudouin had called 'psychophonetics'. It had a 'psychological content' and reflected a 'psychological distinction' between different kinds of 'phonetic opposition' (Trubetzkoy, 1929 [Vachek, 1964: 109]; 1936 [Vachek, 1964: 188]). Phonetics, 'roughly speaking', was concerned with what one actually pronounces; phonology with 'what one thinks one pronounces' ('ce qu'on s'imagine prononcer') (Trubetzkoy, 1933: 232). In the same vein Sapir had written in the 1920s of the 'psychological aloofness' of one 'counter' in the system from another. But by the end of the 1930s this way of talking had become redundant. We take for granted that a community of speakers share a language system or a 'language structure'. This has the same effect as Bloomfield's 'fundamental assumption' (2.2), of establishing the study of such systems as autonomous. The phoneme is one element in their structure, and can be defined by the distinctive oppositions that each phoneme bears to others. If our assumptions are valid there is no need to refer specifically to anything outside our discipline.

Where a Saussurean assumed that there is a language system, a Bloomfieldian assumed, as we have seen in 2.2, that there are units that recur in utterances. Such units were distinguished by sound features, and a phoneme, as Bloomfield defined it, was a 'minimum unit of distinctive sound-feature' (Bloomfield, 1935 [1933]: 79). A phoneme too is thus a unit that recurs in utterances.

Suppose then, for the sake of illustration, that I say 'The little bottle is still full.' The phoneme 'l' recurs, in this sense, five times: at the beginning and the end of 'little', and so on. Its precise phonetic quality varies, even in positions that are similar, in '-ittle' and '-ottle'. What 'recurs' is thus again a 'unit of . . . sound-feature', not literally a sound. But by the same token it can also be seen, as Jones had seen it, as a 'family of sounds'; and it is as such that, in practice, the next generation in America went on to define it. For the method that had been developed has in essence two steps. The first is one of segmentation. Thus, in this and other utterances in English, we identify the shortest 'sounds' that contrast: in that way we segment 'The little . . .' into [ð] followed by [ə] ('the') followed by a clear [l], and so on. The second step is one of classification. We class together, into a single family in Jones's sense, the clear [l] at the beginning of 'little', the dark [ɫ] of 'full' and the similar post-consonantal sound in 'bottle', with (in my speech) the slightly clearer sounds of 'still', following [ɪ] instead of [ʊ], and '-ittle'. All that remained, then, was to define this 'family' formally by operations on our data. To that end, the first need was for watertight criteria which, when applied to the analysis of utterances, would in principle identify contrasting segments. From the end of the 1930s segments were, in a term that was usual in America, 'phones'. Every 'phone' was then an 'allophone' of a phoneme. Hence there was a further need for watertight criteria which, when applied to sequences of contrasting segments, would in principle group different phones as allophones either of the same phoneme or of different phonemes.

The 'in principle' is important. The object was no longer to develop practical methods of analysis, but to set out the ideal procedures by which phonemes might be operationally defined. But it is clear, from Jones's definition in particular, that a phoneme as a class would have to meet two main criteria. One was that its members never contrast. In the terminology used in America in this period, allophones of a phoneme had to be 'in complementary distribution': the 'distribution' of one, defined by the positions in which it is found or of the sounds preceding or following it, must not overlap that of another. There were problems in making this criterion watertight, exceptions had to be taken care of, and so on. But in an account which was to pass into textbooks in the 1950s, the phoneme was defined, in part, as 'a class of allophones in complementary distribution'.

The other main criterion was that its members must be alike. In Jones's terms they were 'related in character'; or, as the American tradition put it, they would have to meet a test of 'phonetic similarity'. Again there were problems and, in particular, a requirement that all variants of a phoneme should share a distinctive set of phonetic features, which was implicit in Trubetzkoy's account in the 1930s, could not always be sustained. But if, once more, the criteria by which phones are established were watertight, and these and other principles of classification were made watertight in turn, the phoneme needed no other definition. It was precisely the unit that, in the analysis of a body of data in any language, would result from the rigorous application of the criteria which had been set out.

We will return to phonology in the next chapter, where we must consider its implications, in the 1950s especially, for historical linguistics. From then on its development, however fascinating, is that of one branch of linguistics, and need detain us only in passing. But in its formative period phonology was the heart of structural linguistics. In the 1870s Sweet had believed already that 'phonetics', in the sense in which that term was used in his day, was 'the indispensable foundation of all study of language': be 'that study', he went on, 'purely theoretical or practical as well'. This, he said, was 'generally admitted' ([1877], cited with similar passages in Sweet, 1971: vii). In the early twentieth century many of the best minds in linguistics worked in this field, and it was in the theories of Trubetzkoy and his contemporaries that what we now see as the main ideas of Saussure's *Cours* were first applied fruitfully. In later chapters we will see how these ideas were also extended to other aspects of language. But, again and again, when faced with problems of theory or method in another domain, linguists were to turn to current phonological theories, to concepts such as that of distinctive oppositions, or to the practical methods of analysis that phonologists had developed, both for general inspiration and for specific models.

The study of sound systems has in consequence remained a popular and influential subject. The editor of *Language*, which is the leading general linguistic journal, reported in 1996 that in that year, of the hundred or so typescripts sent to him, more than a quarter were in phonology as it has later come to be understood ([Aronoff], 1997: 466). The figures for 1995 and later years, though lower, were still high. To observers in other disciplines, the fascination of so many linguists with this aspect of language may at first seem puzzling. Systems of sounds are, after all, but one quite small part of the total 'language structure'. But it derives from a tradition of research and teaching that was the centre of linguistics throughout one crucial and exciting phase.

3.3   'Structuralism'

By the end of the 1930s Bloomfield's 'newer trend of linguistic study', as he had called it in the early 1920s, was formally christened. It is not known exactly when or by whom the terms 'structural' and 'structuralism' were coined. But Trubetzkoy referred in German to 'the language or the language structure' ('die Sprache oder das *Sprachgebilde*') (again Trubetzkoy, 1939), and this usage can be traced back in the Prague School for ten years. For the Danish linguist Viggo Brøndal, 'structuralism' was by then already known by that name (Brøndal, 1943 [1939]: 95). It seems that the term clicked at once for everyone.

Its sense is made clear in the same year, in an introduction to phonology by the Dutch linguist N. van Wijk. A language, as he explains in the preface, is 'a collective possession of a community' ('een collectief bezit van een gemeenschap'). This clearly follows Saussure. 'In the mind of each member' of such a community 'the language exists as a system with a determinate structure' ('leeft de taal als een system van een bepaalde structuur'), and the task of a linguist is to work out such 'structures'. The history of a language is also necessarily the history of its 'structure'; not that simply of the individual words and other units, in abstraction from their mutual relations (Van Wijk, 1939: xiii). Phonology itself is accordingly described in his title as 'a chapter of structural linguistics' ('een hoofdstuk uit de structurele taalwetenschap'). In an article of the same year, H. J. Pos distinguishes the 'structuralism' of Trubetzkoy and other phonologists from the 'nominalism', as he describes it, that had informed earlier descriptions of speech-sounds. In the 'nominalist' view, such sounds were no more than noises, studied individually without reference to the mind of the speaker ('sujet parlant') who produces them. Structuralism, in contrast, has both placed them in the larger system to which they belong and made clear that their reality lies in their relation to the consciousness ('conscience') of individuals who speak and understand what is spoken (Pos, 1939: 72–4). Pos was writing in Trubetzkoy's memorial volume in the *Travaux* of the Prague Linguistic Circle, and phonology is central to his argument. But similar insights would be fruitful in the study of meaningful units (74ff.).

It is perhaps a coincidence that Van Wijk and Pos were both writing in Holland. But it is no accident that both took their inspiration from phonology. For Jakobson, commenting on Van Wijk's book, this was not only the first part of structural linguistics to be realised; the phoneme, as its fundamental concept, had thereby become 'a touchstone of structuralism' generally ('und gerade deshalb fiel dem Phonem als einem phonologischen Grundbegriff die Rolle eines Prüfsteins des Strukturalismus zu') (Jakobson, 1962 [1939]: 284).

Its extension beyond phonology belongs more to the 1940s and 1950s. But let us return, by way of introduction, to the principle of contrast. In comparing *hill* with, for example, *hit* and *hid* we establish contrasts between (in a broad notation) [l], [t] and [d]. In the same way, if we compare *Walk up the hill* with *Walk down the hill* and *Walk over the hill*, we establish contrasts between *up*, *down* and *over*. In both cases, we are performing operations in which something is held constant and other things are changed. Thus, holding constant *Walk — the hill*, we replace *up*, in the position marked by a dash, with *down* or *over*. Likewise, holding [hɪ] constant, we replace [l], in the position following, with [t] or [d]. When the replacements are made the meanings of the whole are altered. Therefore the results in one case show that [l], [t] and [d] must realise, or be members of, three different phonemes. In the other they establish that there are differences, of some sort, between *up*, *down* and *over*. Of precisely what sort we have not said: we will return to that problem later. But the method of comparison is the same.

If we hold [ɪl] constant, we can replace [h] in initial position (— [ɪl]) with [p] (*pill*) or with [s] (*sill*); if we hold — *up the hill* constant we can replace *walk* with, for example, *run* or *climb*; and so on. We thus establish a structure in which units are related on two axes. On the one hand, they are related to others that precede or follow. For example, there is a relation in *hill* between [h] and [ɪ]; likewise between [p] and [ɪ] in *pill*, [h] and [ʌ] in *hull* and any other elements that can individually replace either. There is also a relation between *walk*, *run* or *climb* and *up*, *down* or *over*. This kind of relation had been described, in Saussure's *Cours*, as 'syntagmatic' (see again Saussure, 1972 [1916]: 172f.).

On the other hand, each unit is related to the others that can replace it. In the initial position in, for example, — [ɪl], [h] is related to [p], [s], [f], and so on. In the second position in *Walk — the hill*, *up* is similarly related to other units such as *down* and *over*. Relations on this axis are said, from this period onwards, to be 'paradigmatic'. Our basic method, therefore, is to take a stretch of speech in which we assume that units are related syntagmatically, and to look for contrasts in specific positions. We do not know at first how many positions will be established. Thus we can only guess, ahead of our analysis, that [hɪl] realises three successive phonemes; or that *Walk up the hill* is made up of *walk*, *up*, *the* and *hill*. But, by our analysis, we will validate relations on both axes. In establishing that [h], [ɪ] and [l] stand independently in paradigmatic relations we confirm that just these segments are related syntagmatically. In establishing that *up*, for example, is related paradigmatically to units such as *down* and *over*, we also establish that it is itself a unit, which is therefore related syntagmatically to, as we will establish similarly, *walk*. In failing to establish paradigmatic relations between segments like *up* with a shorter time span (*u-*, say, or *-p*) we confirm that it is a minimal unit. When we get down to basics, the method that distinguishes phonemes and the one by which we validate larger units like *up* seem to be similar.

The term 'paradigmatic' was first introduced by the Danish scholar Louis Hjelmslev, in a conference paper in 1936 (Hjelmslev, 1938: 140). In the *Cours* Saussure had called relations of this kind 'associative' (thus, for an example involving sounds, *Cours*, 180), and many commentators, following Hjelmslev himself, have implied that 'associative' had the same sense. But Saussure's concept was in reality much wider. A prominent diagram (175) shows four series of associative relations in which the word *enseignement* ('teaching') is linked first to, among others, *enseigner* 'to teach' and *enseignons* 'we teach'; then to other nouns whose meaning is similar (*apprentisage* 'training', *éducation* 'education'); then to others that are formed with *-ment* (*changement* 'change', *armement* 'armament'); then to words of other kinds which end with the same syllable (the adjective *clément* 'clement' or the adverb *justement* 'justly, precisely'). In short, Saussure meant what might be expected from the term 'associative'. The relation is in general between any units that may be 'associated' in the minds of speakers.

In proposing the new term Hjelmslev said that his motive was to avoid the 'psychologisme' (n. 3) of the old. But by the end of the 1930s structural linguistics was not only autonomous. It was a technical discipline concerned with problems of method and definition that Saussure could scarcely have formulated. They had been solved, as we have seen, for phonemes, and the next step was to solve them for other units. Of the relations that Saussure had originally called 'associative', only those that formed the axis of contrast were relevant.

The American school did not in general use this terminology. But it was in America, in the 1940s, that the basic operation was most rigorously developed. In *Walk up the hill*, a grammarian will also see a close relation between *the* and *hill*, forming a larger unit called a 'phrase'. But why do *the* and *hill* form a phrase and not, say, *up* and *the*? The issue was explicitly addressed by Zellig Harris, in work first published in 1946. In *Walk up the hill* we can replace *the hill* with *it*, with *Ben Nevis*, with *the mountain over there*, and with many other such forms. We can also replace it, with the same forms, when it is in other positions: for example, in *The hill is too steep*. There are no replacements, on the same scale and applying so generally, for *up the*. For 'replacement' Harris talks of 'substitution'. The method by which we analyse a sentence will accordingly 'require . . . no other operation than substitution, repeated time and again' (Harris, 1946: 161).

4   Diachrony

From the 1940s onwards structural linguists were increasingly distinct from linguists in general. Structuralist schools were not established equally in all countries: scarcely at all, for example, in Italy or in Germany. But in the United States especially to be 'a linguist' was increasingly to be a structuralist. Above all, it was to be a 'descriptive' linguist. The term 'descriptive' has many resonances, and can easily be misunderstood. But for Americans its sense was like that of Saussure's 'synchronic'. In a leading introduction to linguistics, '*descriptive* or *synchronic* linguistics' was the study of 'how a language works at a given time, regardless of its past history or future destiny' (Hockett, 1958: 303). It deals with 'the design of the language of some community at a given time' (321).

But Saussurean linguistics also had a 'diachronic' or historical branch. How was that affected?

When the *Cours* appeared this branch was dominant. Saussure himself had been young in Leipzig in the 1870s, when the so-called 'Junggrammatiker' or 'neogrammarians' formulated basic principles of change in language. It was through their work above all that, we are told, 'linguistics in the true sense' ('la linguistique proprement dite') had been born (Saussure, 1972 [1916]: 18f.). It is not surprising therefore that the chapters of the *Cours* devoted to its diachronic side (Part 3, 193ff.) say so little that was new. Of the structuralists who followed, Bloomfield had been trained in the tradition of the neogrammarians, and his masterly account of language change, which forms most of the latter half of *Language*, was based firmly on their principles. They were applied above all in his brilliant work on the Algonquian family in North America, summarised in one of his last papers (Bloomfield, 1946).

But the foundations of linguistics were by then seen differently. For Hermann Paul, in the 1880s, the only 'scientific treatment of language' had been historical. 'The moment one goes beyond the mere registration of details, the moment one tries to grasp the way they are related and to make sense of the phenomena, one is at once in the field of history, even if perhaps one is not clear about it' ('Sobald man über das blosse

Konstatieren von Einzelheiten hinausgeht, sobald man versucht den Zusammenhang zu erfassen, die Erscheinungen zu begreifen, so betritt man auch den geschichtlichen Boden, wenn auch vielleicht ohne sich klar darüber zu sein') (Paul, 1920 [1880]: 20). For the Danish scholar Otto Jespersen, the historical view had 'brought about a vast change in the science of language'. 'Instead of looking at such a language as Latin as one fixed point', and then 'fixing' another, like French, 'in one classical form', nineteenth-century linguistics 'viewed both as being in constant flux, as growing, as moving, as continually changing'. It 'cried aloud like Heraclitus "Pánta reî" . . .' (Jespersen, 1922: 32f.).

But if one followed Saussure, Latin, for example, had indeed to be a fixed point. It may be that, in the maxim of Heraclitus, 'all things are' in reality 'in flux'. But, to study the history of a language, we must first abstract successive stages through which, like the pieces in his image of the chess board, it has passed. Each stage can be described synchronically, and each description can stand, as a treatment of one 'state of the language', on its own. A diachronic account is secondary.

Bloomfield's definition of a language was not, as we have seen, Saussure's (2.2). But for him too 'all historical study of language is based upon the comparison of two or more sets of descriptive data'. To describe a language 'one needs no historical knowledge whatever'; if indeed we have such knowledge and we allow it to influence our description, it 'is bound to distort the data' (Bloomfield, 1935 [1933]: 19f.). For a later Bloomfieldian, linguistics in a narrow sense could be divided into descriptive linguistics, which was concerned with 'descriptive grammars', and 'contrastive linguistics', in which different descriptive grammars were compared. Historical linguistics was a branch of contrastive linguistics (Trager, 1949).

This new view gave rise to new insights and new problems. The earliest concern the history of sound systems: we will therefore take that field first (4.1). But for a more general orientation it will help if we return to Saussure's parallel with a chess game (2.1). Each player, once again, moves one piece at a time; similarly changes in a language were individual, and each led from an old 'state of the language' ('état de la langue') to a new one. Between moves the pieces form a determinate pattern on the board. Similarly, a language was at any moment in one state of 'equilibrium', which the next change would replace with a new 'equilibrium'. The only important difference, we are told, is that moves in chess are made intentionally. 'A language', in contrast, 'has no intention' ('la langue ne prémédite rien'). Changes occur 'spontaneously and by chance' ('spontanément et fortuitement') (*Cours*, 125ff.).

But is that always so? We must grant, of course, that no supervisory agent alters languages deliberately. But speakers are agents, and changes in a language system must originate in and be sanctioned by their speech. Is it likely, therefore, that all changes are fortuitous? In a game of chess, the players calculate their moves with reference to the present and future position of the pieces. A queen is threatened and for that reason it may be moved or the piece that threatens it may be taken. Now, once again, a language does not calculate; nor do its speakers as a body change it consciously. But might some changes come about not blindly but, in part at least, as a response to the state its system is then in?

Let us take a famous example, based on studies contemporary with the *Cours*, by the dialectologist Jules Gilliéron. From the findings of the French Linguistic Atlas, published by Gilliéron and his assistant Edmont, it was clear that in Gascony, from the Garonne southwards, a consonant that was *ll* in Latin had changed, at the end of a word, to *t*. For example, Latin *coll(um)* 'neck' had become *cot*. It was also clear that, in the west of this region in particular, the word for 'cock' was an innovation. In surrounding dialects it was derived from Latin *gall(us)*; so, in the area of this sound change, we would expect *gat*. But in the region around Bordeaux the word for 'cock' was instead related to French *vicaire* 'curate'; further south, to French *faisan* 'pheasant'. It seemed, then, that these dialects had undergone two separate changes. By a change in their sound systems Latin *-ll* was now *-t*. By change in their vocabulary, the expected word for 'cock' had been replaced.

But in Gilliéron's account these changes were connected. For, in the same dialects, the word for a 'cat' (Latin *catt(us)*) had the form *gat*; and, by the sound change, an earlier *gall* ('cock') would also, as we have seen, become *gat*. In rural communities this would have led to misunderstandings, which speakers could avoid only by replacing at least one of these forms. Now alongside *gat* 'cat' there was a feminine: *gata* 'female cat'. Its form was simple and transparent (masculine *gat* + feminine ending *-a*). Alongside the word for 'cock' there was also a feminine ('hen'), but its form was less transparent. In Latin it had been *gallina*: *gall(us)* + *-ina*. But *ll* did not change to *t* between vowels; instead it changed to *r*: *garina*. The relation of *gat* 'cock' to *garina* 'hen' would thus have been obscure, while that of *gat* 'cat' to *gata* 'female cat' remained clear. Hence, it is argued, *gat* 'cat' was retained, while *gat* in the sense of 'cock' came to be avoided. Speakers then found new ways to refer to cocks.

Gilliéron was no structuralist and his general ideas must be inferred from detailed analyses of these and other findings. But in Saussurean terms the first sound change must be seen as one move on the chess board. By it the expected word for 'cock' would become, in the new 'state of the language', a homonym of *gat* 'cat'. But the language would then be dysfunctional, since speakers need distinct forms with these meanings. In a metaphor that runs through Gilliéron's own writings, the dialects affected are or would be in a partly 'pathological' state ('un état pathologique'). Therefore 'therapy' was needed; and this too was in part determined by the state the system was then in. For by another move on the chess board an original -*ll*- between vowels became or had become *r*; and, in the state of the 'langue' that that gave rise to, the forms for 'cock' and 'hen' would be at best obscurely related. The 'therapeutic' adjustment was made at a point where the relations within the system were weak. The replacement of *gat* ('cock') is not, in this account, 'spontaneous', and all that was 'fortuitous', in the next move, was the particular form (related to *vicaire* or to *faisan*) that groups of speakers had recourse to.

Gilliéron died in the 1920s and was, to repeat, no structuralist. But the image of pathology and therapy, or the general way of thinking that goes with it, was to inspire many others.

4.1   Diachronic phonology

If each language has a determinate structure, its history, as Van Wijk remarked at the end of the 1930s, is the history of that structure (3.3). It was in phonology that the synchronic study of this structure was first fully realised. It is not surprising therefore that it was in phonology, in the work of Van Wijk and his contemporaries, that a structuralist theory of diachrony was first proposed.

One early essay is by Roman Jakobson. In the 'traditional' account, as he describes it, every sound is treated in isolation. Thus, in our example from Gascony, the consonant derived from earlier -*ll* would have been at one time like that of surrounding dialects; its articulation then changed, in a way that we can treat with reference to this consonant alone, to that of -*t*. But for phonologists a speech-sound is not isolated: each 'phonological fact' is treated as a 'partial whole' related to other 'partial sets' at higher levels (Jakobson, 1949 [1931]: 316). The 'first principle' of historical phonology is, correspondingly, that 'each change must be treated in relation to the system within which it takes place' ('*toute modification doit être traitée en fonction du système á l'intérieur duquel elle a lieu*'). Thus, in the example from Gascony, the change of -*ll* to -*t* would have to be considered with reference to the relations, within the system, that this unit bore to other units.

The nature of a phonological system was by then becoming clear (3.2). Its elements were phonemes, each characterised, in the account of Trubetzkoy and other members of the Prague School, by a set of distinctive features. In my form of English, for example, the vowel 'ɪ' (in *pit*) shares one feature with, among others, 'ɛ' (in *pet*) and 'a' (in *pat*). In a phonetician's classification these are all 'front' vowels, produced with the front part of the tongue nearest the roof of the mouth. It is also distinctively 'close' (produced with the lower jaw raised and the tongue near the roof of the mouth). This feature it shares with, among others, the 'back' vowel 'ʊ' (in *put*). Among the front vowels 'ɪ' is then distinguished from 'mid' 'ɛ' (with the jaw more open) and 'open' 'a' (with full opening). As a back vowel 'ʊ' can be distinguished in parallel from a 'mid' 'ɒ' (in *pot*) and an 'open' 'ʌ' (in *putt*). This part of the system is thus formed by a network of relations in which 'ɪ' (*pit*) is to 'ʊ' (*put*) as 'ɛ' (*pet*) is to 'ɒ' (*pot*) and 'a' (*pat*) is to 'ʌ' (*putt*); this is shown diagrammatically in Fig. 1.

ɪ   ʊ

ɛ   ɒ

a   ʌ

Figure 1

Suppose then that in such a system a distinction between phonemes is lost. For example, every speaker of this form of English once distinguished 'ʊə' (in *moor* or *poor*) from 'ɔː' (in *more* or *pour*). Like 'ʊ' and 'ɒ' these were respectively close back and mid back, and opposed as in Fig. 2 to close front 'ɪə' (in *pier*) and mid front 'ɛː' (in *pear*).

ɪə   ʊə

ɛː   ɔː

Figure 2

But many speakers now no longer distinguish them. In Jakobson's terminology (1949 [1931]: 319), a former distinction is becoming 'dephonologised'. But this does not merely reduce the number of phonemes. It also alters the system. Where there was once symmetry, with a pair of front vowels balanced by an equal pair of back vowels, there would now be asymmetry, with two front vowels, 'ɪə' and 'ɛː', but just one back vowel corresponding to them.

In other instances a new distinction is 'phonologised' (321). But that, in turn, does not mean simply that the number of units is increased: we must again ask how the system at large is affected. Now it is obvious that, in either case, some changes will impair its symmetry: thus, for speakers who have lost the contrast between 'ʊə' and 'ɔː', front vowels are no longer balanced equally by back vowels. But others will enhance it. Consonant systems, for example, often distinguish series of consonants with the features 'labial', 'dental'/'alveolar', 'velar'. These are produced respectively with the lips, as English 'p'; with the tip of the tongue behind the upper teeth, as English 't'; and with the body of the tongue raised to the roof of the mouth, as English 'k'. Let us suppose then that at a certain stage a language has three labials ('p', 'b' and 'm') and three dental/alveolars ('t', 'd' and 'n'). As 'p' is to 't' and 'b' is to 'd' so 'm', which is distinctively 'nasal', is to the corresponding nasal 'n'. But there might be no distinct nasal in the velar series: just 'k' and 'g' with no 'ŋ'. So, as shown in Fig. 3, there is what is often called a 'gap' or 'hole' in the system.

p	t	k
b	d	g
m	n	

Figure 3

By a later change the gap might then be 'filled' and the asymmetry eliminated. It may seem tendentious to use words like 'impair' and 'enhance'. But might it not be that, all else being equal, systems change in ways that will reduce asymmetry? In Gilliéron's metaphor, a lack of balance is 'pathological'. A change which leads to greater balance will be 'therapeutic'. It will bring the system closer to an ideal 'healthy' state.

These are Gilliéron's terms, not Jakobson's; and, for the most part, Jakobson did little more than set out logically the ways in which a change within a system might be classified. But in the final section of his paper he insists that 'when we look at a linguistic change in its synchronic context' it is within the scope of teleology. ('*Quand nous considérons une mutation linguistique dans le contexte de la synchronie linguistique, nous l'introduisons dans la sphère des problèmes téléologiques*' (334).) This implies again that changes are not blind and fortuitous; they have a purpose which, we are then told, may be obvious. Thus a specific change might be preceded by 'a disturbance in the balance of a system' ('une rupture de l'équilibre du système'). The change might then result in a removal of the imbalance ('une suppression du déséquilibre'). If so, Jakobson said, we have no difficulty in discovering ('aucune peine à découvrir') its 'function'. 'Its task is to *restore the balance*' ('sa tâche est de *rétablir l'équilibre*'), which had earlier been lost.

These brief remarks will not perhaps bear too much commentary. But if we take this view the obvious question is 'whose purpose'? There is again no agent that watches over language systems and ensures that an 'imbalance' is corrected. So what precisely did this mean?

One thing it might mean is that phonological systems are self-regulating. Let us compare, for example, a thermostat. It is set to maintain a stable temperature: so, if the temperature falls below that level, the heating will switch on. The 'purpose' of this adjustment, if we must speak teleologically, is to 'restore' the correct temperature. If the temperature then rises too high, the heating will switch off. The 'aim' is still to keep the temperature steady. This analogy will not have been so obvious in the 1930s. But, similarly, for each part of a language system there are properties that will, in general, be maintained or maximised. In the case of phonology these are, or include, those of 'balance'. But just as in a building there are many factors, both internal and external, that continually affect the temperature, so there are many factors that, as they impinge on phonological systems, can lead to 'imbalance'. A system will continually initiate adjustments whose 'purpose', if we must again speak in that way, is to 'restore the balance'.

If this were so, we would have no need to speak teleologically. The system simply conforms to laws that govern it. To the extent that they are satisfied its structure is 'in balance'. Where they are not it is 'unbalanced', and there is pressure to correct it. But new 'imbalances' will continually arise. Sometimes they will be brought about by changes that originate outside the system. But they may also result from changes that the system has itself made in response to earlier pressures. Thus, in correcting a 'disequilibrium' at one point, it may create a new 'disequilibrium' at another. In Jakobson's words, this 'often' leads to 'a whole series of stabilising changes' ('toute une chaîne de mutations stabilisatrices').

This is certainly one interpretation of what Jakobson said. But if we take it literally the 'pressures', as we have called them, are exerted directly on the system. The Saussurean 'langue', of which the phonological system is a part, is seen as monitoring and adjusting its own state, independently of the community of speakers, who at any time will simply instantiate it, in acts of 'parole', as it stands. The obvious objection is that 'languages' do not exist as independent entities. There would be no chess game if there were no players. There would be no language system if there were no speakers; and it is surely on them that the 'pressure' truly bears.

The pressures implied were made clear in the early 1950s, in a series of brilliant studies, written at first in exile in New York, by the French linguist André Martinet. At the most general level speakers need, above all, to be understood; therefore they are under pressure to maintain distinctions between phonemes and, in this way, between words and other units of meaning. But, as Martinet saw it, they are also constrained to spend as little energy, in speech as in other things, as they can. 'Linguistic evolution' is accordingly governed by 'the continual paradox' ('l'antinomie permanente') that, on the one hand, people have a need to communicate and express their feelings ('des besoins communicatifs et expressifs de l'homme') and, on the other hand, they tend to make do with the minimum of physical and mental effort ('de sa tendance à réduire au minimum son activité mentale et physique') (Martinet, 1955: 94). Such pressures are permanently opposed and never wholly reconciled. The more clearly speakers try to distinguish between one sound and another, the greater the effort they must make. But, if they make too little effort, the distinction will be at risk.

We may therefore expect sound changes to reflect both pressures. Sometimes, when in practice there is no risk of misunderstanding, a distinction will no longer be kept up. Thus, in my form of English, there was no serious danger, in most contexts where these words are used, that *poor* might be mistaken for *pour*, *moor* for *more*, and so on. But other changes tend to enhance distinctions. In the history of Spanish, for example, a consonant that was historically a [ts] had changed, by the early seventeenth century, to [θ]: thus [katsar] 'to hunt' (spelled *cazar*) became, as in present-day Castilian, [kaθar]. In the same period another, that was historically like [ʃ] in English *ship*, changed to [x]: for example, [bjeʃo] 'old' (*viejo*) became, as generally in modern Spanish, [bjexo]. Before these changes, the relations into which these phonemes entered could be displayed as in Fig. 4

p	t	ts		tʃ	k
b	d				g
f			s	ʃ	

Figure 4

(compare Martinet, 1955 [1951–2]: 323). Their effect was to replace it with the system in Fig. 5,

p	t		tʃ	k
b	d			g
f	θ	s		x

Figure 5

in which, as Martinet points out, the consonants are more clearly differentiated. In its former state, both [ts] and [ʃ] were phonetically similar to other sibilant (or 's-like') units: a [tʃ] (*ch*), as in modern *fecha* 'date', and an [s], as in *casa* 'house', which is produced in modern Castilian with the extreme tip of the tongue against the teeth-ridge. In Martinet's words, the system 'suffered' from a concentration of sounds in this region ('ce système souffre de trop de concentration dans le domaine des sifflantes'), while 'other articulatory possibilities', which were plainly open in a language with relatively few phonemes, were not exploited (323). In the new system, the phonemes are more clearly distinguished.

In cases like this we can see how a system might be represented as, in effect, 'correcting an imbalance'. Thus, in terms of the features that these tables imply, the change of [ts] to [θ] also fills a 'gap' in the 't' series and that of [ʃ] to [x] a corresponding 'gap' in the 'k' series. But the locus of change lies in the habits and perceptions of successive groups of speakers. To distinguish the consonants in *viejo* or *cazar* some would have shifted their articulation, at first slightly and at first sporadically. But the system could, at that stage, still be said to be the one they had inherited. Such shifts were soon familiar; they would have become less slight and more frequent; and finally new generations, as they learned to speak from the example of their elders, would have interpreted what they commonly heard as [θ] or [x] as indeed, in terms of their distinctive features, 'θ' and 'x'. Their language had, we can then say, the new system. An important factor, in Martinet's general theory, is the 'attraction' of an 'integrated system' ('l'attraction exercée par le système intégré') (Martinet, 1955: 80). Thus, in the case of 'gaps' or 'cases vides' (80ff.), the system in general, in which series of phonemes stand in parallel relations, exerts a pull on sounds that are not 'fully integrated'. But the pull is exerted on a changing population of speakers, and in particular, as in Martinet's discussion of a later change in Spanish (84f.), on new speakers.

In the same way systems can be seen as influenced by other systems. 'Les langues', as Martinet remarks at one point, 'do not evolve in an ivory tower' (89). People who speak one language or dialect will engage with people who speak others; many are bilingual. Nor are the boundaries of a speech community established for all time. A population may speak language A; but then, through contact with a population that speaks language B, they may more and more speak that instead. Later generations may lose A altogether, as, for example, many descendants of Welsh speakers now speak only English. We all know that, in learning a new language, we will speak it with a foreign accent. 'Habits of pronunciation' will be carried over from the one we speak already. So, when language A gives way to language B, we might expect that habits of this kind might sometimes be retained. For example, aspects of the English spoken in Wales or Ireland might reflect specific features 'carried over' from the Celtic languages.

When Martinet was writing this had long been familiar. But here too a structuralist will look at systems and not simply at sounds. In mediaeval Spanish, for example, there had also been a phonological distinction between voiceless and voiced sibilants: voiceless 'ts', 'tʃ', 's' and 'ʃ' were thus opposed to voiced 'dz', 'dʒ', 'z' and 'ʒ'. But over the centuries Castilian in the north gained many speakers from Basque; and in contemporary Basque, as Martinet reconstructs it (1955 [1951–2]: 317), voiced sibilants were not separate phonemes. Let us imagine, following Martinet, a community of Basque speakers who learn Spanish as a foreign language. They would hear a word in Spanish with, for example, a 'ts'; this they would identify, as a phoneme, with the 'ts' in their own system. But they would also hear words with a Spanish 'dz' and, since [ts] and [dz] did not realise different phonemes in Basque, they would identify that too as realising their 'ts'. They would accordingly pronounce both consonants alike; and, in practice, native Spanish speakers, though themselves distinguishing 'ts' and 'dz', might not usually misunderstand or need to correct them. Their descendants then progressively speak Spanish more than Basque, and in time Spanish only. But the dialect of these descendants, on the northern boundary of the larger area in which Spanish is spoken, would be one in which pairs such as 'ts' and 'dz' were no longer distinguished. Now it was from these speakers that, as the use of Spanish continued to spread, still further generations of Basque speakers would learn it. That dialect of Spanish would thus become more widespread. It was also from the very north, as Martinet reminds us in another section of his study, that the Christian Reconquista started. For speakers to the south this dialect then became 'a model to imitate' (310), and, for other Spanish speakers, the distinctions were in time lost.

The explanation for these changes is 'external'. Martinet was invoking the impact, on the system of Spanish, of another system. For those cited earlier, by which [ts] became [θ] and [ʃ] became [x], it is 'internal'. We were invoking an inherent 'imbalance'. In each case, when we speak in that way, we are dealing with an abstraction. 'Spanish', qua 'langue', was not directly under pressure, at one stage, to adapt to 'Basque' any more than, later, it was directly under pressure to enhance its symmetry. But the mapping of one system onto the other is essential to a structuralist understanding of what happened.

4.2   System and norm

Let us return, in the light of these insights, to Saussure's analogy of the chess game. It was now in one way more exact, in that not all change in language is, in the words of the *Cours*, 'spontaneous' and 'fortuitous'. But in another way it was too simple. To describe a move in chess, we need say only that piece A was on one square and is now on another square. Nothing more is relevant. Likewise, we might say, a consonant that was 'ʒ' in an earlier 'state' of Spanish became, in a subsequent 'state', 'ʃ' and, in a still later 'state', 'x'. But these changes were in practice neither instantaneous nor separate; both spread gradually, over many years, through a large community. 'It is inconceivable', as Martinet remarks, 'that the whole nation, from Burgos to Granada' should have pronounced a word like *viejo*, in which *j* had earlier been [ʒ], in one way 'in 1550', and in a new way, with [x], 'in 1625' (1955 [1951–2]: 319f.). What do we suppose, he asks, of a speaker whose lifetime spans this period? As the changes spread the usage of successive speakers will have varied, with their age, with the region in which they lived, and with their social status. For it is also clear that the ruling classes were the last to give up the old forms (320).

Let us take another, somewhat simplified illustration, this time from the order of units in sentences. In modern English one does not say, for example, *Then rode Alfred to Winchester*. The verb must instead follow the subject (*Then Alfred rode to Winchester*). But the order of *Then rode . . .* is normal in related Germanic languages and was once normal in English also. Therefore, in Saussurean terms, the system has changed: what was once required is now excluded. But we can hardly imagine that at a certain moment every speaker switched from the inherited order to the new. For a time both would have been heard; and, at first, the new arrangement might have been rare. Then, gradually, it began to prevail: fewer speakers used the old one, they used it less often, and the range of words with which they used it narrowed. Eventually the modern order was so normal that, as children learned the language, they would hear the old one only in a range of residual uses. Therefore they would learn it only as an exception; and, for later generations, its scope was set to narrow further.

In both cases we must envisage a gradual shift in usage: in which, at first, more Spanish speakers normally said [ʒ] and, by the end, more normally said [ʃ] or [x]; in which the majority of English speakers may, in one period, have preferred to say *Then rode Alfred . . .* and, in a later period, to say *Then Alfred rode . . .* It is further evident that, in phonetics at least, there can be shifts of usage that will leave the system unchanged. In an article in the 1930s, Archibald Hill had remarked that, in the Southern United States, 'the whole . . . vowel system' would strike a phonetician coming from New England as 'a notch higher' (= closer) than in other parts of the country. These differences must have their origin in earlier changes, by which usage in one population diverged from that of others. But between the dialects there were 'no striking differences in phonemic pattern' (Hill, 1936: 15). Therefore, in Hill's terms, the historical shifts had been 'phonetic', not 'phonemic'. In the terms that Jakobson had used a few years earlier, there was no change to the phonological system: no difference between sounds was either 'phonologised' or 'dephonologised', and the features that distinguished phonemes were also unaffected. All that had shifted were the precise vowel qualities by which the system of oppositions was realised.

The problem for Saussurean theory is clear and is central. For, in the view that had been presented in the *Cours*, each 'language' is a system of invariants; and it is to such a 'langue' or language system, which exists in each community as a 'fait social' or social reality, that an individual speaker has to conform. Change in a speaker's 'language' is thus change in the system. But at the level of speech a change will not be instantaneous, either across a community or for each individual in it. There will instead be periods in which usage varies from one form of realisation to another; and, even where it is claimed that the system does not change, similar patterns of variation may be found. These patterns too are part of the 'social reality' to which speakers conform. An American born and bred in Charleston or Atlanta will be socially constrained to speak like others in the Southern states, a Bostonian like others in Boston. A grandee born in Spain in the 1540s would have spoken throughout his life like others of his age and social standing; a peasant born in 1600 like others of his district. Each individual's 'language', in an ordinary sense, will conform in such ways to the usage of the community in which they are at home. But there is a discrepancy between a 'language' in that sense, and the processes of change in such a 'language', and the Saussurean notion of a system, and of change as a transition from one system to the next.

The most constructive critique was that of the Romanian Eugenio Coseriu, in work first published in Montevideo in the early 1950s. For Saussure, the term 'parole' had referred to concrete acts of speaking: to individual acts of utterance by individual speakers in individual circumstances. A 'langue' was, in contrast, at once abstract and a social construct. There was in this way 'an initial identification' of what was 'individual' with what was 'concrete' ('parole') and what was 'social' with what was, as Coseriu put it, 'formal' or 'functional' (Coseriu, 1962 [1952]: 53). But we can see now that Saussure's dichotomy had conflated things that are logically separate. A distinction, for example, between phonemes is indeed both 'functional' and 'social'. The way in which a phoneme will be realised is, however, social but not *'functional'*: it does not have 'relevance', again in Trubetzkoy's sense, to the phonological system. But it is not simply 'individual'. In realising 'l' in English, speakers do not freely articulate a 'clear' [l] or a 'dark' [ɫ] as each individual is inclined. Instead they follow a set of 'norms' by which it is clear or clearer in some positions in a word and dark or darker in others. The term 'norm' is Coseriu's, and norms too are 'social'.

Coseriu's solution was to recognise not one but two successive levels of abstraction. At a higher level we can establish a system. But it is no more than 'a system of possibilities' ('es sistema de posibilidades'), of 'coordinates' specifying what is open to speakers and what is excluded ('que indican caminos abiertos y caminos cerrados') (98). Our example from syntax has no parallel in Coseriu's own illustrations. But, in a simplified story, English as a system may at one time have allowed both orders. In this construction one could, in principle, say *Then rode Alfred* . . . ; and one could also, in principle, say *Then Alfred rode* . . .

But the system is then not the primary abstraction from speech. What in reality is 'imposed on' an individual ('que . . . se impone al individuo') is instead conformity to a 'norm'. Let us take, from among Coseriu's illustrations, the words in Spanish for 'actress' (*actriz*) and for 'manageress' (*directora*). One is formed from *actor* 'actor' with *-iz* and the other from *director* with *-a*; and, in general, the system of the language, as a system of 'possibilities', allows feminines to be formed with either of these endings. Hence the word for 'manageress' could, in principle, be *directriz* and the word for 'actress' could, in principle, be *actora*. Now any speaker, naturally, will learn from other members of the community to say *actriz* and *directora*. But in using these forms, they are constrained not by the system, which would equally allow these meanings to be carried by *actora* and *directriz*, but by what Coseriu calls the 'normal realisation' of the system. Only at this level of 'realisation', as he puts it, are the forms that speakers actually learn and use 'preferred' (79). In our example from syntax, it is possible that, for a period in which the system allowed either order, different speakers were constrained by norms that varied. Conservative speakers may have usually realised such constructions, though perhaps not always, with the verb before the subject. Perhaps, in particular, they put the verb first when a word like modern *then* preceded. Others may have usually realised it, though perhaps again not always, with the verb after the subject.

The norm which constrains a speaker is thus, 'in effect, a system of prescribed realisations' ('un sistema de realizaciones obligadas'), 'of social and cultural requirements' ('de imposiciones sociales y culturales') (98), at a level of abstraction (95f.) between 'speech', as a representation of individual concrete acts of utterance, and the 'system' in a Saussurean sense. The preferences it imposes are, of course, not absolute. For the essence of creativity in language, as Coseriu explains in various places, lies in exploiting the possibilities that the system will leave open in a way that goes beyond the limits that the norm prescribes. Furthermore norms vary 'according to the community' (98).

Coseriu's account was based on a critique of fundamental concepts, without specific reference to diachrony. But, among its many applications, it was claimed to be especially revealing for our understanding of linguistic change (106f.). Some changes, we can now say, affect only the norm. In Southern British English, the vowel in words like *hair*, which earlier phoneticians represented with a diphthong ([ɛə]), is now more usually a monophthong ([ɛː]). But its place within the system, in relation to the vowels of *hear*, *hire* and so on, has not altered. Some Spanish speakers might create new feminines in -*ora*: *senadora* ('female senator') is one that is not in my dictionary. If such a word became part of the norm, the 'language', in an ordinary sense, would have a new form. But its creation would have followed a route that in the system, as Coseriu describes it, was already open.

In other cases changes will affect the system also. It is the norm, as we have seen, that is directly 'imposed' on individuals. But every member of a speech community has knowledge of the system ('tiene conciencia del sistema'); and, in speaking, will remain within the limits that it sets ('[se mantiene] dentro de las posibilidades del sistema'). Individual speakers then, in addition, either 'know or do not know' the norm and, in their speech, 'either obey or do not obey' it. Within the system, as we have said, there is scope for originality in expression; and what is at first original in a single speaker (the use of *senadora*, for example, or a sporadic monophthongisation of [ɛə]) may be taken as a model by other speakers. In consequence, what was at first an isolated error or an isolated act of creation may in time become part of a new norm, to which each individual will in turn conform and sometimes not conform. But norms cannot change without affecting what Coseriu calls 'the balance of the system' ('el equilibrio del sistema'). At any specific moment the norm 'reflects' this balance. So, as the norm changes, the balance of the system is in turn altered, to the point at which, in the end, it 'overturns completely to one side or another' ('hasta volcarse totalmente de un lado o de otro') (107). In this way, Coseriu argued, changes that originate at the lowest level of abstraction, in the speech behaviour of specific individuals, can successively change both the norm, which is an abstraction at an intermediate level, and the system, at a level still higher.

Our example from syntax is again not modelled on one that Coseriu gave. But, in these terms, we could speak of a moment of 'overturning' when, as the norm had shifted more and more to the order of *Then Alfred rode* . . . , and the 'balance' of the system had in turn altered, it finally became the only order that, exceptions apart, the language allowed. In the history of Southern British English, to return to an earlier example, the 'normal realisations' of the vowels in *moor* and *more* have shifted gradually from [ʊə] and [ɔː], which were once distinguished clearly by all speakers, to variants that are increasingly convergent. This will at first have been a matter of realisation only. But in time the system may allow no opposition.

Neither the monograph cited (Coseriu, 1962 [1952]) nor a later important book on change in language (Coseriu, 1973 [1958]) had the attention, or the critical review, that they deserved. But the role of variation was to catch the imagination of many linguists in the 1960s, through the work of the American sociolinguist William Labov. For Labov argued both that variant realisations could themselves form structures, and that variation could be striking even in quite tight communities.

It will be obvious at once that, in any community, the speech of any member will differ slightly from that of any other. This is in part, but only in part, because they are physically different. Hence, for example, Coseriu had spoken of an 'individual norm' as well as a 'social norm' (Coseriu, 1962 [1952]: 96f.). But Labov claimed that, if it was studied in isolation, the speech of an individual might make no sense on its own. The 'dialect' of an individual is often called an 'idiolect'; and in the city of New York, where his classic study was carried out, 'most idiolects do not', in phonology at least, 'form a coherent system'. They are 'studded', he goes on, 'with oscillations and contradictions, both in the organization of sounds into phonemes, and the organization of phonemes into larger systems' (Labov, 1966: 6). The same speakers might on one occasion have an 'r' in their pronunciation of a word like *car* or *card*; on other occasions they might not. The quality of the vowel in word *a* might sometimes be recorded as identical to one recorded in word *b*; at other times as different. We cannot, of course, recover the facts from past stages of a language. But through Labov's and later studies it became clear that, as sounds change, the speech of individuals may be inconsistent. In our example from Spanish, 'ʒ' changed, in an overall perspective, to 'ʃ' and then 'x'. But, as the changes spread, the realisation of the consonant in a word like *viejo* may at any time have ranged, for a certain group of speakers, between [ʒ] and [ʃ]; for another, between [ʃ] and [x]; for another, over all three.

The 'most coherent system', in New York at least, was 'that which includes the . . . community as a whole' (7). But a system, for Labov as for Saussure, was simply 'a set of differences'. Within the New York system, the vowel of, for example, *bad* is different from, or is opposed to, that of *bed*. But how these vowels are realised is another matter. In fact, among the speakers Labov studied, the phonetic quality of 'a' was found to vary strikingly according to, in particular, the social 'class' to which he assigned them and the 'style', as he described it, in which they were speaking. The lower a speaker's 'class' the more its realisation was towards one end of a scale; the higher their 'class' the more it was towards the other. For speakers of any given class, the more casual their speech the greater would be the percentage of 'lower' variants; the more careful, the greater that of 'higher' variants. To put this in Coseriu's terms, we could still speak of a 'norm' for each individual. It might be represented by a frequency distribution, correlated with 'styles'. But the distribution would reflect a larger pattern which is systematic in the community. Only when the whole community is studied can its order be revealed.

Labov was a pupil of Uriel Weinreich, whose own thesis, on the effects of contact between different language systems, had been supervised by Martinet (Weinreich, 1963 [1953]: x). It is perhaps not surprising, therefore, that he was 'particularly interested' (318) in cases where there was evidence of change. Let us suppose that, as historically in the example of the Spanish consonants, a sound change is spreading through a community. As Spanish changed, we would have expected the distribution of variants to be different, at any stage, in different places and at different levels in society. But at any moment there would also have been differences among speakers of different ages. The older the speaker the more often, at least, we might have expected to hear [ʒ] or [ʃ]; the younger the more often at least, all other factors being equal, [x].

Such findings are, as Labov describes them, in 'apparent time'; and from them we can conjecture, even without evidence of earlier stages, that a change is happening in 'real time' (319f.). In New York 'r' was variably realised after vowels – in words, as we have said, like *car* or *card*. It was found, among other things, to be less frequent in casual 'style' and among speakers lower in 'class'. But its frequency also varied with the age of speakers; and this confirmed what was indeed known in advance of Labov's investigation, that it had spread quite recently to this area. In Labov's terms, this was a change that was still 'in progress'; also one that, as was attested by the distribution across 'classes' and 'styles', had spread 'from above'. The details of this case need not concern us (see Labov, 1966: 342ff.). What is important is the overwhelming evidence that, in phonology at least, the process of change is reflected in the patterning of variation. Before his death in 1967, Weinreich had begun a major paper on the theory of change in language; in its completion, which reflected Weinreich's thinking, Labov laid down the principle, among others, that 'all change involves variability and heterogeneity'. It is thus 'transmitted within the community as a whole'; not 'confined to discrete steps' between parents and children. 'Linguistic and social factors' are again 'closely interrelated' in it (Weinreich, Labov and Herzog, 1968: 188).

But, for the community as a whole, Labov still spoke of a system. In New York, for example, the vowel of *bad* was still 'different', in the Saussurean sense, from that of *bed*. Their realisation might vary systematically, but both entered into a system of 'differences' constant across 'the New York speech-community'. By the end of the 1960s the terminology of Saussure was increasingly supplanted by that of Chomsky, which we will come to later. A system was accordingly a set of 'rules', and a 'linguistic variable' was then an element 'within the system controlled by' such a rule (Weinreich, Labov and Herzog, 1968: 167). The quality of a vowel was one such variable; the presence or absence of an element, such as 'r' in *car* or *card*, another. But the system as a whole, including the variables, would again be the same for every member of the speech community whose language it represents.

A famous illustration was that of 'copula deletion' in northern American 'Black English'. A speaker of this variety of English could in principle say, for example, *He is a fool*, with a form of the copular verb 'to be', or *He a fool*, without it. Therefore the system, for all speakers, allows both. In Labov's account, the set of rules includes one for the 'deletion' of *is*. But it was not a 'categorical rule': one that speakers have to follow always. It was a 'variable rule', controlling a 'variable' (*is* present or *is* absent) which is a function of all the factors that determine the frequency of one value or the other (Labov, 1977 [1969]: 93ff.; compare Weinreich, Labov and Herzog, 1968: 169–72).

The system of 'Black English' must then be different from those of other varieties of English, by which *He a fool* is excluded. It would also change, as a system, if in the future *He a fool* were to become the only possible form. In our own example from syntax, the original system would have had to change at one stage to allow the order of elements in *Then Alfred rode* . . . In Labov's terms we could claim that there was then a 'variable rule' by which the order was rearranged. Though the facts can at best be surmised, the frequency with which it was followed would have been explained by various factors, and their influence would again have changed successively from one period to another. At a later stage we might claim that the rule itself changed: while the rearrangement had at first been from *Then rode Alfred* . . . to *Then Alfred rode* . . . , now it was the opposite. There would then be a new system, though the rule, at that stage at least, was still 'variable'. In such accounts, linguistic change is in reality continuous: it is not just a matter of discrete moves on a Saussurean chess board. But at a more abstract level the transitions from one 'state of the language' to another are still there.

4.3   'Universals'

The theory that had been developed in the 1950s was one in which change in a language system, towards, for example, greater symmetry of vowels or consonants, originates in changes in the behaviour of individual speakers. It is on individuals that, in particular, 'pressures' operate. Where sound change was concerned this theory had been taken, by 1960, as far as then seemed possible.

But words and grammar also change and here too change can be transparently of systems. In Latin, for example, *hic* (translated 'this') was basically opposed as a 'first person' pronoun ('this' in the sense of proximity to or association with the speaker) to both 'second person' *iste* (proximity to or association with whoever the speaker is addressing) and 'third person' *ille* (proximity to or association with neither). But the languages that have descended from Latin have in general a two-way distinction similar to that in English: thus, for Italian, *questo* 'this', *quello* 'that'. In the history of Italian, it is not the forms alone that have changed. The system of 'differences' has also been transformed.

The example is one explored in the 1940s by the Romanist Walter von Wartburg (Wartburg, 1969 [1943]: 208ff.). But here and elsewhere Wartburg tends to talk as if a language system governed itself. At a certain stage 'the language can try to maintain a distinction' ('la langue peut tenter de maintenir la distinction') by 'looking elsewhere' for a new element to supply it ('en cherchant ailleurs un remplacement'). Alternatively, it can 'buy peace' ('elle peut acheter sa tranquillité') at the 'price' of sacrificing it ('au prix de la renonciation à toute différentiation') (209). A language can again be said to 'have avoided' the weakening of a distinction ('. . . a obvié à cet affaiblissement . . .') (210). This way of talking seems once more to suggest that language systems are self-regulating. Like, for example, thermostats (4.1), they monitor and adjust their own states. Alternatively, such talk is figurative; but a figure for what, precisely?

The image of self-regulation has been taken from an essay on structuralism in general, by the Swiss psychologist Jean Piaget (Piaget, 1968: 13ff.); and, though rarely made explicit, it has remained, and remains, tempting. It is not surprising, therefore, that the issue was raised again in the 1970s, by theories that proposed laws regulating patterns of word order.

The origin of this idea lies in the early 1960s, in work in America by Joseph H. Greenberg. It was purely descriptive, and his findings were not absolute. But let us assume that, in any language, we can identify the elements 'subject', verb and 'object'. In some, they are normally in that order: thus, in English, subject *Mary* plus verb *saw* plus object *Jim*. But in others their order is different. Let us also assume, for example, that we can identify a category of what are described as 'adpositions': either prepositions, like English *to*, which precede a noun (*to Cambridge*) or 'postpositions', with a similar role but coming after it. We can then ask if there is a correlation between the order of adpositions (preposition versus postposition) and that of, in particular, verbs and objects. In a sample of thirty languages examined by Greenberg, some had as their 'dominant order' VSO (verb first, then subject, then object). Such languages, he found, were 'always prepositional' (Greenberg, 1963: 78). This correlation was accordingly described as a 'linguistic universal', or 'universal of language'. Others had the 'normal' order SOV (first subject, then object, then verb); such languages were found, 'with overwhelmingly greater than chance frequency', to have postpositions. This too was a 'universal' (79). In all, Greenberg postulated forty-five such 'universals', some absolute and some not, involving these and other syntactic elements.

Let us assume, for the sake of argument, that the assumptions underlying this study were valid. Thus, in particular, all languages 'have', in an equivalent sense, subjects and objects. But why, we then ask, should there be such correlations? A tempting answer is that 'universals' reflect laws that govern the evolution of language systems. Suppose that a language has the 'normal' or 'dominant' order SOV; but, unlike the majority with that order, it has prepositions. By law, we claim, it should have postpositions. Therefore it might be expected to change in conformity with the 'universal'. Perhaps it too might, in time, become 'postpositional'. Alternatively, the ordering of S, O and V might change: perhaps to that of English (SVO). In either case, the change is 'explained' (we would claim) by pressure to conform to a law that every language system must ideally obey.

This line of thought was developed in particular by Winfred P. Lehmann and by Theo Vennemann. In Lehmann's account, the order of prepositions or postpositions was one of several features that covary with, specifically, the order of the verb and object. Another of particular importance is the position of an attributive adjective. In French, for example, *blanche* 'white' is attributive in *une maison blanche* 'a white house'; and the noun to which it is related (*maison* 'house') comes first. This is the order we expect, from Lehmann's theory, if, as again in French, the verb precedes the object. A language was then said to be 'consistent' if such expectations are met. So, in these terms, French is a consistent 'VO language' insofar as (*a*) the object normally follows the verb, (*b*) it has prepositions instead of postpositions, and (*c*) the position of most adjectives is after the noun. A language was 'inconsistent' to the extent that expectations are not met. Thus English is, in one respect at least, an 'inconsistent' VO language. Once more (*a*) the object normally follows the verb; (*b*) it has prepositions; but (*c*) the normal position of adjectives, as in *a white house*, is before the noun and not after.

Various arguments followed. For example, from the 'aberrant position' of adjectives in English we 'may propose the hypothesis' that it is 'a language which has been changing from OV structure', in which we would expect an adjective to come before the noun, 'to VO structure' (Lehmann, 1978: 37). But what if the order in English were to change, so that this 'aberrancy' is eliminated? In the same volume Lehmann speaks of 'a drift' in languages 'towards consistency' (408). Studies of syntactic change show that, as 'patterns of the new type . . . gradually become established', 'the language becomes increasingly consistent' (409). 'In change, languages of a given type are modified in accordance with the principles' that he proposes (431); such principles 'permit explanations'. So, if the position of the adjective in English were to change, that might be explained by pressure for 'consistency' to be enhanced.

The term 'drift' had been used much earlier by Sapir (n.d. [1921]: 150, 154ff.). But in what exactly does the current on which a language drifts, or the pressure by which it is impelled in that direction, consist? In Lehmann's account, the 'basic patterns of any language' are 'governed by simple but powerful principles' (396). In, for example, *I saw a white house*, the attributive adjective (*white*) comes between the verb (*saw*) and the object noun (*house*). But by a principle that he formulates (19), the sequence of verb and object noun 'must not be interrupted'. If English were to change, the language would be responding to that principle.

In Vennemann's account, the role of *white* in relation to *house* was that of an 'operator' to an 'operand'. So too was that of an object in relation to a verb; also, among others, that of a noun in relation to a preposition or a postposition. He therefore proposed a general principle, by which 'languages tend to serialize' such elements 'unidirectionally'. In English, objects are among the operators that must follow verbs: so, taking 'X' as any operator of this sort, it is a 'VX language'. In tune with this, an operator such as *Cambridge* in *to Cambridge* follows a preposition; if the tendency were perfect, attributive adjectives should also follow nouns. In 'XV languages' the pattern will be the opposite. Operators such as objects come before verbs; 'adpositions' like *in* are instead postpositions; attributive adjectives precede nouns. 'The history of the word order syntax of each language can be understood to a large extent', according to

Vennemann, 'as a development toward consistent implementation of this principle' (Vennemann, 1975: 288).

The principle is said to be of 'natural serialization'. The development of languages is accordingly, all other factors being equal, towards greater 'naturalness'. But where again is the pressure that will propel or guide them in that direction? Those who speak a language such as English do not themselves find its 'inconsistency' unnatural. There seems no reason why, in a construction like *I saw a white house*, the noun should not continue to come after the adjective, simply because that is the pattern that each speaker will learn. How could the application of this principle lead, in appropriate circumstances, to change?

In the paper cited, Vennemann considers in particular the motives for a change from XV order to VX. There is a tendency, he claims, for languages to be of the first type (XV) when the subject and object are reliably distinguished by case endings: for example, in Latin by a nominative ending (*servu-s* 'slave' or *puella* 'girl') and an accusative (*servu-m* or *puella-m*). Where there are no such endings, as in English, they tend to be of the other (VX). Now that as it stands is no more than a finding, generalising one of Greenberg's (288f.). But suppose that a case system breaks down, so that subjects and objects are no longer distinguished effectively in that way. This can happen, for example, through sound changes that affect the endings. If the language is, as we expect, an 'XV language' it then 'changes', according to Vennemann, 'to VX' (289). But why, he asked, should that change follow?

His answer (289ff.) was that, when the cases are lost, the roles that nouns play can be obscured. In English, for example, it is clear that, in *the man who Mary saw*, the subject of *saw* must be *Mary*. It is clear because English is an 'SVX language'; hence, if *Mary* were the object, the order would be *the man who saw Mary*. But what if a language has the order 'SXV'? So long as it retains its cases there is no difficulty. If the word for 'Mary' is the subject it will be nominative and the word for 'who' accusative: thus, using English words for clarity, *who*-accusative *Mary*-nominative *saw*. If the word for 'Mary' is the object, it will be the opposite: thus, with 'XV' order, *who*-nominative *Mary*-accusative *saw*. What then if the cases are lost? If *Mary* is the subject it will again precede *saw*: *who Mary* (S) *saw* (V). But its position will be no different when it is the object: *who Mary* (X) *saw* (V). Sometimes, when such phrases were uttered, hearers would still understand, in practice, what the speaker meant. But quite often they would not.

This is one of several 'ambiguities and perceptual difficulties' (290) to which Vennemann points. An 'XV' language without cases is, in brief, dysfunctional. Its speakers will accordingly find other ways to make their meaning clear; and, in Gilliéron's terms, apply 'therapy' to it. But in explaining such changes Vennemann had not invoked a specific law of naturalness. Speakers are simply under pressure to make clear what they mean. Hence, as Martinet argued, they are under pressure to preserve distinctions between phonemes (4.1). Hence too they are under pressure to preserve distinctions in syntax. In phonology this may lead to changes, for example, in the structure of a consonant system. In syntax it may lead, for example, to changes of word order.

What was the status, then, of principles like that of 'natural serialisation'? On one view they are still no more than summary findings. We find that there are correlations between one construction and another: typically, in Greenberg's formula, 'with overwhelmingly greater than chance frequency'. This is just a matter of observation. To explain it we must look much deeper, in the need for speakers to make clear what they are saying, for their hearers to understand them with as little effort as possible, and so on. Likewise when we look for explanations of change. We might find that, all else to the best of our knowledge being equal, changes are in the direction of greater 'consistency'. That would again be no more than a finding. We cannot explain it by hypostatising laws that govern systems independently of their speakers. To propose such principles is merely to restate the initial findings. We must again look deeper, at the pressures bearing on speakers.

But that was not apparently what Lehmann, in particular, was claiming. Just as Wartburg, for example, could talk of 'a language' finding ways to avoid the weakening of a contrast, so 'a language', on a literal reading of what Lehmann said, is under pressure to maximise 'consistency'. Was that just a convenient way of talking? Or were 'languages' to be seen as, in reality, autonomous systems, subject to constraints that, if no countervailing factors intervene, require consistency?

5   The architecture of a language system

Let us return to synchronic linguistics. By the end of the 1930s, the description of sound systems had a theoretical foundation in the work of Trubetzkoy and others, and its method was increasingly codified. But the phonology of a language is again just one part of the total 'language structure'. How do phonemes relate to, in particular, units of meaning? By what methods can these in turn be identified securely? What kinds of relation does each unit of meaning bear, in turn, to other units of meaning?

These were technical questions, and the elaboration of techniques of description, which is the most striking feature of linguistics in the decades that follow the Second World War, was not at first accompanied by new general or philosophical ideas. For the most part European linguists tended to found their work on those of Saussure, and linguists in America on Bloomfield's. The most exciting problems were of method, and those that concerned the detailed structure of a language system. For Trubetzkoy the 'language structure' had already been not one system but 'several partial systems' ('mehrer Teilsysteme') (Trubetzkoy, 1939: 6). These components 'hold together, complement each other, and stand in mutual relations' ('so daß alle Teile einander zusammenhalten, einander ergänzen, sich aufeinander beziehen'). The main task for his successors was to say exactly how they do so, and exactly what the components are. It was in America especially that answers were given, and much of what was worked out in this period has found its way into textbooks and been taught for decades to generations of students. It is therefore a large part of what structural linguistics has concretely achieved.

We must begin, however, with the theory of Louis Hjelmslev, who was more nearly Trubetzkoy's contemporary. Its roots lay in the 1930s, and at the time it was felt to be so original that a new name, 'glossematics', was coined for it. With other Europeans of this period, Hjelmslev found his inspiration in the *Cours de linguistique générale*, and it was by him that the overall design of language systems, seen as systems of linguistic signs as Saussure had conceived them, was most rigorously and systematically worked out.

74

5.1   Expression and content

The definitive account was published in the war years, in a monograph
'On the foundations of linguistic theory' (Hjelmslev, 1943). It was never
easy, and in the 1950s was already the subject of a secondary exposition longer than the original (Siertsema, 1965 [1955]). But at the heart
of Hjelmslev's theory lay an analysis of the 'sign relation', or what he
called the 'sign function', that linked the two sides of a sign. For Saussure,
as we have seen, each sign had been a unit with two faces: on the one
hand, what the *Cours* had called an 'acoustic image', or a mental representation of sounds, and on the other a 'concept', or mental representation of meaning. Thus the sign *tree*, to return to our earlier example,
united an acoustic image, which we might now represent as '[triː]', with
a concept 'tree'. Each sign was, to repeat, a unit. In another of its seductive images, the *Cours* had compared the analysis of a language to cutting a sheet of paper. One cannot cut one side of the paper without
cutting the other; similarly, one cannot distinguish either 'signifiants', like
'[triː]', or 'signifiés', like 'tree', unless, at the same time, one distinguishes
both (Saussure, 1972 [1916]: 15). It was for that reason, as we saw, that
the 'sign' could not, as in ordinary usage, be the 'signifying' element
alone.

But to say that a unit has two faces is to say that, between one face and
the other, there is a relation. Thus, in this example, '[triː]' stands in a
relation of mutual implication to 'tree'. In Hjelmslev's formulation, one
term in the sign relation is, by definition, an 'expression' ('udtryk') and
the other is, again by definition, a 'content' ('indhold') (Hjelmslev, 1943:
44). That, to repeat, was simply a matter of definition. In using the word
'expression' Hjelmslev did not imply that signifiers had any other properties; it refers quite simply to a term in a relation whose other term is
referred to by the word 'content'. In using that word in turn he did not
imply that what was signified had any property other than that of entering formally into a relation whose complementary term is referred to by
the word 'expression'. Thus, in particular, expressions were not in principle acoustic images, and contents were not in principle concepts. But the
relation is in other respects as Saussure, in effect, conceived it. We cannot
talk of units of expression, such as, in the same notation, '[triː]', except
by virtue of the contents that they 'express'; nor of units of content,
such as 'tree', except by virtue of the expressions whose 'content' they
are. For Hjelmslev too the relation is one of mutual implication. In his
terminology, which often does not translate very easily into ordinary
usage in English, the sign relation or 'sign function' is a 'solidarity' (45),
in which each term or 'functive' depends on the other.

This formulation may seem merely to restate, in a way yet more removed from the realities of speech, what Saussure had been saying in his lectures thirty years earlier. But by defining the relation as fundamental, we can understand the nature of such systems much more clearly.

Let us consider still the sign *tree*. It is formed by a relation between expression and content, in which one term is specifically what Hjelmslev calls a 'sign-expression' ('tegnudtryk'): let us continue to represent this as '[triː]'. The other is specifically a 'sign-content' ('tegnindhold'), which we will continue to represent by 'tree'. These terms or 'functives' are paired symmetrically, and in that sense the analogy in the *Cours* with two sides of a sheet of paper is still applicable. But each term is a unit that can then be related to others in its own domain. On the one hand, there is what Hjelmslev called a 'plane' of expression, and at this level sign-expressions can be found to form relations, independently of any among the corresponding sign-contents, with other sign-expressions. Thus, in particular, '[triː]' can be related to other units of expression, like '[friː]' (*free*) or '[trʌɪ]' (*try*), with which it will be found on analysis to share smaller elements. On the other hand there is a 'plane' of content, and at that level a sign-content like 'tree' can be found, as we will see in a moment, to form relations with other sign-contents. Such relations will again be independent of any obtaining between the corresponding sign-expressions. There is a point at which analogies cease to be illuminating; but, having cut up Saussure's sheet of paper, we can then in effect take either side of any of the separate pieces, and study it in comparison with the same side of any other piece.

Both the cutting and the comparison depend crucially on a procedure that Hjelmslev called 'commutation'. Let us take, first of all, the expression unit realised, in a phonologist's terms, by [triː]. This is distinct, as a whole, from, among others, the one realised by [hɪɫ]. But on what evidence are units on this level distinct? The answer is that, in the sign relation, the exchange of one sign-expression for another carries with it an exchange of corresponding sign-contents. Thus the exchange of '[triː]' and '[hɪɫ]' on the level of expression must entail, on the level of content, the exchange of 'tree' and 'hill'. In the same relation, an exchange of one sign-content for another carries with it an exchange of corresponding sign-expressions. Thus 'tree' is distinct from 'hill', on the level of content, because, conversely, their exchange entails, on the level of expression, that of '[triː]' and '[hɪɫ]'. In Hjelmslev's terminology both units in the sign relation 'commute'; and they are separate units only if this 'commutation test' is met. As he presented it, the test applies equally and symmetrically on both planes.

As for the initial cuts, so for all subsequent analysis. Let us compare, for example, the expression units '[triː]' and '[friː]'. In part they are similar ('[riː]'), in part different ('[t]', '[f]'). But replacing '[t]' with '[f]' again entails, at the level of content, the replacement of 'tree', as a whole, by 'free'. Likewise the exchange of '[iː]' and, let us say, '[uː]' entails the exchange of 'tree', as a whole, and 'true'; that of '[r]' and '[l]' ('[fliː]') that of 'free', as a whole, and either 'flee' or 'flea'. By the same test of commutation, we distinguish units of expression, like '[triː]', as wholes and we analyse each, on its own level, into smaller units like '[t]', '[r]' and '[iː]'.

Hjelmslev's formulation of this test was contemporary with the codification of procedures in phonology (3.2); and, as applied to the analysis of expression units, it was plainly similar. In a phonologist's account, two sounds must realise different phonemes if they distinguish words with different meanings. In Hjelmslev's account, two smaller units of expression must be distinguished if their commutation entails a commutation of contents. But just as 'sign-expressions' can be analysed by this criterion into smaller expression units, so in his view could 'sign-contents', by a symmetrical procedure, be analysed into smaller content units. In Hjelmslev's terminology, units such as '[t]' or '[r]' were 'expression-figurae' ('udtryksfigurer'). Likewise, on the level of content, we could establish 'content-figurae' ('inholdsfigurer').

'Till now', Hjelmslev points out, 'such an analysis has never been made or even attempted in linguistics' (Hjelmslev, 1943 [1953]: 61). The consequences have, he says, been 'catastrophic', since, without it, the description of content has appeared unmanageable. But the method, as he sees it, is 'exactly the same'. Let us compare, for example, *tree* and *bush*. In ordinary terms, they are words whose meanings are partly similar: both 'woody plant', but one 'large' and the other 'small'. Therefore, in Hjelmslev's system, just as *tree* and *free* have part of their expression in common, so *tree* and *bush* would, correspondingly, have part of their content in common. Let us call this shared part x. At the same time their content would also, in part, be different. Just as *tree* and *free* are differentiated, in their sign-expressions, by '[t]' versus '[f]', so these must be differentiated by parts of their sign-contents. Let us call these parts y and z. In exchanging y and z, we exchange, on that level, the sign-contents xy ('tree') and xz ('bush'); and at the same time, on the level of expression, the sign-expressions '[triː]' and '[buʃ]'.

Hjelmslev's own brief illustration (63f.) is of nouns distinguished by sex. 'Ram' and 'ewe' are, as wholes, distinct sign-contents; so are 'man' and 'woman', 'boy' and 'girl', 'stallion' and 'mare', and so on. In a straightforward inventory, these are simply different content units; likewise 'he' and 'she', 'sheep', 'human being' (Danish 'menneske'), 'child' or 'horse'. But, by the commutation test, we can 'eliminate' the first eight by resolving them into combinations. 'Ram' can be analysed as 'he-sheep'; 'ewe' as 'she-sheep'; likewise 'man' and 'woman' as 'he-human' and 'she-human', 'boy' and 'girl' as 'he-child' and 'she-child', 'stallion' and 'mare' as 'he-horse' and 'she-horse'. For Hjelmslev the exchange of 'he' and 'she', as parts of sign-contents, was parallel to that of parts of sign-expressions. In replacing '[iː]' in '[triː]' with '[uː]' we effect, on the associated plane, a change of 'tree' to 'true'. Likewise, in replacing 'he' in 'he-sheep' with 'she' we effect, on the associated plane, a change of '[ram]' to '[juː]'.

The symmetry between the two sides of the paper, or the two 'planes' that make up the structure of a language system, was now perfect. But this was not the only way in which the theory took Saussurean ideas to an extreme. Sign-expressions and sign-contents, expression-figurae and content-figurae, all were identified, as we have seen, by their relations to one another. But did they then have any other properties?

It might have been natural to take for granted that they did. For Saussure, a 'signifiant' was again the 'acoustic image' of some complex of sounds; a 'signifié' a 'concept' as an element of thought. For Trubetzkoy, a 'signifier in the language structure' was constituted by distinctive features of sound (3.2); a 'signifié', one might analogously suppose, would be defined by features of meaning. In explaining Hjelmslev's system of relations, I have myself relied on an implicit link between, in particular, the sounds transcribed [triː] and the abstraction '[triː]'. But in Hjelmslev's own account such links were of realisation only. A sign-expression is characterised just by its relation to a sign-content, a sign-content just by its relation to a sign-expression. Quite literally, as Hjelmslev said when these terms were introduced (45), neither of the terms 'expression' or 'content' meant any more than that.

In developing this idea, Hjelmslev cited (46) a passage in Saussure's *Cours* in which, independently of language, 'thought' and 'sound' are both said to be formless. Independently of its expression by words, thoughts are a shapeless continuum ('notre pensée n'est qu'une masse amorphe et indistincte'). There are no divisions between ideas until language comes into play. Nor are sounds any less shapeless. 'Sound substance' ('la substance phonique') is 'a plastic material' ('une matière plastique') that is in turn divided only to supply 'the signifiers that thought needs' ('les signifiants dont la pensée a besoin'). A language can therefore be represented by a series of divisions made simultaneously in both domains (Saussure, 1972 [1916]: 155f.). The 'linguistics of a language system' does not deal with either separately. It operates 'in the boundary area where elements of both orders combine' ('La linguistique travaille donc sur le terrain limitotrophe où les élements des deux ordres se combinent', 157). Their combination, we are then told, *'produces a form, not a substance'* (*'cette combinaison produit une forme, non une substance'*).

This last sentence is found only in part in the written material on which the *Cours* is based (see De Mauro's note in the edition referred to). But the formula is repeated at the end of the chapter. From whichever side a language is approached, we find a 'complex equilibrium of terms that condition each other reciprocally' ('ce même équilibre complexe de termes qui se conditionnent réciproquement'). 'In other words, *the language system is a form and not a substance*' (169).

What Saussure meant is perhaps not so important. We must again remind ourselves that this is a book which he did not write. But what Hjelmslev meant was exactly what that formula says. One cannot talk of 'phonic substance', even as shapeless, independently of language systems. Nor can one talk independently of a 'substance' of thought. The sounds of speech exist only as a manifestation or projection, in a domain outside the language system, of purely formal distinctions among expression units. The substance of 'thought' is likewise a projection, in a domain again outside the language system, of purely formal distinctions among content units.

To understand this, it may help if we look in a different way at our analogy, in 2.1, of coinage. I can pay someone ten pounds by, for example, handing over several bits of metal. But I do not always have to pay in that way. I might instead write a cheque, or use a credit card, or transfer the money electronically from my account to theirs. In each case I am paying ten pounds: that is constant. But all else is variable. In one case a sum of money is realised, we may say, by coins. In another it may be realised only in an exchange between computers. So what, independently of these variable realisations, is 'ten pounds'? It is evidently no more than a numerical value. It is defined, in a specific monetary system, by its relation to all other possible sums: as ten times 'one pound', a hundred times 'ten pence', and so on. Coins are one of the physical means by which it can be transferred; and, in general, coins would not be coins if it were not for the units of value that they represent. But there is no necessary connection. We can easily imagine a system of money with no coins.

As for money so, though the analogy is not Hjelmslev's own, for language. On the expression plane the role of sounds, like that of coins, is contingent. A distinction between expression-figurae might be realised, or manifested, by [t] versus [f]. But the mode of realisation is again a variable. Writing, in particular, is an alternative 'substance' in which the same units would be realised by marks on a flat surface: 't' versus 'f', or 'T' versus 'F'. In Hjelmslev's definition (Appendix, §52), substance is 'the variable in a manifestation'. Only the system is constant, and it is for him no more than a network of relations, or Saussurean 'differences', among units.

By a parallel definition, 'form' is 'the constant in a manifestation' (Appendix, §51). We might therefore say that, in Saussure's *Cours*, 'form' was constituted by a relation between constant mental images of sounds and constant 'concepts'. But just as sign-expressions and expression-figurae have no intrinsic connection, at their level, with sounds, so, in Hjelmslev's system, sign-contents and content-figurae have, at their level, no intrinsic connection with concepts or thoughts. 'Thought' too is a substance, and as such contingent. 'Form', in content as in expression, is a system of relations only.

In summary, then, a language is structured on two planes: plane A, let us say, which Hjelmslev called that of 'content'; plane B, which he called that of 'expression'. But 'plane A' and 'plane B' would be perfectly adequate, since these are merely terms in a bilateral implication. The 'form' of plane A ('content') is a network of relations, which structures a 'substance'; the 'form' of plane B ('expression'), likewise. On each level, substance implies form: there could not be a substance without the form that structures it. Form does not, conversely, imply substance. It exists as a pure system of relations: like, for example, those of mathematics. A substance, in contrast, exists only as the projection of a form, and it is only when the substances of different languages are compared that we can talk at all of, for example, speech sounds in general or of 'thought' in general. In a passage that we have not yet covered, Hjelmslev defined a 'purport' (Danish 'mening') that can be abstracted from the 'content' substances of different languages. Thus there is a 'purport', in his illustration, common to the 'thought substances' of English *I do not know*, of its French translation *Je ne sais pas*, of the Danish *Jeg véd det ikke*, and so on (46f.). There was similarly a 'purport', though the term is now acknowledged to be 'unusual', that can be abstracted from different 'sound substances' (51). But neither 'content-purport' nor 'expression-purport' exist independently of language systems.

The symmetry of Hjelmslev's scheme immediately attracted comment. The 'main idea', in the words of the Polish scholar Jerzy Kuryłowicz, was to pinpoint 'structural features common to the two planes' (Kuryłowicz, 1949: 48). The method Hjelmslev had envisaged was that of an 'internal comparison' (60), establishing what Kuryłowicz describes as a resemblance in form, or 'a remarkable *isomorphism*' (48), between them. Though Hjelmslev did not himself speak of 'isomorphisms' in that sense (compare Hjelmslev, 1943: 100f.), the term has often been taken to characterise his and similar theories.

What is perhaps less obvious than the symmetry itself was the role of abstraction in achieving it. If by 'expression' we mean sound and by 'content' we mean meaning, there is, on the face of it, no parallel between these domains and no way, in particular, of manipulating 'meanings' as the commutation test required. The symmetry was only possible in that Hjelmslev was in fact manipulating neither sounds nor meanings, but purely abstract counters which were established solely as terms in the relations that the test defined. Nor, on the face of it, do sounds and meanings correspond in any simple way. But the 'solidarity' between 'contents' on our plane A and 'expressions' on our plane B had nothing literally to do with either. The relation of sign-contents to the 'purport' of thought was indirect: it had to be if different languages, with different systems at that level, project 'substances' that are correspondingly different. The relation of sound 'purport' to sign-expressions, whether similar or not, was also indirect. The connections in general between, literally, sound and, literally, thought or meaning, were accordingly very complex. But by abstraction to a system of pure 'form' the mediating 'sign relation' could be made very simple.

5.2   Phonology and grammar

Glossematics was debated actively in the years that followed the Second World War, especially after Hjelmslev's account was published in English. But by the time of his death in the 1960s its influence was no longer direct. The treatments that were dominant then had different origins, and had been developed with the full insight of synchronic phonology, either of the Prague School or of the Bloomfieldians, behind them. They are also more complex.

Let us begin by looking back to a scheme inherited from antiquity. In a formula that appears to have originated with the Stoic philosophers, language is, in general, 'articulated sound'. The term 'articulated' is from the Latin word for a 'joint' ('articulus'); and what was meant is that, in distinction as it was then thought to the cries of animals, or to other 'inarticulate' sounds emitted by human beings, speech was organised into distinct units. Its smallest unit was the 'letter' (Latin 'litera'): as we have already noted (3.1), this was traditionally a spoken and not just a written unit. Thus, in a standard formula transmitted in the fourth century AD by the grammarian Donatus, the letter is 'the smallest part of articulated vocal sound' ('pars minima vocis articulatae') (in Holtz, 1981: 603). Other units form a hierarchy in which units at each level are composed of units at the level below it. Letters first combine to form a syllable (Latin 'syllaba'). For example, in English the letters 's' and 'a' form the syllable 'sa'. Syllables then combine to form a word (Latin 'dictio'). For example, 'sa' and 'tin' form the word 'satin'. Finally, at the highest level, words combine to form an utterance or sentence (Latin 'oratio'). Of these units, a word or a sentence also has a meaning; a letter or a syllable does not. But that apart, they are related throughout by simple composition. As Priscian put it a couple of centuries later, 'just as letters combining appropriately form syllables, and syllables words, so too do words form a sentence' ('quemadmodum literae apte coeuntes faciunt syllabas et syllabae dictiones, sic et dictiones orationem') (Priscian in Keil, 1855–9, II: 108).

For the ancient 'letter' we can read, by the 1930s, the phonologists' 'phoneme'. But, in addition, it had long been clear that words can be divided into other units. Take, for example, *unkindnesses*. We might imagine, once more, that we are investigators to whom the structure of English is unknown. So, in a form such as *his many unkindnesses* we will want to work out where, as Bloomfield put it (2.2), there are recurring likenesses in form and meaning. We might find that *many* recurs in, for example, *her many friends* or *They were many*; also that, holding *his — unkindnesses* constant, we can replace *many* with *few* (*his few unkindnesses*), or indeed remove it (*his unkindnesses*). On such evidence, we establish that *his*, *many* and *unkindnesses*, as wholes, all meet our criteria. But we will find that they are also met by smaller units. The form *kind* recurs in *He was kind* or *a kind man*; *un-* can also be removed (*his many kindnesses*); as we removed *many* so we can also remove *-es* (*his unkindness*); *-ness* recurs in, say, *his sadness* or *his happiness*. On such evidence *un-*, *kind*, *-ness* and *-es* can be identified as other recurring likenesses.

Since the Renaissance, units like *un-*, *-ness* or *-es* had been described as 'affixes', and in a more recent tradition, which was to persist among French linguists in particular, were one kind of (to use for the moment the French term) 'morphème'. Thus, for Joseph Vendryes, 'morphèmes' were elements that expressed 'relations among ideas'. In the same example, *kind* is a 'root' or (again in French) a 'sémantème'. 'Sémantèmes' were said to represent 'ideas' themselves: thus, in this case, it would be an 'idea' which all words that include it, such as *kind* or *kindness* or *unkindness*, have in common (compare Vendryes, 1968 [1923]: 92f.).

For Bloomfield, and most other linguists since the 1920s, *un-*, *kind*, *-ness* and *-es* are indifferently 'morphemes'. But, whatever the terminology, this result must clearly complicate the ancient hierarchy. Take, for example, *uneasy*. It has three successive syllables: in the usual analysis, [ʌ], [niː] and [zi]. It can also be analysed into three successive morphemes: *un-* ([ʌn]), *eas(e)* ([iːz]) and *-y* ([i]). But at no point in this word do the boundaries of syllables and morphemes coincide. We can say once more that its component phonemes are combined in syllables and the word in turn is formed from these. We can say instead that they are combined in roots and affixes, and the word is then composed of those. But in this word as in many others, syllables and morphemes cannot both be units in a single hierarchy.

The obvious answer is that, within words at least, there are two hierarchies. As the ancient grammarians had said, speech is articulated into units like [ʌ], [n] or [iː]. The phonemes that these realise form syllables, which like them are units without meaning. But speech also realises, and is in that sense articulated into, units like un-, eas(e) and -y, which, independently of syllables, form words. As 'letters' or phonemes are the smallest units that do not have meaning, morphemes, at the lowest level in a parallel hierarchy, are the smallest that do.

In Europe at least, the classic account is that of André Martinet. Suppose, to follow his argument from the beginning, that one has a headache. One might perhaps groan, which, as ancient writers would have put it, is to emit a sound that is 'inarticulate'. But one might also, if one is French, say j'ai mal à la tête 'I have got a headache.' Unlike the groan, this is articulated into distinct units, written j(e), ai, mal and so on, each identifiable, like the un-, kind or -ness in English, by their recurrence in other utterances. In the tradition of Saussure and the Prague School, each is a minimal 'linguistic sign'. Within each, a specific 'vocal form' (thus, for the sign mal, the form [mal]) is linked to a specific meaning (in Martinet's notation, "mal"). I am citing from a textbook published at the end of the 1950s (Martinet, 1970 [1960]: 13f.), in which minimal signs were, in his terminology, 'monemes' ('monèmes') (15).

The division into minimal signs was Martinet's 'first articulation'; and its practical advantage, as he pointed out, is that by combining discrete units of meaning, which together number no more than 'some thousands', speakers of a language can communicate many more things than they could by millions of unarticulated groans, cries, and so on. But then, at a subsidiary level, 'vocal forms' like [mal] are themselves not shorter groans or cries; but are articulated, in turn, into phonemes. Thus the vocal form [tet], which is the signifying side of the sign tête, is articulated in turn into the phonemes [t], [e] and again [t]. This was Martinet's 'second articulation'; and its practical advantage, once more, is that, by virtue of it, a small number of these ultimate sound units can combine to distinguish the thousands of vocal forms that 'signify', or have meaning, in the first (15). Thus the initial [t], on its own, distinguishes [tet] from, for example, [bet] (bête); the final [t], on its own, distinguishes it from, for example, [tel] (tel), and so on. If language were not articulated on both levels, it would not be nearly so efficient.

These important insights were first set out clearly at the end of the 1940s (Martinet, 1949). But they were also central to the work of Charles F. Hockett and the other Bloomfieldians. In his own much longer introduction to linguistics, Hockett pointed to seven properties that potentially distinguish human language from communication in other species (Hockett, 1958: 574ff.). The first was a similar property of 'duality' or 'duality of patterning'. It would be 'inconvenient', as he pointed out, if our system of communication were not structured in this way; and, of his seven, it was the only property that he could discover, on the evidence then available, in man only.

In any language, as Hockett conceived it, an utterance 'consists of an arrangement of the phonemes of that language'; 'at the same time', it also 'consists of an arrangement of the morphemes of that language'. Any sentence would accordingly be structured on two levels. On one level morphemes, which were the nearest Bloomfieldian equivalent to Martinet's 'monèmes', would be related syntagmatically (in Saussure's terminology) to other morphemes. Such relations were the nearest equivalent of what Bloomfield called 'grammatical forms' (Bloomfield, 1935 [1933]: 264); and, for Hockett, morphemes and their arrangements constituted the 'grammatical system'. On another level phonemes would be related syntagmatically to other phonemes. This was the equivalent of Martinet's 'second articulation'; and, for Hockett, phonemes and their arrangements constituted the 'phonological system'. We can see that, despite differences in terminology, both scholars were, in these respects at least, describing components or levels of a 'language structure' in essentially the same way.

'In linguistics', Hockett had already declared in his mid twenties, 'there are . . . two basic levels, *phonological* and *grammatical*' (Hockett, 1942: 3). One has the phoneme as its elementary unit; the other the morpheme. But what exactly was the nature of this second unit in '-eme', and how was it related to the first?

We have seen Martinet's answer. A morpheme, or rather a 'moneme', was a sign in Saussure's sense. One side was a signifier, and was analysable directly into phonemes. Martinet's account agreed thus far with Hjelmslev's, and with others generally in continental Europe. It was also not unlike, in spirit, Bloomfield's. But in Bloomfield's system of terminology, a morpheme had been, in Saussurean terms, a 'signifier' only. It was a unit that 'had' a meaning, not one that itself consisted of both a form and a meaning. For Hockett and the other Americans of his generation it was a unit of form, in Bloomfield's sense, only; and, in one extreme view, meaning was to play no part in its definition. Nor could we assume that, when a morpheme had been identified, any single meaning could in reality be associated with it. Nor, finally, was a morpheme composed of phonemes. We have seen that, by the end of the 1930s, phonemes were not literally speech-sounds. They were instead abstractions realised by sounds

(3.2). By the end of the 1940s, morphemes were a still more abstract unit, not composed of phonemes but in turn realised through them.

This view developed very quickly, and to see why we must think back to the period in which it was formed. The theory of the phoneme was still new and still very exciting; and in America especially a method had been developed by which the phonemes of any language could be rigorously identified. The criteria were objective: different linguists could, in principle, apply them independently to the same material and obtain equivalent results. The next step was to develop rigorous criteria for other units. Just as, at one level, an utterance could be analysed, exhaustively so far as a linguist was concerned, into phonemes, so at another level it could be analysed exhaustively into, in Bloomfield's sense, morphemes. How could these in turn be objectively identified?

First we needed criteria for segmentation. Why, for example, is *unkindnesses* to be divided into *un-*, *kind*, *-ness* and *-es*, and not, say, into *unk-*, *-indne-* and *-sses*? Then, at some level, we had to identify invariants. In words like *unkindnesses* or *peaches* ([piːtʃɪz]) the plural ending, to return for the moment to older terminology, is [ɪz]. In, for example, *apples* or *pears* it is [z] ([aplz], [pɛːz]); in *nuts* or *currants* it is [s] ([nʌts], [kʌrənts]); in irregular plurals, such as *children* or *men*, we find yet more variation. But behind it, all grammarians will agree, there is the constant or invariant that we are calling 'plural'. How were we to identify that, and what sort of unit is it? In *Come in*, the verb is phonetically [kʌm]; in *He came in*, the past tense of the same verb ('to come') is phonetically [keɪm]. But all grammarians will agree that these are indeed forms of the same verb. How was that unit ('to come') to be identified? And, again – what sort of unit? What was it?

In Martinet's account, the 'signifié' was constant but was 'realised in forms that vary' ('se manifest[e] . . . sous des formes variables') (Martinet, 1970 [1960]: 102). The variation is thus in the 'signifiant'. Martinet also talked of 'variants of the signifying side of monemes' ('variantes des signifiants de monèmes') or, more briefly, 'variants of monemes' ('variantes de monèmes') (106). By implication, the 'moneme' itself was constant. Thus, to take his own example from French (102), "aller" ('to go') is a 'signifié' realised variously in the forms [al] (*aller*), [va] (*va*), and so on. By implication, [al] and "aller" form one variant of a 'moneme', [va] and "aller" a second variant of the same 'moneme'.

For the Americans, whose work Martinet knew well, the invariant had to be the morpheme. In phonology, as we have seen, the phoneme was a class of 'allophones' (end of 3.2) in complementary distribution. But our variant endings, for example, are also in complementary distribution. The plural [ɪz] is found only after a certain set of consonants ([tʃ] in *peaches*, [s] in *unkindnesses*, and so on); and, after these consonants, we do not find either [s] or [z]. Where [s] is found, after among others the [t] of *nuts* or *currants*, we do not find [z]; nor vice versa. The irregularities in *men* or *children* are precisely irregularities, found only in specific words. The parallel was, by the later 1940s, obvious. In a phonologist's terms, the procedure by which we establish phonemes involved, first, the segmentation of recorded utterances into 'phones'; then the classification of 'phones' as 'allophones' of their respective phonemes. Each utterance could then be represented as a sequence or, more generally, 'arrangement' of phonemes. The next step after that was to segment such representations into smaller arrangements such as, in the case of *peaches*, [piːtʃ] and [ɪz]. In the terminology that Hockett now proposed, these were analogously 'morphs' (Hockett, 1947). In a further step 'morphs' would be classified, by among others a criterion of complementary distribution, as 'allomorphs' of their respective 'morphemes'.

A further criterion was, on the face of it, that 'allomorphs' should share a meaning. Thus there is a meaning (Martinet's 'signifié') common to *come* and *came*, or to French *va* and *aller*, or to all the plural endings. But the morpheme itself was now identified by a procedure operating solely on arrangements of phonemes. If defined by that procedure, it was again a unit that 'had' meaning, not a unit, like that of Martinet and others in the Saussurean tradition, that was itself, in part, 'of' meaning. But neither was it a unit composed of phonemes. 'Come', we could now say, represents one morpheme, realised in both [kʌm] (*come*) and [keɪm] (*came*). The category 'plural' was another morpheme, realised by [ɪz] and so on. But only their realisations could be divided into parts; the morphemes themselves are formally primitive.

These were technical details, and a reader may well feel that, in a history that has hitherto dealt largely with more general ideas, they might helpfully have been skipped over. But the result is fundamental to most later theories of a language system. In earlier treatments, units like Saussure's 'signifiants', or morphemes as Bloomfield had represented them, had been related directly to 'signifiés' or units of meaning. Even in Martinet's, a variant like [al] in *aller* was still directly related to "aller". But the morpheme as defined by Hockett had the properties of neither an 'expression' nor a 'content'. It was not Saussure's mental representation of sounds; nor made up of distinctive features of sounds; nor even of Hjelmslev's 'expression-figurae'. It could indeed be realised by allomorphs, like [va] and [al] in French, which were phonetically very different. At the same time it was not a unit of meaning: not even Hjelmslev's abstract combination of 'content-figurae'. It was simply an unanalysed whole, by which sounds and meanings were related through a mediating level. As a unit on that level, 'come' can be related, on the one hand, to a form [kʌm]; on the other, to a meaning represented for the moment by 'come'. But these relations are separate, and there is no longer a direct link between [kʌm] and 'come'.

The entire scheme was set out in Hockett's general introduction to linguistics, ten years after the article I have referred to. A language was as a whole a system, which 'can be broken down', he said, 'into five principal subsystems' (Hockett, 1958: 137). Three were 'central': a '*grammatical* system' and a '*phonological* system', and a third which linked them. Two others were 'peripheral'. When Hockett was writing, the term 'interface' was not yet in fashion; but the peripheral subsystems formed two opposite interfaces with domains outside language.

Morphemes, such as 'plural' or 'come', were the basic units of the grammatical system. It consisted, therefore, of 'a stock of morphemes, and the arrangements in which they occur'. At this level, then, the word *peaches* may be represented by the arrangement 'peach + plural'; *came* by the arrangement of 'come' with, as a further morpheme, 'past tense'. The phonological system was, in parallel, 'a stock of phonemes, and the arrangements in which they occur'. So, at this level, *peaches* and *came* may again be represented by arrangements of '[p]', '[iː]', and so on. It was by virtue of these systems, then, that language has the property, as we saw earlier, of 'duality'. The third central component was 'the code that ties together the grammatical and the phonological system'. By this system, 'peach' as a single morpheme would be related to the arrangement of phonemes '[piːtʃ]' and, by reference to the '[tʃ]', 'plural', as a morpheme following it, would be related by the 'code' to '[ɪz]'; an arrangement of 'come' with 'past tense' would in the same sense be related as a whole to '[keɪm]'. Since this code related morphemes to phonemes Hockett called it the '*morphophonemic* system'.

Finally, one interface was formed by a peripheral '*semantic* system', which associated the units and arrangements of the grammatical system with 'things and situations, or kinds of things and situations' (138). Meanings, therefore, were 'associative ties' (139) between linguistic units and the world that speakers are talking about. The opposite interface was formed by a '*phonetic* system' which related arrangements of phonemes to produced or perceived sounds.

For a final twist to this part of our story we can return to the ancient scheme with which this section began. For the ancient 'letter' we can again read 'phoneme'; and by the 1930s, as we have seen, phonemes were already abstractions. At that stage, however, it could still make sense to say that words and sentences were sequences of phonemes. In the schemes developed by the end of the 1950s this was drastically modified.

The phoneme, as the basic unit of one level of articulation, was matched by the morpheme, or by Martinet's 'moneme', as the basic unit of another. At this new level of abstraction, sentences were formed ultimately of morphemes or of signs corresponding to them. Thus, following Hockett, a sentence *The women came in* might be represented at that level by an arrangement of morphemes 'the + plural + woman . . .' and so on. But what then of, in particular, the word? Traditionally the sentence would have, as its smallest units of meaning, four words. But if morphemes or monemes now had that role, did this traditional unit still have a place in the system?

Martinet was one structuralist who thought not. In the introduction I have been citing he put the term 'word' ('mot') in inverted commas, and argued that it should be discarded (Martinet, 1970 [1960]: 114ff.). Take, for example, French *nous courons* 'we are running'. By tradition, this is a sequence of two words: *nous* 'we' and *courons*, which is a first person plural of the verb *courir* 'to run'. The first person plural is distinguished by the ending -*ons* and, still in the traditional account, the verb 'agrees' with *nous* as its subject. But for Martinet (104) the monemes that make up this form were just two. One was, as we might expect, *cour*-: that is to say, the 'signifiant' [kur] in conjunction with the 'signifié' "courir". The other united a 'signifié' "first plural" neither specifically with [nu] (*nous*) nor specifically with [õ] (-*ons*), but with a discontinuous 'signifiant', [nu . . . õ], that includes both. In that way the analysis cut clean across the traditional boundary between words, which was therefore invalid. In the next section (105), Martinet also put 'agreement' ('accord') in inverted commas.

Not everyone was an iconoclast to that degree. But the logic of such treatments could not be ignored. If the phoneme and the morpheme were the first great technical gains that structural linguists might claim, the word was beginning to look like the first casualty.

5.3   Deep structure and surface structure

The British linguist C. E. Bazell remarked in the 1950s that, 'if it is possible to discover any aim common to all linguistic schools', it was 'the reduction, by terminological devices', of what he called 'the fundamental asymmetry of linguistic systems'. If, for example, there are phonemes and allophones it is assumed that 'there must also be' morphemes and allomorphs. 'If there is a form and a substance of the expression, then there must also be a form and a substance of the content.' If phonemes can be analysed into 'relevant phonic features', then morphemes (as we will see more clearly in a later chapter) were analysed into 'relevant semantic features'. No single scholar might subscribe to all specific proposals current, but the relation between them was 'unmistakable' (Bazell, 1953: iii).

These were the comments of a critic, and most structuralists would have protested that the symmetries which they saw between the two sides of the linguistic sign, or the parallels that they explored between descriptive method in phonology and in grammar, were not figments. But the passion for isomorphism, as Kuryłowicz had described it, was then rampant; and, if Bazell had been writing towards the end of the next decade, he could have added yet more instances to his list. Of the new schemes in the 1960s, the most influential by far was that of Noam Chomsky. When he proposed it he was still in his late thirties, and much of both its substance and its terminology has since changed. But Chomsky's reputation, in linguistics and still more outside it, had then reached its zenith. This scheme was therefore widely known and widely pondered, often by commentators who knew little or nothing of those that had preceded it.

Its sources lay, in part, in Chomsky's earlier account of syntax. By 'syntax' grammarians have traditionally meant the study of relations among units that make up the sentence. Originally these were words: thus, to describe the syntax of *The women came in*, a grammarian would relate the noun *women* to the article *the*, the verb *came* to the preposition or adverb *in*, and so on. But by the 1950s they were widely taken to be morphemes. In the same example, *the* and *in* were indivisible units; but *women* and *came* could both be represented by two: 'woman + plural', 'come + past'. Syntax was accordingly concerned with the 'arrangements', in Hockett's sense, of morphemes. Hockett's scheme was published later than the earliest work by Chomsky. But Chomsky had been a protégé of Zellig Harris, and these results were taken for granted by most structuralists of the American school.

How then were morphemes arranged in sentences? The answer given was, in part, that they form hierarchies of intermediate units. Thus, at the lowest level, 'woman' and 'plural' form one intermediate unit which we write as '*women*'. We can show this, in a common notation, by enclosing them in square brackets: [woman plural]. Both larger units and the morphemes that compose them are of various classes. Thus *women* is, in the traditional classification into parts of speech, a noun. We may show that as follows: $_N$[woman plural]. In this notation, which translates easily into others, successively larger units are enclosed throughout in brackets and their class is indicated by a symbol, such as 'N' for 'noun', subscript to them.

In the same way 'come' and 'past tense' form a verb: $_V$[come past]. But then, in our example, that in turn will form a unit with *in*: [[come past] in].

Traditionally this is a 'predicate', and predicates were said to have verbs as essential elements; therefore they were described in the 1950s as 'verb phrases'. So, with a subscript 'VP', $_{VP}$[$_V$[come past] in]. In the same way units like *the women* were described as 'noun phrases': $_{NP}$[the $_N$[woman plural]]. Finally, in a still larger pattern of arrangement, the sentence as a whole (S) would then be made up of the noun phrase plus the verb phrase: in summary, $_S$[$_{NP}$[the women] $_{VP}$[came in]]. In this way, any sentence could be represented by a sequence of morphemes, such as 'the + woman + plural . . .', combined, stage by stage, into a hierarchy of larger units.

The basic insight precedes Chomsky. But it was in his work in the 1950s, and in particular in his monograph *Syntactic Structures*, that the nature of this system was most rigorously explored. To describe the syntax of a language was to set out, in a series of statements as simple and as general as possible, all the ways in which a unit of one class can combine with units of others. Thus by one statement, or in Chomsky's terms one 'rule', a sentence (S) can, in English, consist of a noun phrase (NP) followed by a verb phrase (VP). By another rule, a noun phrase can consist of an article, such as *the*, followed by a noun; by another, a noun may consist of a morpheme like 'woman' followed by the 'plural' morpheme; and so on. I referred briefly, at the end of 2.2, to the concept of a generative grammar. A 'grammar' taking this form could be seen precisely, in the way that Harris had foreshadowed, as 'a set of instructions' by which sentences are generated (again Z. S. Harris, 1954: 260). If we begin with 'S' as the largest unit, we could take the first of these rules as an instruction to derive a more detailed structure 'NP + VP'. We could take the second as an instruction to derive from that a structure in which 'NP' is in turn divided: 'article + N + VP'. By successive steps we would eventually reach a point at which all elements are classes of morphemes. Any sequence of morphemes which would satisfy that structure represents one utterance that is possible in the language.

In Chomsky's account, a generative grammar in which all rules were of this form was, more precisely, a 'phrase structure' grammar (Chomsky, 1957: 26ff.). But, having made their form explicit, he then argued that, on their own, they were inadequate. He did 'not know' (34) whether English, for example, literally could not be generated in this way. But, as soon as we 'consider . . . sentences beyond the simplest type' and, 'in particular, . . . attempt to define some order among the rules that produce' them, 'we run into numerous difficulties and complications' (35). The remedy, as he saw it, lay in adding rules of a quite different kind, by which one hierarchical structure, like that of *The women came in*, is 'transformed' into another.

Let us take a classic illustration, which concerns 'the active–passive relation' (42). In, for example, *John eats lunch* the verb *eats*, which is traditionally 'active', had two elements: the 'eat' morpheme plus, in Chomsky's notation, an '*S*' morpheme. But in *Lunch is eaten by John* the form *is eaten*, which is traditionally 'passive', had two more: first 'be', which now combines with '*S*' to form *is*; then 'en', combined with 'eat' and realised, in this instance, by -*en*. These further morphemes went together (39). They could not be added when a noun or noun phrase, like *lunch*, follows directly: thus one cannot say *John is eaten lunch*. Neither could they be omitted, or replaced by others, in a context such as *Lunch — by John*. One cannot say *Lunch eats by John*; nor, for example, *Lunch is eating by John*. Finally, 'in a full-fledged grammar', we would need to place restrictions on nouns in the positions of *lunch* and *John*. Such restrictions would 'permit', for example, an active sentence such as *John admires sincerity* or *Sincerity frightens John*, while 'excluding the "inverse" non-sentences' *Sincerity admires John* or *John frightens sincerity*. Likewise, in the passive, they would have to permit both *Sincerity is admired by John* and *John is frightened by sincerity*, while excluding both *John is admired by sincerity* and *Sincerity is frightened by John*. 'If we try to include passives directly', alongside actives, in a phrase structure grammar, we will have to state all such restrictions once, for one construction, and then restate them all, 'in the opposite order', for the other (43).

'This inelegant duplication', with all the 'special restrictions' affecting 'be' and 'en', 'can be avoided only', Chomsky argued, if we introduce a new rule by which, for any active sentence, there is automatically a corresponding passive sentence. So, given *John eats lunch*, with a hierarchical structure of the sort already outlined, it will follow that there is another sentence *Lunch is eaten by John*, whose structure will in part reflect it. By this new rule 'be' and 'en' would be obligatory: therefore there cannot be a passive construction, like '*Lunch eats by John*', that does not include them. They would not be specified, as a unit, by the rules for actives: therefore there is no active sentence '*John is eaten lunch*'. If there is an active *John admires sincerity*, it followed that there is a passive *Sincerity is admired by John*. Since passives were formed only by this rule, then, by excluding an active '*Sincerity admires John*', we also exclude '*John is admired by sincerity*'.

This new rule was a 'grammatical transformation' (44), and a phrase structure grammar plus transformations was a 'transformational grammar'. Its attraction, once more, was that in this way we could avoid inelegancies, complications, duplications, and so on. But Chomsky also claimed that such rules would explain some aspects of meaning. This was argued, in particular, for examples of what was often called 'grammatical ambiguity'.

A famous example was *the shooting of the hunters* (Chomsky, 1957: 88f.). This 'can', in Chomsky's words, be 'understood ambiguously', in a sense which is either like that of *the growling of lions* (the hunters are doing the shooting, the lions are doing the growling) or like that of *the raising of flowers* (the hunters are being shot, the flowers are being raised). For other grammarians these were examples of 'subjective' and 'objective genitives': *the hunters* is related to *shooting* in the sense of either a subject (compare *The hunters shoot*) or an object (compare *They shoot the hunters*). For Chomsky, therefore, they reflected different transformations by which forms in *-ing* could be derived. 'Careful analysis . . . shows that we can simplify the grammar' (89) if we 'set up' rules by which, in one case, 'any sentence' like *The lions growl* would 'carry . . . into the corresponding' phrase *the growling of lions*; and, in the other, any sentence like *They raise flowers* would carry into a superficially similar *the raising of flowers*. In what Chomsky had earlier called 'a full-fledged grammar', there would, by implication, be restrictions which exclude 'non-sentences' such as '*The flowers raise*' or '*They growl the lions*'. But both *The hunters shoot* and *They shoot the hunters* would 'carry', by different transformations, into *the shooting of the hunters*. This was, in Chomsky's words, 'a clear and automatic explanation' (88f.) of the 'ambiguity'.

That is as far as Chomsky had got by 1957. The parts of a generative grammar were therefore, first, a set of rules for phrase structure; then a set of transformations; then, finally, a 'morphophonemic part' which, like Hockett's 'morphophonemic system' (5.2), related abstract representations of words, such as 'be + S' or 'admire + en', to sequences of phonemes such as 'ız' or 'ədmʌɪəd' (Chomsky, 1957: 45f.). In terms of 'some more general theory of language' (102) we could also study 'correspondences' between the formal structure of sentences, as generated by such a grammar, and features of meaning.

But in the 1960s it was assumed that grammars should themselves give an account of meanings. 'It is quite obvious', Chomsky said in one work of this period, 'that sentences have an intrinsic meaning determined by linguistic rule' (Chomsky, 1973 [1967]: 115). To know a language was to control 'a system constituted by rules that interact to determine the form and intrinsic meaning' of its sentences (1973 [1968]: 71). A generative grammar was 'a system of rules that relate [phonetic] signals' to what are called 'semantic interpretations of these signals' (1966: 12). Such a grammar would again have parts or components (Trubetzkoy's 'Teil-systeme'). So what exactly were the levels at which sentences would be represented?

Two were seen as given. If a grammar relates 'signals' to meanings of signals it must, first, represent the signals themselves. These were not Chomsky's main concern; but a natural proposal, developed by his colleague Morris Halle, was that successive segments should be represented, in the tradition of the Prague School, by phonetic features. Halle had been a colleague of Roman Jakobson, who had escaped from Europe to America in the Second World War; and in the 1950s had contributed to a theory of phonology in which phonemes were defined as 'bundles of concurrent features' (Jakobson and Halle, 1956: 5). In his representations of signals segments correspond more nearly to 'phones' (3.2); except that, as Chomsky and Halle make clear in a joint work, grammars were concerned not with physical sounds, but with 'signals' as they are 'mentally constructed' by the speakers of a language (Chomsky and Halle, 1968: 14). The features of which they were said to be composed refer by 1968 to postures of the vocal organs by which speech is produced. But that aside, such representations were in the tradition of Saussure's 'acoustic images' (2.1).

As a grammar must by definition represent the 'signals', so, again by definition, it must represent 'semantic interpretations'. The problems here were still 'veiled', as Chomsky put it, in 'their traditional obscurity' (Chomsky, 1966: 13). But in the same passage he referred to work by colleagues, notably Jerrold J. Katz, which implied that meanings might be 'intrinsic' if they did not reflect the particular circumstances in which sentences are uttered. 'Semantic theory' was, in the words of Katz and Jerry A. Fodor, 'a theory of the semantic interpretation of sentences in isolation' (Katz and Fodor, 1963: 177). We will return to their theory in another chapter. But when a sentence is uttered it will be in a specific 'setting' (176ff.), and will have its meaning in that setting. Its meaning 'in isolation' was one assumed to hold independently of 'settings'.

A generative grammar would then mediate between these, just as, in Hockett's 'design of a language' (1958: 137), central systems mediate between peripheries. How then did the parts that Chomsky had established in 1957 fit in?

The answer was superbly simple. As Chomsky expounded it, the next step was to posit a 'neutral technical notion of "syntactic description"' (Chomsky, 1966: 13). This would mediate the relation between forms and meanings, in that any such description would 'uniquely determine' both a 'semantic interpretation' and a 'phonetic form' that corresponds to it. So, whatever the intrinsic meaning of, let us say, *She was disturbed by the growling of lions*, it would be 'determined' by a representation of the syntax of this sentence which would also 'determine' that, phonetically, its first segment is [ʃ], its second [iː], and so on. A sentence like, say, *She was disturbed by the shooting of the hunters* would, naturally, have two semantic interpretations. These would accordingly be determined by two different syntactic descriptions, each, however, determining the same phonetic 'signal'.

The form of a 'syntactic description' is now sufficiently obvious. In the first of our examples the structure of a sentence like *The lions growl* 'carries through', as Chomsky had argued in the 1950s, into that of *the growling of lions*. The structure of an active, like *The growling of lions disturbed her*, was in addition transformed to that of a passive. Its syntactic description would accordingly relate two representations. One was an initial structure generated only, following *Syntactic Structures*, by rules for phrase structure. This would include a smaller structure in which *lions* is the subject of *growl*: [*lions growl*]; and, although this had the form of a sentence (s[*lions growl*]), it would occupy the same place as a noun phrase in, for example, *The noise disturbed her*. It was in that sense both a sentence and a noun phrase: NP[s[*lions growl*]]. The initial structure as a whole would thus be one in which this smaller sentence is in turn the subject of *disturbed*.

The other representation was the structure that, by transformations, this would 'carry into': thus, in part, s[*she was disturbed by* NP[*the growling of lions*]]. But two further points will now be clear. First, it was this second representation that specifically 'determines' the phonetic form of the sentence. To be exact, a grammar would include rules that relate 'she' to a phonetic representation [ʃiː], 'be + past' to [wəz], and so on, in the order in which successive morphemes appeared in it.

Likewise, it was the initial representation that, to all appearances, 'determines the semantic interpretation'. In our second example, *the shooting of the hunters* would be related to initial structures in which *hunters* was variously a subject (NP[s[*the hunters shoot*]]) or an object (NP[s[*someone shoot(s) the hunters*]]); and, on that basis, we could posit rules by which it was 'interpreted' in different ways. But the structure that was derived by transformations would be in either case the same. Therefore, while the latter would 'determine' the phonetic signal, it would seem that it was irrelevant to the meaning.

In Chomsky's famous terminology, the semantic interpretations were determined by 'deep' structures. As he defined it at this stage in the development of his theories, the 'deep structure of a sentence' was precisely the 'aspect' of a syntactic description to which, by the rules of what he called the 'semantic component' of a grammar, a representation of meaning was assigned (Chomsky, 1966: 16). Phonetic representations were instead determined by 'surface' structures. The 'surface structure of a sentence' was thus correspondingly the 'aspect' of a syntactic description to which the rules of a 'phonological component' assigned what were also called 'phonetic interpretations'. This phonological component was in part the equivalent, it can be seen, of his or Hockett's earlier 'morphophonemics'. The central part was a 'syntactic component' that, as in *Syntactic Structures*, included transformations. This 'generates [syntactic descriptions] each of which consists of a deep structure and a surface structure'.

The work I am citing is the published version of a series of lectures delivered in 1964. But the scheme was summarised in Chomsky's *Aspects of the Theory of Syntax* (Chomsky, 1965: 16), and it was from that account, in a chapter that in later sections dealt inspiringly with issues in the philosophy of language and the general history of ideas, that it first caught everyone's imagination. It was therefore tempting to read into the term 'deep', in particular, far more than was actually there. But its interest is again as part of a technical scheme of levels, by which, as in Hockett's, a relation between forms and meanings could be mediated. Famous as it was, the scheme was of the 1960s and within ten years was already drastically revised.

But, as a scheme of the 1960s, it is of great historical importance. With many others, it assumed that meanings can be abstracted as invariants: the basic relation was accordingly between an abstract level of phonetic representation (Chomsky's 'signals') and a similarly abstract level of 'semantic interpretation'. These levels interfaced, by implication, with real sounds and real meanings. But semantic representations were not just the 'signifiés' of individual signs. They were the meanings, as determined by a generative grammar, of whole sentences. Nor were parts of meanings related one to one to parts of signals. Phonetic representations were paired first with surface structures; and this relation was already not as simple as sign theories had at first implied. Surface structures were in turn paired with deep structures; and the 'arrangements' of morphemes on these levels, to borrow again Hockett's terminology, could be as different, both in the units themselves and in their order, as need be. Finally deep structures were paired with semantic representations; and, when the 'veils of obscurity' were lifted, that relation might be as complex. For any sentence, the relation between the 'signal' and its 'meaning', via the mediating level of syntax, could in principle be very indirect.

Such schemes were therefore apt to be rejected by any structuralist for whom the Saussurean link between the two sides of the sign remained central. By the same token, of course, anyone who took that view would, from a Chomskyan viewpoint, be concerned with syntax only at a surface level.

6   Internalised language

By 1960 structural linguists could look back on thirty or more years of progress. The theory of the phoneme was now widely accepted; and, although there were disagreements in detail between most Americans and most Europeans, few disputed that it was one central unit of language. For many linguists the morpheme or a unit like it was another, and the identification of these units in '-eme', as the elements of articulation on two different levels, was increasingly a basis for the practical description of languages. Such findings had begun to work their way from technical publications into textbooks. I have referred to Hockett's general introduction to linguistics (Hockett, 1958). But it had been preceded by at least one specialist textbook in descriptive linguistics, by H. A. Gleason, whose table of contents gives a clear view of how students, in at least part of the English-speaking world, were taught (Gleason, 1961 [1955]). Martinet's introduction, to which I have also referred, was to have a similarly wide success in continental Europe (Martinet, 1970 [1960]).

These achievements were ostensibly founded in the thought of Saussure, in lectures that had last been given in 1911, and of Bloomfield, formulated in its mature phase in the 1920s. A linguist was therefore describing either an underlying system whose reality was supra-individual (2.1), or a set of potential utterances (2.2). But both accounts had naturally reflected the preoccupations of their own day and, with hindsight, though the structure of a language system had been worked out in some detail, it was time to ask again exactly what reality such systems had. A new answer was given by Noam Chomsky, and the Chomskyan 'revolution' in linguistics, as it has been widely described since the 1960s, rested on it. How then did this revolution unfold?

In an account in the 1980s Chomsky himself distinguishes 'two major conceptual shifts' (Chomsky, 1986: 6). The first 'inaugurated', in his words, 'the contemporary study of generative grammar'; and consisted in 'a shift of focus', as he puts it later in the same book, from a view of language as 'behavior and its products' to the study of 'systems of mental

96

representation and computation' (51) underlying behaviour. Such systems of mental representation constitute an individual speaker's 'knowledge' of a particular language, and a 'generative grammar', as he then defined it, is a theory of the state in which the 'mind/brain' of a person knowing a language must be (3). The second conceptual shift is said to be 'theory-internal' and to be 'in process' as he was writing (6). It led to a specific theory of genetic factors in the acquisition of this knowledge, or the development of these systems of mental representation, which had by then, in the 1980s, become the centre of this thought. Now the theory to which this was internal is that of, in general, 'generative grammar'. Therefore it is with that notion that we should begin.

6.1   Generative grammars

The term 'generative grammar' had in origin a perfectly transparent sense, and did not at first bear the construction that, in passages like the one I have just cited, Chomsky would eventually put on it. We have seen, to begin, how Bloomfield had defined 'a language' as a totality of poten-tial utterances (again 2.2). Each utterance in a language could then be represented by an arrangement of smaller units, up to the limits of, again in Bloomfield's account, a sentence (2.3). So, for example, 'English' would be a set of which the arrangement of words *I + (a)m + hungry* is one member. By implication, other arrangements would not belong to the language. For example, there would be no potential utterance *Am hungry I*; or, splitting *hungry* into morphemes, *I'm -y hung(e)r*. A grammar was a description of 'a language'; and, under this definition, it described such a set. It could therefore be interpreted, in the words of Zellig Harris (2.2), as a set of 'instructions' by which a language is 'generated'.

A set is in a mathematician's definition any collection of members. We can accordingly define 'a language' in that spirit, in a sense whose applica-tion to the real world is potentially much wider than to languages in the ordinary sense, in which we are interested. The members of such a 'language' are by definition its 'sentences', and their number may in prin-ciple be either finite or infinite. But each individual 'sentence' is in turn a finite sequence of elements, and the number of such elements, for any 'language', will itself be finite. Now a 'language' as a mathematical object bears as much relation to a language as conceived by Bloomfield as, for example, a mathematician's concept of a 'triangle' bears to an actual object whose shape is triangular. For that reason, I have scrupulously put both 'language' and 'sentence' in inverted commas. But all 'natural languages', as Chomsky called them, '. . . [we]re languages in this sense'. The 'natural language' English, for example, would be, in its 'written form', a set of sentences each 'representable as a finite sequence' of the letters of the alphabet (Chomsky, 1957: 13).

Likewise, in its 'spoken . . . form', each sentence would be 'representable as' a finite sequence of phonemes. Just as *I'm hungry* would in writing be a sequence of orthographic characters, so the spoken sentence corresponding to it may be represented by a sequence 'ʌ + ɪ + m + h + ʌ + ŋ + g + r + i', made up of the phonemes 'ʌ', 'ɪ' and so on. In Bloomfield's terms, this would have represented a 'potential utterance': something that a member of an English speech community could say. In Chomsky's terms, the 'natural language' could be represented by a set of sentences of which that is one member. But this formulation also made explicit that some sequences of phonemes are not sentences. Thus the 'natural language' English would not be represented accurately, in its 'written form', by a set of which one member is the sequence *Am hungry I*; or, in its 'spoken form', by one which had a member 'a + m + h + ʌ + ŋ + g + r + i + ʌ + ɪ'. In Bloomfield's terms, this would by implication not have represented a 'potential utterance'.

I have explained this with a care that is in part derived from hindsight. At that stage, for example, Chomsky did not systematically distinguish 'sentences' and 'utterances'. But if 'natural languages' could be represented in this way, the 'fundamental aim in the linguistic analysis' of a language was, in his words, 'to separate the *grammatical* sequences' which were its sentences 'from the *ungrammatical* sequences' that were not. It was also, Chomsky added, to 'study the structure of the grammatical sequences'. But an essential task was to indicate what members the set had. 'The grammar' of a language 'will thus', as he defined it, 'be a device that generates all of the grammatical sequences of [the language] and none of the ungrammatical ones'. So, for example, we can imagine a grammar of English, as represented in its written form, that would generate a set with members such as *I'm hungry*, *You are thirsty*, *Are we hungry?*, *He's not thirsty*; it would also say what structure each of these has. But the set would not have among its members such sequences as *Am hungry I*, *Are you -y thirst?*, or *Not's angry he*. Ideally it would generate all the sequences, and only the sequences, that represent what Bloomfield would have called the potential utterances of English.

This is from one page of Chomsky's first book, and for most readers it was a bombshell. For no one else had taken that to be the 'fundamental aim' of linguistic analysis. In the view then dominant in America it had been precisely that of analysis: of the controlled division of utterances into phonemes, morphemes, phrases, and so on. The overall description of a language was a synthesis to which, as Harris put it at one point, 'the work of analysis leads . . . up' (Z. S. Harris, 1951: 372). A few years later

Harris too was talking, as we have seen, of grammars 'generating' sentences. But it was his pupil Chomsky who now took that goal as primary.

A generative grammar of a language such as English 'is essentially a theory', as Chomsky put it in a later chapter, of that language (Chomsky, 1957: 49). Like any 'scientific theory', it was 'based on a finite number of observations'; and, in our case, these were observations of what people say. A grammar of English was thus 'based on a finite corpus of utterances', taken to be in English. Any theory 'seeks to relate the observed phenomena' and, 'by constructing general laws', 'to predict new phenomena'. Similarly, a grammar would contain 'grammatical rules' which 'express relations' among both 'the sentences of the corpus' and 'the indefinite number of sentences generated by the grammar beyond the corpus'. These were in turn its 'predictions'. But how was the adequacy of such a theory to be assessed?

One obvious test was whether the sentences predicted did count as 'potential utterances'. In Chomsky's terms, we had to determine 'whether or not [they] are actually grammatical, i.e., acceptable to the native speaker, etc.' (13). The 'etc.' was important, and supplying what Chomsky called 'a behavioral criterion for grammaticalness' was never supposed to be easy. But one 'external condition' of adequacy (49) was that 'the sentences generated', those predicted as well as those observed, 'will have to be acceptable to the native speaker'. A grammar of English which allowed a sentence like *Am hungry I*, or excluded *Am I hungry?*, would accordingly be less adequate, in that respect at least, than one which did not. Another external condition was illustrated in a later chapter with the famous example of *the shooting of the hunters*. We saw earlier (in 5.3) how this phrase was said to be 'understood ambiguously', and how, if a grammar were simplified by the addition of transformations, its ambiguity could be 'explained'. In Chomsky's terms, the transformational grammar would treat it as a 'constructional homonym'. Such homonyms existed, by definition, whenever 'a given phoneme sequence is analyzed in more than one way on a given level' (86). Another criterion of adequacy, he suggested, was 'whether or not each case of constructional homonym[y] is a real case of ambiguity and each case of the proper kind of ambiguity is actually a case of constructional homonym[y]'. By this criterion, then, a grammar of English which did not 'analyse' *the shooting of the hunters* in two distinct ways was less adequate, in that respect, than one which did.

A grammar was accordingly expected to predict the 'sentences' or 'utterances' of a language, and 'explain' certain properties that they have. But Chomsky also imposed a 'condition of generality'. It was not sufficient that a grammar of English or any other language should be 'externally' adequate. For that requirement might be met in many different ways.

Therefore, he argued, we must also prescribe the form a grammar may take. Each grammar should, as Chomsky put it, 'be constructed in accordance with a specific theory of linguistic structure' whose terms were 'defined independently of any specific language' (50).

In a footnote to this passage Chomsky referred to a paper published three years earlier, in which Hockett had proposed criteria for 'models' of description. For Hockett too descriptions had to be such that, 'following the statements' that they made, one could 'generate any number of utterances in the language'. They were thus predictive or, as Hockett said, 'prescriptive'; and the test for their predictions was, as he put it, that of 'casual acceptance by a native speaker' (Hockett, 1954: 232). A 'model of description' was defined by Hockett as 'a frame of reference within which an analyst approaches . . . a language and states the results of his investigations' (210). This frame of reference would therefore have to allow an analyst to formulate descriptions by which predictions were made. It must, as Hockett put it, 'be *productive*: when applied to a given language, the results must make possible the creation of an indefinite number of valid new utterances' (232).

The requirement that a description should be predictive was a criterion for descriptions; that a model of description should be 'productive' was accordingly a 'metacriterion' (232f.), and one of four that Hockett had considered essential. The others were, first, that it 'must be *general*'; secondly, that it 'must be *specific*'; thirdly, that it 'must be *inclusive*'.

To say that a model must be 'general' was to require that 'it must be applicable to any language, not just to languages of certain types'; and Chomsky, similarly, required that grammars should accord with a general 'theory of linguistic structure'. In arguing for this condition, Chomsky said that, to assess the 'external adequacy' of a grammar, we need to assume no more than a 'partial knowledge of sentences and non-sentences'. We would know, for example, that *I'm hungry* is an English sentence and *I'm -y hung(e)r* is not; but there would be many 'sequences of phonemes' about which we were not sure. Thus, to hazard an example, could one or could one not say to someone *Be hungry, you!*? 'In many intermediate cases we shall be prepared', he said, 'to let the grammar itself decide', when it 'is set up in the simplest way so that it includes the clear sentences and excludes the clear non-sentences'. But '[for] a single language, taken in isolation', this was 'only a weak test . . . , since many different grammars may handle the clear cases properly'. To make it stronger he insisted that they should 'be handled properly for *each* language by grammars all of which are constructed by the same method' (14).

To say that a model must be 'inclusive' was to require that 'when [it is] applied to a given language, the results must cover all the observed data and, by implication, at least a very high percentage of all the not-yet-observed data' (again Hockett, 1954: 232). But we may make this more precise if we think again of languages as sets to be generated. A 'model' could be seen as specifying, among other things, the form that, switching now to Chomsky's terminology, a generative grammar of a language must have. A general model would have to be such that any 'natural language' can be generated.

To say that a model must be 'specific' was to require that 'when [it is] applied to a given language, the results must be determined wholly by the nature of the model and the nature of the language, not at all by the whim of the analyst'. Hockett added that such a model might require us to 'subsume . . . facts more than once, from different angles'. But there would be 'a lack of specificity' if it '*allowed* us to take our choice, instead of *forcing*' one or another solution. Now the purpose of Chomsky's 'condition of generality' was to reduce the multiplicity of grammars that, for any language, might be 'externally adequate'. Therefore a 'specific theory of linguistic structure', as he described it, had to be specific in precisely that sense.

In Chomsky's early thinking, that translated, in particular, into the requirement that a 'linguistic theory' should provide 'an *evaluation procedure*' (Chomsky, 1957: 51) for grammars. From what we have said already, it was 'necessary to state precisely . . . the external criteria of adequacy'. This was in Chomsky's account the first of 'three main tasks' in the programme he suggested (53). The second was to 'characterize the form of grammars in a general and explicit way' (54): to specify the kinds of ways in which, as we have seen, they were to 'express relations' among sentences. But for any given 'corpus of utterances', there may still be more than one alternative grammar, each in the prescribed form and equivalent as to 'external adequacy', between which, if our theory was to meet what Hockett called the 'metacriterion' of specificity, it would have to choose. The third task, therefore, was to 'analyse and define' a notion of, in Chomsky's term, 'simplicity' that 'we intend to use in choosing among grammars all of which are of the proper form' (54). The theory would thus 'tell us', for any 'corpus' and any two such grammars, 'which is the better grammar of the language' (51).

This was without doubt a tall order. A grammar was, once more, a theory like, as a rave review proclaimed, a theory in the natural sciences (Lees, 1957). But on top of that we then required a higher-order theory of, in general, grammars. This not only specified the form that theories of each individual language would have; it also had to show how one was better than another. Such a theory would indeed have been a remarkable achievement. For, as Chomsky himself remarked, 'there are few areas of science in which one would seriously consider the possibility of developing a general, practical, method for choosing among several theories, each compatible with the available data' (53).

But it is easy to see why Chomsky did consider it. The science of 'descriptive linguistics', as it was then called by Harris, Hockett and other American scholars, had as its aim the description of languages, and a grammar, in Chomsky's sense, was such a description. But 'describing' a language is not like, for instance, describing a physical object. If I describe a tree, say, or a picture, someone else might then in principle examine it and judge directly how far my account is adequate. But to 'describe' a language is not so straightforward. We may describe, in something like the same sense, the behaviour of two people who on a particular occasion happen, among other things, to be making certain noises. But the language they are speaking, however one defines it, does not lie open to observation in the same way. For Saussure it had been a system whose existence was not concrete. For Bloomfield in the 1920s it had been a set of utterances; but, even if that definition is taken very literally, we can never observe, and so describe in the ordinary sense, a language in its entirety. So how is what we are calling a description to be validated?

The problem was faced by structural linguists from the beginning, and the programme of controlled analysis, as envisaged by Chomsky's American predecessors, had been one intended solution. It had led, in particular, to operational definitions of the phoneme (3.2), of the morpheme (5.2), and increasingly, as Chomsky himself came onto the scene, of larger units. Now for Chomsky a 'description' was a grammar, and a grammar was, more exactly, a theory. But his 'fundamental concern' was still, he said, that of the 'justification of grammars' (49). A 'linguistic theory' had accordingly to be a higher-order theory, which in some way validated object theories.

The second of Chomsky's three tasks was, as we have seen, to 'characterize the form of grammars' in general. But for this there was another motive. For any linguist naturally had an interest both in the description of individual languages and in the properties that distinguish languages, in general, from other systems that are not languages. In Chomsky's terms, a particular 'natural language' was the subject of a particular grammar. This was, as we have seen, a 'theory' of the language. The properties of languages in general would in turn be characterised by a higher-order theory satisfying his condition of generality. Now the primary aim was, once more, to select for any language a particular grammar from the multitude that would in principle be possible. But the requirement was 'reasonable', Chomsky added, 'since we are interested not only in particular languages, but also in the general nature of Language' (14).

This last quotation is worth pondering. For structural linguistics had been, from the beginning, a science of language systems. It was in essence a 'linguistique de la langue'; and implicitly, in any study of the wider phenomena of 'langage', the findings of this discipline, concerning among other things the character of 'langues' in general, would be central. For Chomsky it was similarly implicit that a theory of 'the general nature of Language' (singular and with a capital letter) would be, at its heart at least, a theory of the general properties of (in the plural) 'languages'.

6.2 'Knowing a language'

When Chomsky wrote *Syntactic Structures* he was still in his twenties; and, however brilliant and original his ideas, the problems with which it overtly dealt were still those of his older American contemporaries. But by his own account his real goals were already changing.

A full exposition came in the 1960s, and began with a famous distinction between linguistic 'performance' and linguistic 'competence'. By 'performance' Chomsky meant 'the actual use of language in concrete situations'. So, if I come into the kitchen at a specific time and say 'I'm hungry', that is an instance of 'performance'. But for me to say this, and for whoever else is in the kitchen to understand me, we must share a knowledge of the language I am speaking. This constitutes my or their 'competence'. Competence is thus 'the speaker–hearer's knowledge of his language' (Chomsky, 1965: 4); it is acquired in childhood by any normal individual, and in Chomsky's first 'conceptual shift', as he was later to describe it, it became the central object of study.

There was a parallel, as Chomsky remarked, in Saussure's theory of 'langue' and 'parole'. 'Performance' or 'parole' was constituted by what Bloomfield had called 'acts of speech': my act of speech on coming into the kitchen, another act of speech by Bloomfield's child who does not want to go to bed, and so on. The study of 'a language' as potential acts of this kind had developed, as we have seen, into the proposal that a grammar should generate 'utterances'. But, for followers of Saussure, linguistics 'in the strict sense' was a theory of the nature and structure of 'langues'. In the *Cours* a 'langue' existed in the minds of a community of speakers, each of whom 'passively registers' it (Saussure, 1972 [1916]: 30). To describe it was to describe the sum of what could be so registered. For Chomsky, 'competence' was instead directly individual. But to describe it was to describe the knowledge of a language that an ideal 'speaker–hearer', as an individual member of the community, would have.

For scholars educated in the tradition of Bloomfield this shift was striking and controversial. But it is remarkable how smoothly ideas were transferred from Chomsky's earlier perspective to his new one.

In what, first of all, did competence consist? A grammar was, as we have seen, a theory of a language. But to 'know' a language native speakers must, in Chomsky's analysis, have formed analogous 'theories': they must as children have worked out, from the speech they heard around them, what are sentences that can be said in it and what structures they have. In the 1950s, therefore, Chomsky had already suggested that, to have learned a language, a child has 'in some sense constructed a grammar for himself' (Chomsky, 1959: 57). This was again a 'generative grammar'; and 'obviously', as he now said, 'every speaker of a language has mastered and internalized' such a grammar (Chomsky, 1965: 8). 'Generative grammars' were thus, in the title of the section which includes this last quotation, 'theories of linguistic competence'. In a later passage, Chomsky suggested that 'the term "grammar"' could be used with 'systematic ambiguity'. In one sense, a grammar was 'the native speaker's internally represented "theory of his language"'. This was what children were taken to construct or master or internalise; and it was 'a system of rules that determine how sentences are to be formed, used, and understood'. The architecture of this system was at the time the one described in our last chapter (5.3): so, in 'constructing' their 'theory', children had to work out the deep structures that the sentences of their language have, how structures at that level are related to surface structures, and so on. But in Chomsky's other sense a grammar was 'the linguist's account' of this system. So, in developing as linguists our own 'theory' of, for example, English, we would be formulating an 'account' (or 'grammar' in the second sense) of an internally represented 'theory' (or 'grammar' in the first sense) that must be in the mind of anyone who 'knows' English.

But if Chomsky's theory 'of a language' was now a theory of a speaker's 'competence', what of the higher-order theory, bearing on 'the general nature of Language'? This specified the form that grammars of a 'natural language' must take and a procedure that would justify a choice among alternatives. But when children learn a language they were themselves seen as constructing grammars. Those too would be theories based on evidence of what people say: on 'observation', in Chomsky's words, 'of what we may call *primary linguistic data*'. So, faced with this, a child 'must have a method for devising an appropriate grammar'. 'As a precondition for language learning, he must possess', according to the sentence that immediately follows, both 'a linguistic theory that specifies the form of the grammar of a possible human language' and 'a strategy for selecting a grammar of the appropriate form that is compatible with the primary linguistic data' (Chomsky, 1965: 25). A later section made the parallel between children and descriptive linguists still more precise. 'A child who is capable of language learning must have', Chomsky said:

'a technique for representing input signals' (compare a linguist's phonetic transcription of utterances); 'a way of representing structural information about these signals' (compare a linguist's representation of, for example, phrase structure); 'some initial delimitation of a class of possible hypotheses about language structure'; 'a method of determining what each such hypothesis implies with respect to each sentence'; and, finally, 'a method for selecting one of the (presumably, infinitely many) hypotheses that are allowed . . . and are compatible with the given primary linguistic data' (30).

On that basis the term 'theory of language' could in turn be used with 'systematic ambiguity' (25). Just as a 'grammar', or 'theory of a particular language', could be a system 'constructed' in the minds of speakers, so a 'theory of language' in general would be in a corresponding sense what speakers, when they are children, need in order to construct it. It was 'the innate linguistic theory that provides the basis for language learning'. But in another sense it was 'a linguist's account' of what is innate, just as a linguist's grammar was an account of what has been learned. In this way the whole programme of the 1950s, aimed at characterising languages as sets of utterances, converted beautifully, if Chomsky's reasoning was accepted, into a programme for investigating both the 'knowledge' that each speaker of a language acquires and what Chomsky called 'the child's innate predisposition' to acquire it.

I have introduced these ideas as they were introduced by Chomsky himself, and in the words he used in the 1960s. It will be noted, in particular, that the argument rested simply on the fact that people, in an ordinary sense, 'know languages'. 'Knowing a language' was then interpreted as 'having a theory' of a set of sentences; therefore people 'must', when they are children, form such theories. A theory of a language was by definition a 'generative grammar'; therefore children 'must' construct or internalise generative grammars. They must be predisposed to do so; therefore, it was argued, they 'must' have foreknowledge of what languages in general are like, they 'must' have a way of choosing between grammars, and so on. So far, then, the reasoning was purely philosophical. It started from the initial statement that each language is known to its speakers. From that one could not rationally dissent. The rest was an analysis of what it means to have this knowledge and to come to have it.

But could there also be evidence that an 'innate linguistic theory' exists? Let us assume that Chomsky, as a linguist, had formed a correct account of what an ideal 'speaker–hearer' of, say, English must, as such a speaker–hearer, know. This knowledge has to be acquired in childhood: therefore competence in English must develop in that form, from an initial state in infancy in which a child has none (call it 'S_0') to an eventual steady state (call it 'S_S') in which, ideally, it is complete. How then do the minds of learners get from S_0 to S_S? Now it might be that, if S_0 were blank, we could see no way by which, in principle, that could happen. Therefore S_0 could not be blank: we would have to ascribe to it specific features that are needed if S_S is to be reached. These features must be part of just such an 'innate theory'.

An innate grammatical theory was alternatively a 'Universal Grammar', and by the 1980s, in the period of what he called a second 'conceptual shift', Chomsky had long been convinced that there were overwhelming arguments for it. 'In many cases that have been carefully studied . . . it is a near certainty that fundamental properties' of the grammars that children attain 'are radically underdetermined by evidence available' to them, and 'must therefore be attributed to U[niversal] G[rammar] itself' (Chomsky, 1981: 3). This is cited from a technical monograph, in a passage to which I will return. But the argument, as he had often put it elsewhere, was from 'poverty of stimulus'. The stimulus for acquiring a language is formed by what he had called 'the primary linguistic data'. But the 'evidence' from this is too limited for the knowledge that he ascribed to adult speakers to have developed on that basis alone. Therefore, in his analysis, it must develop by an interaction of the input from a child's environment with specific internal structures. These could only be genetically inherited; or, in a loose sense, innate.

An early illustration was of 'structure-dependency' in syntax. Take, first of all, the sentence *Is Mary coming?* Its construction is that of an interrogative; and in Chomsky's early account of generative grammars, just as passive structures were derived by a transformation from the corresponding actives (5.3), so the structure typical of questions was derived, by an interrogative transformation, from that of statements. The structure of *Is Mary coming?* was thus derived from that of *Mary is coming*. The reason given was that, if we bring out in this way the parallel between these structures, we can 'simplify the description of English syntax' (Chomsky, 1957: 65). But in Chomsky's next phase 'learning a language' meant constructing a grammar. So, as the first step in his argument, we assume that any speaker of English must construct one that includes this transformation.

We also assume that the rule is as general as possible. It must therefore cover not just sentences like this, in which the subject is the one word *Mary*. In other cases subjects are whole sequences of words: thus, alongside *Your sister is coming*, with the subject *your sister*, there is a question *Is your sister coming?*; alongside *The girl next door can't come*, where the subject is *the girl next door*, there is a question *Can't the girl next door come?*; and so on. A child must thus construct a grammar which includes a transformation by which all such sequences are derived. But, in deriving what is 'grammatical', the rule must also exclude what is 'ungrammatical'. Take, for example, the statement *The girl who is invited is coming*. Speakers 'know' that, alongside this, there is a grammatical sequence *Is the girl who is invited coming?* Utterances like these may indeed be in the 'primary linguistic data', for which a particular child internalising such a 'theory' must account. But adult speakers also 'know' that, for example, one cannot say *Is the girl who invited is coming?* The reason (we assume) is that, when they were children, they internalised a grammar that includes (we assume) a transformation, still constructed (we assume) in as general a form as possible, which does not generate sequences of words of that kind. But how, we then ask, were they able to do so?

In one seductive treatment Chomsky imagines a 'Martian scientist' ('call him John M.') who is confronted with this problem. John M. would discover a correspondence between statements and interrogatives: between sentences like *The girl is coming* and *The girl is invited* and others like *Is the girl coming?* and *Is the girl invited?* To be precise, he 'discovers . . . that speakers form' interrogatives 'by moving the verb to the front of the sentence' (Chomsky, 1988: 41). He also 'discovers' that speakers can combine sentences like *The girl is coming* and *The girl is invited* to form more complex structures like *The girl who is invited is coming*. How, he asks, do they form an interrogative from that? 'Evidently, speakers have some rule that they use to form interrogatives corresponding to declaratives'; this 'forms part of the language incorporated in their mind/brain'; so his task as a scientist is to 'construct a hypothesis as to what the rule is' (42).

'The obvious and most simple hypothesis', Chomsky supposes, is that the rule obliges speakers to identify and move the first verb. Thus, in *The girl is coming*, they find *is* and move it to form *Is the girl coming?* But if that were indeed the rule then, from *The girl who is invited is coming*, they would form precisely what they do not form: *Is the girl who invited is coming?* Therefore the hypothesis fails. Is it possible then that they move not the first verb but the last? This too is wrong: thus, to supply an illustration, they do not move the last *is* in the statement *She is the girl who is invited* to form an interrogative *Is she is the girl who invited?* Eventually his Martian discovers that no rule will work if it refers 'simply to the linear order of words'. The rule that speakers 'have' instructs them to move neither the first verb nor the last; but what grammarians call 'the *main verb* of the sentence' (43). But to apply a rule in that form 'one must undertake a complex computational analysis' to identify the verb in question. One must analyse the structure of each statement, to identify the subject phrase (*the girl, she, the girl who is invited*) that the main verb follows. Why, 'one may ask', do speakers 'use a computationally complex rule' (44) instead of one which is much simpler?

John M. is puzzled, and 'might speculate' that they are taught it. Perhaps, as children, they make mistakes and their parents or others correct them. But he 'will quickly discover' that this is not so. 'Children never make errors about such matters and receive no corrections or instruction about them.' Now the rule that Chomsky and his Martian have proposed can be characterised as 'structure-dependent'. Which verb is moved depends on the grammatical structure that each sentence has. It is thus a 'fact', as Chomsky puts it elsewhere, that 'without instruction or direct evidence, children unerringly use computationally complex structure-dependent rules' and not ones that are 'computationally simple' (Chomsky, 1986: 7). The mystery deepens: why do children not make errors and not need instruction?

Chomsky's Martian is left in the end 'with only one plausible conclusion'. There has to be 'some innate principle of the mind/brain', which, given the 'data' that children have, 'yields' this rule as 'the only possibility' (Chomsky, 1988: 44). What is this principle? It is precisely that, in general, 'rules of language . . . are *structure dependent*' (45). They 'operate on expressions that are assigned a certain structure in terms of a hierarchy of phrases': subject noun phrase, following verb, and so on. A child learning any language 'knows, in advance of experience, that the rules will be structure dependent'. Therefore their rule for interrogatives cannot but be as the Martian, or as Chomsky, takes it to be.

Other arguments involved more complex evidence but had essentially the same structure. Knowledge of a certain kind is attributed to state S_S: that of an ideal speaker–hearer who has developed competence, as it was called in the 1960s, in a language. We ask how S_S can be reached; and the only 'plausible conclusion' is that, in an initial state S_0, 'in advance of experience' bearing on its acquisition, certain general principles of language are already genetically determined. By the 1970s, Chomsky was already claiming that 'the growth of language' could be seen as 'analogous to the development of a bodily organ' (Chomsky, 1976 [1975]: 11). Its development depended not just on the environment in which a child was placed. It was not learned, therefore, in the sense in which we learn things by instruction or by experience alone. It 'grew' by the interaction between input from experience and specific structures that were part of our genetic inheritance.

If Chomsky was right this placed linguistics at the forefront of the cognitive sciences. In the 1960s, when the idea was first put forward, it caught the imagination of philosophers, psychologists, and others across neighbouring disciplines, even though, at that stage, most of what he later believed to be the structure of Universal Grammar, and therefore what became his principal evidence for it, had been barely touched on.

Two decades later, he himself suggested that the 'discoveries' he claimed might 'be compared with the discovery of waves, particles, genes, valence, and so on . . . in the physical sciences' (Chomsky, 1988: 91). 'We are beginning to see into the deeper hidden nature of the mind and to understand how it works, really for the first time in history.' One hesitates to cite a scholar when he is blowing his own trumpet, but if the discoveries were genuine this was true. The main task for anyone who wants to understand the nature of language would then be to extend them. It was not to describe each language individually, each simply for its own sake. It was not even to describe each individually, and then, by comparing them, to find out what, if anything, all have in common. It was to study directly the genetically determined structures that, by Chomsky's argument, had to exist.

It was in the 1980s that the implications of this programme finally became clear. There have since been changes of detail: many specific hypotheses, in part modifying or overturning earlier hypotheses, about the structure that the Universal Grammar has. But Chomsky's basic philosophy of linguistics has not altered.

To 'know a language' was, he had said in the 1960s, to have 'constructed a grammar'. Alternatively, we could talk of an 'internalized language', or 'I-language'; so, as Chomsky now expressed what is essentially the same point, a Universal Grammar could be 'construed as the theory of human I-languages'. It was 'a system of conditions deriving from the human biological endowment that identifies the I-languages that are humanly accessible under normal conditions' (Chomsky, 1986: 23). But our problem then is to explain why individual languages, which all 'grow' in minds with the same 'biological endowment', are as different, even in their basic structures, as they are. Let us suppose that, through our study of an individual language, we discover that its speakers 'know' x. This might be, for example, a specific constraint on the movement of a unit which belongs to a specific class. We are once more convinced that their knowledge of x could not have been acquired without the mediation of some 'universal' principle. But suppose that x itself is found not, in reality, to be universal. Thus, in some other languages, we find that units of a similar class are subject not to x, but to another constraint y. Let us suppose moreover that, for y to 'grow' in speakers' minds, we must again invoke some 'universal' principle. How can both x 'grow' and y 'grow', if the biological endowment of all speakers is the same?

The problem was in effect anticipated by the end of the 1970s. On the one hand, Universal Grammar had to be inherited by every member of our species; and, since any infant can be found in practice to be capable of learning any language, there was no reason to suppose that it might vary from one population to another. So, in Chomsky's words, a theory of it had to be 'compatible with the diversity of existing (indeed possible)' individual grammars (Chomsky, 1981: 3). On the other hand, it would have to include whatever he considered necessary for the development of any individual I-language. In Chomsky's words, it had to be 'sufficiently constrained and restrictive in the options it permits so as to account for the fact that each of these grammars develops in the mind on the basis of quite limited evidence'. In the next sentence, which I cited earlier, Chomsky said that it was 'a near certainty' that many 'fundamental properties' of individual grammars had to be attributed to Universal Grammar. But by then it was known that many of the arguments that justified that statement had been based on rules that varied from one language to another, even within Europe.

The conclusion was that the inherited Universal Grammar had to include variables. By the basic argument, certain structures must originate in S_0; if not, Chomsky could not conceive how speakers' minds attained the steady state S_S that he ascribed to them. The principles that determined these had then to be genetically inherited. But what is inherited had now, in addition, to include explicit alternatives. The minds of children about to develop a knowledge of English would still be initially in the same S_0 as those about to develop one of, say, Japanese. But the task they faced was not just to acquire those aspects of I-language which develop independently of Universal Grammar. Within the Universal Grammar there would have to be specific choices, by which a child faced with 'primary linguistic data' in, say, English would develop an I-language that is specifically of one type; but one faced with 'data' in, say, Japanese would develop another whose type might appear, at first sight, to be inexplicably different.

What 'we expect to find', in Chomsky's own words, is 'a highly restricted theory of U[niversal] G[rammar]' based still on 'a number of fundamental principles that sharply restrict the class of attainable grammars and narrowly constrain their form'; but, in addition, 'with parameters that have to be fixed by experience' (again Chomsky, 1981: 3f.). 'If these parameters', he continued, 'are embedded in a theory of U[niversal] G[rammar] that is sufficiently rich in structure, then the languages that are determined by fixing their values one way or another will appear to be quite diverse, since the consequences of one set of choices may be very different from the consequences of another set'. Five years later, the parameters of such a system were compared to an array of switches. When a child's mind is in its initial state, each switch will be open; and, in the transition from that to a final or steady state, each is 'set' in either of two ways. But for the 'core', as Chomsky called it, of each language that is all that will be necessary. In the light of input from experience, a child learning English will be led to make one series of choices. Each switch in the array will then be set to correspond to one of two alternative values of the relevant parameter. In the light of differing experiences, a child learning Japanese will make choices that, in part at least, are different. The corresponding switches will accordingly be set in ways that correspond, in part, to opposite values. But in either case no more will be needed for the core of their I-language to develop. 'The transition from the initial state S_0 to the steady state S_S' was simply, in Chomsky's words, 'a matter of setting the switches' (Chomsky, 1986: 146).

These passages are cited from the books that mark what Chomsky himself saw as a new 'conceptual shift' (again Chomsky, 1986: 6). It was a shift internal to the theory of 'generative grammar'; and, in the 1990s, terminology from every phase of Chomsky's exposition of his ideas – 'generative grammar', 'competence', 'I-language' – is still woven together (Chomsky and Lasnik, 1995 [1993]: 14–15). But the focus of this theory had significantly changed.

In the beginning, as we have seen, a generative grammar was a set of rules that 'generated', and assigned analyses to, a set of sentences. That was how Chomsky had defined it in the 1950s (6.1), and it was such a grammar that, in his first 'conceptual shift', was said to constitute the competence of speakers of a language. In describing languages, a central aim was thus to separate the sequences of words that were 'grammatical' from others that were 'ungrammatical'. If we did not do this, we could not claim that we had correctly characterised the 'competence', or 'knowledge', that their speakers had. But it was obvious in the 1980s that I-languages include much that cannot develop by the setting of parameters. Speakers of English will know, for example, the forms of irregular verbs: not *thinked* but *thought*, not *haves sinked* but *has sunk*, and so on. They will know that *boiler house* or *boat house* are established combinations with established meanings; but that *bone house* (in a poem by Seamus Heaney) is not. They will know that there is a sentence *It will be raining cats and dogs tomorrow* and that this means that it will rain very heavily; they will know too that there is no corresponding passive *Cats and dogs will be being rained tomorrow*. But details like these will not be determined by the setting of parameters. They must be learned, from experience alone, in just the way that, it was claimed, the 'core' is not 'learned'.

In Chomsky's terms, such knowledge formed a 'periphery'. The 'core' of an I-language was defined as 'a system determined by fixing values for the parameters of U[niversal] G[rammar]' (Chomsky, 1986: 147). This was variously called 'core grammar' or 'core language'; and, in a later account that was given in the 1990s, would consist of 'what we tentatively assume to be pure instantiations of U[niversal] G[rammar]' (Chomsky and Lasnik, 1995 [1993]: 19f.). But 'the systems called "languages" in common sense usage tolerate exceptions: irregular morphology, idioms, and so forth' (again Chomsky, 1986: 147). The I-language that a speaker has developed will accordingly include not just the core, but also a 'periphery' consisting of 'whatever is added on in the system actually represented in the mind/brain of a speaker–hearer'. In the 1990s this periphery was again said to consist of 'exceptions' (Chomsky and Lasnik, 1995 [1993]: 20).

The 'innate linguistic theory', as Chomsky called it in the 1960s, is accordingly focussed on the core part of a speaker's competence. But the core is not a system that alone distinguishes what are sentences and what are 'non-sentences'. That will depend on both it and the periphery; and exactly what belongs to which is not determined by our evidence of any individual language that we might set out to study. What is an 'exception' in the periphery is, presumably, whatever is not part of the core. But what is part of the core can be determined only by a specific theory of 'Universal Grammar', whose 'instantiation', on this hypothesis, it will be.

The primary aim is therefore to engage directly with this aspect, as it is claimed, of man's biological inheritance. But the grounds on which the claim is made will also have to be more complex. In the beginning evidence could come from a single language: if its speakers could be shown to 'know' things that they could not have 'learned' from experience alone, a genetic explanation would be posited. This was made clear by Chomsky in a footnote in the 1960s. 'Paradoxical as it may seem at first glance, considerations internal to a single language may provide significant support for the conclusion that some formal property should be attributed not to the theory of the particular language in question (its grammar) but rather to the general linguistic theory on which the particular grammar is based' (Chomsky, 1965: 209). I can recall one reader who confessed to throwing down the book at this point. But, by the logic of Chomsky's argument, it had to be true.

We have seen how, in the 1980s, Chomsky could still argue in that vein. But the theory of 'Principles and Parameters', as he calls it, is a theory of everything in I-languages that is not an 'exception'. Its parameters will therefore cover many things that can, in principle, be learned from experience alone. One of Chomsky's earliest parameters determined, for example, whether subject pronouns could be 'dropped'. English was one language in which they could not: *She is coming* or *He is coming*, not *Is coming*. In Italian the setting would be the opposite: *Viene*. But there was no argument that, to acquire this one specific aspect of their 'knowledge', children needed anything other than the evidence of speech to which they were exposed. What was claimed instead was that this difference was one of a series by which types of language were distinguished. In Italian, a verb like *viene* can be either preceded or followed by a subject: *Giovanni viene* 'John is coming' or *Viene Giovanni*. In English it can only be preceded. This feature of Italian was then one of a 'clustering of properties' that, in Chomsky's hypothesis, were 'related' to this single parameter (Chomsky, 1981: 240). Others were of a kind that, in the 1970s, had been taken to show that language could not be learned from experience. But, once the parameter was set, through experience that would be immediately decisive, they would necessarily follow. In English the parameter would be set differently, and a different clustering of properties would follow likewise. As the values of this and other such parameters are fixed, 'the languages that are determined' will, in Chomsky's words, 'appear to be quite diverse' (4). If he is right, the explanation for their diversity is that each parameter will have repercussions throughout their core systems.

To justify the theory, it had now to be established that such 'clustering of properties' exists. But to that end it was not enough to look in detail just at English or just at Italian. The validity of the theory depended on the thorough study of the relevant structures in all languages, of every possible type.

6.3   Universal Grammar and diachrony

Chomsky himself has said little or nothing about change in internalised languages. But a theory has been developed by others, notably David Lightfoot. His earliest treatment dates from the late 1970s, before the second of Chomsky's two 'conceptual shifts', and was inspired by accounts of Universal Grammar, or what was at first called an 'innate linguistic theory', from the 1960s. His latest synthesis is, as I write, barely a year old.

For Saussure, as we have seen, change in language was change in a system. In one 'state' a language has, for example, one system of consonants; in a later state it has another. Now a 'state of a language' can, for a follower of Chomsky, be at best a derivative concept. The primary reality is the grammar constructed, in the terms he first used, by an individual speaker–hearer. To say that a language changes from one state to another is accordingly to say that, in a later generation, children construct grammars differing in a certain respect from those constructed in an earlier generation. Change in a Saussurean 'langue' is at bottom change in Chomskyan 'I-languages'.

But for change in systems there must be a reason; and one suggested by work on diachronic phonology (4.1) was that it might correct 'imbalance'. 'Balance', by implication, was a property that systems tend to maximise. Now the properties of grammars were the province of Chomsky's 'linguistic theory': both those that they must have and, since he had talked in the beginning of a method for choosing between alternative grammars, those that are preferred. It was therefore natural, as Lightfoot saw in the 1970s, that such a theory should be taken as a key to understanding change. Suppose, in the extreme case, that a grammar does not respect some limit that is laid down. It would then be 'driven', in Lightfoot's words, 'to a therapeutic restructuring' (Lightfoot, 1979: 123). He has tended not to refer to predecessors in the Saussurean tradition. But, similarly, a theory of phonology might have defined the limits of 'imbalance'. Systems that breached them would be driven to change, therapeutically, in such a way that they conformed.

In syntax Lightfoot proposed, in particular, that grammars were subject to a 'transparency principle'. The simpler their account of the construction of sentences, and the closer the relation between surface structures and underlying representations, the more 'transparency', as he defined it, there would be. Grammars then tend to be restructured in ways that will maximise it. But, as earlier linguists had seen, changes which are therapeutic at one point in a system can create need for new therapy at another. As Lightfoot put it, the restructuring of a grammar will be such as 'to solve essentially local problems' (378). But a local change will not be inhibited if unwittingly it leads to problems elsewhere. '[L]anguage learners do not re-design their entire grammar or practise sufficient prudence to check all the implications of a given change for all other areas of the grammar'. Therefore a fresh problem may provoke another change. 'This means', as Lightfoot said, 'that changes may often take place in implicational sequences'.

The assumption, to elaborate his image, was that 'grammars practise therapy, not prophylaxis' (123). But therapy itself could not be the whole story. 'One is still left to wonder', Lightfoot said, 'why grammars never reach a state of equilibrium or indeed what set off such implicational sequences in the first place' (381). Why do they not simply achieve a state that is most 'highly valued', and stay put?

A similar problem had been implicit in the 1950s, and an answer, as we have seen, was that the 'balance' of a system, at one level, may be disturbed by cumulative shifts, at another level, in what Coseriu (4.2) called a 'norm'. Likewise, in Lightfoot's terms, the causes of change were in part 'extra-grammatical'. Suppose, for example, that an ordering of words falls out of use. Once it was normal; therefore instances of it were part of the 'primary linguistic data' to which children were exposed; therefore the competence they acquired in turn permitted it. But, in performance, other orderings were increasingly preferred: perhaps under the influence of a foreign language (compare Lightfoot, 1979: 381f.), or for reasons of 'expressivity' (384f.). Such causes are beyond the scope of grammars. But children of a new generation would then have increasingly little evidence that the ordering was possible. Therefore they might construct rules that did not permit it; that might lower the value of their grammars as regards transparency; and, through other changes, limits laid down by 'linguistic theory' might no longer be respected.

The picture that Lightfoot presented was accordingly of 'piecemeal changes', such as the exclusion of a specific arrangement of words, that result 'in steady complication of a grammar, rendering it . . . less highly valued' (78). In his main illustration, words in English like *can, may* or *will* were in the beginning verbs like any other. But, by what he described as separate changes, they came not to take an object (one could not say the equivalent of *I can him* or *I may this*); other verbs came to be followed by an infinitive with *to* (modern *I want to do it* as opposed to *I can do it*), and so on (details, 101ff.). Their status as verbs became less and less transparent. What followed, in his account, was a restructuring of the grammar in which they were no longer verbs, but formed a separate class of 'modals'. As such, they were subject to different rules. In Lightfoot's explanation, piecemeal changes can in this way lead up to a 'catastrophic' readjustment (78). As Coseriu would have said, before 'catastrophe theory' was invented, the system in time 'overturns'.

These ideas had been inspired by Chomsky's first 'conceptual shift'; and, since the object of investigation was not speech but a system underlying speech, it is natural that we should be able to find parallels in work that looked back to Saussure. But Chomsky's second 'shift' soon followed, and in Lightfoot's response to that the model of therapy, in particular, is transcended.

For 'a child constructing a grammar' we must now talk of a child 'setting parameters'. To be precise, that is all that will be involved in the 'construction' of a Chomskyan 'core language'. The 'primary linguistic data' that are available to children are accordingly a 'triggering experience' (Lightfoot, 1999: 66f.) for Universal Grammar to develop into the central systems of particular grammars. Changes in the basic structure of a language then reduce to differences in the setting of parameters, in response to different triggering experiences.

That much follows directly from what Chomsky himself proposed. But setting parameters, as Lightfoot makes clear, is a task quite different from the one that children had originally been said to face. According to

Chomsky in the 1960s, children did what linguists had been seen as doing in the 1950s. In Lightfoot's own terms, he 'viewed children as endowed with a metric evaluating grammars which can generate the primary data to which they are exposed, along with appropriate structural descriptions for these data'. This metric had to select the grammar which, among other things, is 'most successful in generating those data' (Lightfoot, 1999: 144).

In that account a child 'selects a grammar which matches his or her input as closely as possible'. But let us assume that the Universal Grammar is as Chomsky has claimed since the 1980s. In the development of 'core' structures, no set of rules will strictly be 'constructed': the possible alternatives derive directly from the system that each child inherits, and all that is going to happen, in the light of what Lightfoot calls the 'triggering experience', is that one instantiation of a Universal Grammar will be activated and the others suppressed. Nor does this require that 'inputs' should be 'matched'. Parameters must be set easily, and the natural process is not one in which alternative 'core' grammars, each derived by different combinations of settings, are compared to see which, with the addition of a 'periphery', generates most successfully the sentences that a child hears. It will be one in which each setting is determined by a minimum of specific evidence.

That insight is the key to everything that follows. In Lightfoot's theory, learning of a grammar, or core language, will be based on 'cues' (149). These are partial structures designated as such by a Universal Grammar; and, in developing their knowledge of a language, children will 'scan their linguistic environment' (206 and elsewhere) for them. To be precise, they will search for fragments of incoming speech that can be seen as instances of them. Once a cue has been found sufficiently often or, as Lightfoot puts it, 'with sufficient robustness' the parameter that it represents will be set. But the Universal Grammar is a system, as we have seen in the last section, in which the setting of a single parameter, which will again be determined by experience, may have a wide range of consequences. Each of Lightfoot's cues could therefore be associated with a series of additional structures. Once the first choice is determined then, without any further analysis of the input that a child receives, their developing grammar automatically includes these also.

For grammars to be different, there must first be a difference in the 'triggering experience'. This must again be due to 'nongrammatical factors' (225), again involving, for example, 'language contact or socially defined speech fashions' (166). No 'theory of grammar or acquisition' (218) will predict shifts in the speech of a community at that level, and Lightfoot says very little about them. But, given that they take place, he now has an even more seductive theory of 'catastrophes'. As speech shifts, the evidence for specific cues may diminish. They may no longer be found 'with sufficient robustness', and the parameters will no longer be set as they have been. The 'expression of the cues' will change, in Lightfoot's words, 'in such a way that a threshold [is] crossed and a new grammar [is] acquired' (166). But each cue is a structure that, once identified, entails others. If it is not fixed, they are not selected either; and, as alternative cues are identified, different structures will be selected, regardless of the remainder of the input, by them. In this way, a small shift in the 'linguistic experience of some children' may have what Lightfoot calls 'dramatic consequences' (111) for the grammars that develop.

It will be clear now why the notion of 'therapy' was no longer needed. We again speak, at the level of abstraction represented by the core of Chomskyan I-language, of change in a system. To explain it, we must again invoke shifts at another level, in the speech that supplies 'triggering experiences'. But the rest appeals simply to the laws of Universal Grammar, which inexorably determine specific structures in response to specific inputs.

7   Structural semantics

The term 'semantics' was coined in the 1880s, by the French linguist Michel Bréal. As 'phonétique' was in its widest sense a science of the sounds of speech, so 'sémantique', from the Greek verb for 'to mean', was a 'science des significations' (Bréal, 1911 [1897]: 8). How Bréal saw this discipline need not concern us. But for a structuralist a language is a system in which determinate forms are related to meanings that are also determinate. 'Structural semantics' is accordingly concerned with meanings as terms in such systems.

Its beginnings lie in Saussure's theory of 'linguistic signs' (2.1). Each sign, as we have seen, had two sides; and just as on the level of expression, to use Hjelmslev's terminology, units were identified in abstraction from the sounds that speakers physically utter, so those on the content level had to be abstracted from the passing meanings that were intended. This second task was therefore, in principle, as important as the first. But when Hjelmslev wrote he was himself among the few who had approached it seriously. We have seen how, by his test of commutation, both expressions and their contents were divided into 'figurae': '[ram]', for example, into '[r]' plus '[a]' plus '[m]'; 'ram', in parallel, into 'he' plus 'sheep' (5.1). Another parallel, as we will soon see, was between semantic oppositions and distinctive phonetic features in Prague School phonology (3.2). But these were ideas that few applications had explored in detail, and by the 1950s it seemed clear to many linguists that a great deal of the basic structure of a language could be described, in practice, without doing so. Structuralists in America, in particular, came to see the 'semantic system' of a language, as in Hockett's scheme of levels in the 1950s, as a field which was separate from its 'central' systems (5.2). Its investigation could therefore, for the moment, be postponed.

For one contemporary commentator it was 'paradoxical and disturbing to find that many structural linguists are uninterested in problems of meaning and reluctant to handle them' (Ullmann, 1957 [1951]: 317). It might likewise have disturbed Saussure, for whom each side of a linguistic sign had presupposed the other. But it was only after this stage had been reached that earlier ideas came finally to fruition. In the section which follows the framework is still that of Saussure and of other structuralists whose ideas were formed before the Second World War. The central problem, therefore, is the identification of what Saussure called 'signs'. In most later treatments the identity of units that have meaning is one problem. The analysis of the meanings that they have can then be treated as another.

7.1   Meanings as invariants

In the beginning, forms and meanings were indissociable. *Ram*, for example, is a word in English, with the meaning given in dictionaries as 'an uncastrated adult male sheep'. But its status as a word depends precisely on its having a meaning. If *rem*, in contrast, is not a word in English, it is because it has no meaning in English. That much was obvious; and it was also obvious, and acknowledged since antiquity, that the forms and meanings of words stood in a conventional or, in the term used since the Renaissance, in an 'arbitrary' relation. But what holds for words held also, in Saussure's analysis, for the meanings themselves. The meaning 'uncastrated adult male sheep' is arbitrarily related to *ram*. But its status as a meaning depends precisely on there being a word whose meaning it is. If, for example, no dictionary in English includes a meaning 'castrated male dog', it is because there is no word in English for it. As the system of the language distinguishes forms that are 'arbitrary', so it also distinguishes meanings that are 'arbitrary'.

The underlying insight was that meanings too are different from one language to another. Their speakers talk, in part, about the same world and the same things and same happenings in it. But any translator knows that what *x* means in one language often does not correspond exactly to what *y* means in another. In Saussure's analysis, the concept 'x' has its place in one system of oppositions; the concept 'y' its own place in a different system. Each system must be analysed, in a later structuralist slogan, 'in its own terms'. In the theory as developed by Hjelmslev, a comparison of different systems will establish common areas of 'purport'. But formal oppositions between 'x' and other content-units of one system structure such an area in one way. Oppositions between 'y' and other content-units in another system structure it differently.

A famous illustration is of words for colours. A speaker of English will describe a certain range of colours as 'red'; another as 'brown'; another as 'pink', and so on. But within each range there are perceptible differences: a reddish brown is objectively not like a greyish brown. Therefore different languages can distinguish ranges that are not equivalent. What is 'brown', for example, in English is not always, in French, 'brun', and what is indifferently 'black' in English was in classical Latin variously 'ater' or 'niger'. To underline the point that he was making, Hjelmslev set four colour terms in Danish beside those that most nearly correspond in Welsh. One range of colours is in Danish 'grøn' ('green'), and of these some are in Welsh 'gwyrdd'. But not all: others, closer to the range of Danish 'blaa' ('blue'), are instead 'glas'. Colours that are 'blaa' in Danish are again 'glas', but so too are some that in Danish are 'graa' ('grey'). Others that are 'graa' are then in Welsh not 'glas' but 'llwyd'; still others that in Welsh are 'llwyd' are in turn 'brun' ('brown'). In Hjelmslev's diagram (see fig. 6)

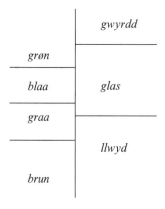

Figure 6

the colour spectrum is again a 'purport', which the oppositions within Welsh and Danish structure, 'arbitrarily' in Saussure's sense, each in their own way (Hjelmslev, 1943: 48f.).

The case for structural semantics rests on such facts. But the particular conclusion that Saussure drew from them was that neither forms nor meanings had an identity independent of a system in which they were paired. One could not talk of words such as *tree* or *horse* independently of either 'triː' and 'hɔːs', as mental representations of sounds, or 'tree' and 'horse', as mental representations of trees and horses (compare again Saussure, 1972 [1916]: 97ff.). Nor could one talk of either independently of the oppositions between each pair and all others. To identify words was to distinguish simultaneously, within an individual language system, what distinctively 'means' (or 'signifies') and what is distinctively 'meant' (or 'signified').

For Bloomfield too the essential first step was to identify recurrent likenesses in form linked to recurrent likenesses in meaning. A speaker of English might say, on a specific occasion, 'I planted a tree yesterday'; another, on another occasion, might say 'Those trees are magnificent.' But to identify their language we must abstract specific forms, like 'tri:', and specific meanings, like 'tree', that are linked consistently across utterances. Now the form 'tri:' was not literally a recurring sound. It was a 'phonetic form' abstracted, as an invariant, from the widely varying sounds that speakers actually produce. Nor was its meaning literally to be identified with any of the varying objects that they may refer to. Our first speaker might have planted, for example, an oak and, for it to be planted, it would have had to be, as trees go, quite small. In Bloomfield's terms, both its species and its size would be features of the 'situation' that 'called forth' the utterance that is produced (Bloomfield, 1935 [1933]: 139). The other speaker might instead be talking, in a very different 'situation', of a grove of mature redwoods. But the features that concern us are just the invariants that constitute the 'likeness'. We have therefore to 'discriminate', as Bloomfield put it, 'between *non-distinctive* features of the situation', such as the species, size or state of a tree or trees referred to, 'and the *distinctive*, or *linguistic meaning* (the *semantic* features) which are common to all the situations that call forth the utterance' (141) of, in this example, the distinctive form 'tri:'. The problem for semantics, as for phonology, was to identify such invariants.

A 'concept' of a tree is one thing; features of the 'situations' in which *tree* is uttered are another. Nor, for that matter, is an 'acoustic image' in the minds of speakers the same thing as a unit physically identified in sounds. But, whether one was a 'mentalist' or a 'physicalist', the application of such theories could be less straightforward than it might seem in this instance. Take, for example, the *-ed* at the end of *planted*. For grammarians it is an ending of a category that they describe as 'past tense'; this is also the tense of, among others, *painted* in *I painted a tree yesterday*, or *decorated* in *I decorated a tree yesterday*. But what establishes this category as a sign? If we take these sentences alone the problem is sufficiently simple. The ending 'ɪd' is constant, and in uttering it a speaker will refer to what has happened earlier than the time of speaking. But a past tense does not always have the ending 'ɪd': compare, for example, *bought* or *came*. Nor are forms of this category always different from those of other categories. In *I have planted a tree* an identical ending 'ɪd' is assigned instead to a category that is traditionally the past participle; in *I bet you £10*, said in making the bet, the form of a present is identical to that of the past tense in *I bet you £10 last week*. Nor does the past tense, whether in 'ɪd' or otherwise, refer always to things that have happened in the past. Compare, for example, its use in *If I planted a tree tomorrow.* The time reference is future, as it also is in *If I plant a tree tomorrow.* The difference lies instead in the likelihood, as the speaker intends or perceives it, of the planting taking place. Nor is the past the only tense that can refer to things that have already happened: compare, for example, the narrative present in *Then, last week, I plant a tree.* If 'past tense' is to be identified by a direct relation between forms and their meaning, the meaning cannot simply be 'past'.

As conventional dictionaries list different 'senses' of words, so conventional grammars list different 'uses' of such categories. In our last example, the present *plant* is said to have a 'historic' use; in *I plant a tree every autumn* its use is 'habitual'; in *I plant it tomorrow* it is used to refer to the future; and so on. To establish categories as terms in a sign system we must therefore identify a meaning that is invariant across each range of uses; by which present and past tense, for example, stand in a constant opposition. But how abstract must such meanings be?

The problem was clear in the 1930s, and was addressed in particular in two articles by Roman Jakobson. Both dealt with Russian, one with categories of the verb, including tenses; the other, longer and more contentious, with the system of cases. For cases too, grammarians distinguish different uses or 'individual meanings' ('Einzelbedeutungen'), and there is again no simple relation between the forms that different words take and the categories to which, despite this independent variation in both forms and uses, they are nevertheless assigned (compare Jakobson, 1971 [1936]: 24f.). The same problem arises; and the solution, as Jakobson saw it, was to establish a system of oppositions between 'general meanings' ('Gesamtbedeutungen'), by which each case is consistently distinguished from all other cases. 'Individual meanings' would then be explained by reference to these general meanings, and the individual contexts in which they are found.

As categories are opposed to categories so, in the phonology of the Prague School, phonemes are opposed to phonemes. In English, for example, 'm' was a phoneme distinguished from 'b', among others, and characterised in part by a phonetic feature 'nasal'. Similarly, accusative in Russian was a category to be distinguished from among others nominative, and characterised by a general meaning that had to be discovered. But let us look further at the features by which phonemes are defined. One features of 'm' is, as we have said, 'nasal'; 'b' and 'p', which are also articulated with the lips, can be contrasted as 'non-nasal'. In the same way nasal 'n', which is alveolar, is opposed to non-nasal 'd' and 't', and nasal 'ŋ' (*ng*) to non-nasal 'g' and 'k'. What then is meant by the term 'non-nasal'? In Trubetzkoy's account, it meant precisely that one set of phonemes could be characterised, in part, negatively. The three nasals ('m', 'n' 'ŋ') were characterised positively, by what he called a 'mark' ('Merkmal') of nasality. Their place in the system was as consonants produced specifically with air flowing through the nose. In opposition to these, the non-nasals ('b', 'p'; 'd', 't'; 'g', 'k') were distinguished by the absence of this mark. Their place in the system was accordingly as consonants that were not produced specifically in that way. 'Correlations', as he called them, were defined by parallel oppositions of this kind, in which the phonemes of one set are 'marked', and the others are in contrast 'unmarked' (Trubetzkoy, 1939: 77ff.).

This doctrine was new when Jakobson wrote the first of his articles, and he at once seized on it as a clue for the analysis of meanings. Take, for example, the distinction in word-meaning between *duck*, which can be used of either females or males, and *drake*, which is used specifically of males. The latter is the 'marked' term, the 'mark' being the specific feature by which it is so used. The other is 'unmarked' and in consequence it might be said to have two uses. If someone points to a female mallard and asks if it is the drake, one might reply 'No, it is the duck': in that case *duck* is used specifically of one sex. But if they point to a mixed flock and say 'Look at those ducks', it is used of the species, or the kind of bird, in general. Does it follow then that *duck* has two distinct meanings? If we follow the logic of markedness it does not. *Drake* is the marked term and is used specifically of male ducks. *Duck* is, in contrast, unmarked. But that means simply that it is not specifically restricted in the way *drake* is restricted. Therefore it can be used freely, both, in one set of circumstances, of ducks that are female and, in another, of ducks in general.

The argument is modelled on Jakobson's own treatment of a contrast in Russian, between a word for a donkey and another specifically for a female donkey (Jakobson, 1971 [1932]: 4). Let us therefore return, in this light, to the distinction between past and present tense. In Jakobson's account of Russian, a past tense makes clear that, specifically, 'the action belongs to the past'. But the opposing present constitutes instead a 'typical unmarked category'. It does not indicate specifically that actions are in present time; nor even that, in contrast, they are not in past time. It simply does not indicate specifically what the past tense indicates. Therefore it has, inherently, no temporal restriction ('an sich zeitlich unbestimmt ist') ([1932]: 8).

Let us suppose that the present is similarly unmarked in English. *Plant(s)*, for instance, does not in itself have a specific time reference. Therefore, in *I plant it tomorrow*, it can combine with an expression that refers to the future; and, in that way, is used, in one 'individual meaning', of an event in the future. It can also combine with an expression such as *every autumn*; hence the 'habitual' use, which is another individual meaning, in *I plant a tree every autumn*. In *I plant a tree on Tuesday* it might be used with either meaning: 'next Tuesday' or, conceivably, 'every Tuesday'. But which it has depends entirely on the 'situation', to use Bloomfield's term, in which this is said. A present can again combine, in narration, with an expression such as *last week*. Hence one could say either *Then, last week, I planted a tree*, where *planted* is in the marked tense; or, with the 'temporally unrestricted' present, *Then, last week, I plant a tree*. That would be the equivalent, in grammar, of referring to a male of the family of anatinae as either a (marked) drake or an (unmarked) duck. Similarly, in Jakobson's account of case in Russian, the accusative is marked in opposition to the nominative. In his initial formulation, the accusative 'always indicates that some *action* is as it were *directed* to the object referred to . . .' (1971 [1936]: 31). Thus, in the Russian for 'to write books', the word for 'books' will be accusative, since it refers to the objective of the writing. But a nominative, in contrast, indicates neither the presence of 'a relationship to an action' nor the absence of such a relationship (32). In some uses, therefore, its meaning does involve one: thus the word for 'books' will be nominative in the passive 'Books were written.' In others it does not. Thus, as the term 'nominative' implies, it may simply name things: 'books' (nominative), 'newspapers' (nominative), and so on.

Unmarked terms can thus have a wide range of uses. But what of those that are marked? In English, as we have seen, the past tense is not always used of events in past time. Compare again the conditional *If I planted a tree tomorrow* . . . In Russian, an accusative can also be used with prepositions: 'onto the table (accusative)'. These uses are again in specific contexts. Thus, in the example in English, it is relevant both that *tomorrow* follows and that *if* precedes. But the general meanings of the marked past and the marked accusative must allow for them.

It follows that, in grammatical systems, the 'marks' may be very abstract. In particular, they may themselves be negative. Thus, in an analysis of tense in English, we might begin by talking of a reality that is subjectively before the speaker: this includes both things perceived and things anticipated. Let us call this 'R'. The meaning of the past tense might accordingly be characterised as 'not R'. In *I planted a tree yesterday*, the planting is removed from this reality in one way, because the speaker remembers the event objectively as something that has happened in the past. But in *If I planted a tree tomorrow* . . . it is removed in another way, in that it is not likely. Both uses of the marked term are then covered. The unmarked present is in contrast, more precisely, 'not specifically "not R"'.

This analysis of English is not Jakobson's; but in his own account of Russian cases the level of abstraction was breathtaking. In the system in general, the relation of the nominative to the accusative is also that of the instrumental to the dative: in his terminology, this is a 'Bezugskor-relation' or correlation, we may translate, of 'relationship'. What is indicated by, in general, the 'relationship cases' ('Bezugskasus') is 'the non-independence of the object referred to' (65): this implicitly subsumes the non-independence, in 'to write books', of the books from the writing. In the passage referred to Jakobson remarked that it is characteristic of his oppositions that the marked term is in reality 'throughout *of a negative type*'. The nominative and instrumental, which are unmarked in the 'relationship' correlation, are then characterised as not specifically indicating this non-independence. In opposition to the nominative and the accusative, the instrumental and the dative are marked terms in an 'edge correlation' ('Randkorrelation'). As such, they indicate that the noun occupies 'a *peripheral position* in the overall meaning-content of the utterance' (46). Peripheries, as Jakobson points out, imply centres: nouns in the nominative and accusative are thus characterised in effect as not specifically having a non-central position. As the nominative and accusative are to the instrumental and the dative so the genitives are to the locatives: locatives 'peripheral', genitives not specifically 'peripheral'. These in turn form the marked terms in an 'extent correlation' ('Umfangskorrelation'). A locative indicates a locality within which something happens: for example, in Moscow. But such a locality 'is not represented to its full extent in the utterance' (59). A locative is thus a marked term in an 'extent correlation', as, he argues earlier (38), is a genitive. For example, in 'Ivan's (genitive) book', Ivan is represented only to the extent that the book belongs to or is written by him. Now the genitive has, in an 'atomic' treatment, many different, often contradictory, meanings (37). Only by this degree of abstraction, to a 'mark' whose characterisation is again essentially negative, can they be united.

This tour de force was for a long time unique. But if forms and meanings were direct terms in a sign relation, a category with varying 'signifiers', as in our example from English, could be identified only by an invariant meaning that is 'signified'. 'The question of general meanings' had to form the natural foundation, as it was for Jakobson, of all study of grammatical systems ([1936]: 23). If each category has a multiple set of varying meanings, 'the *interrelation between the signs and the meaning*' is, as he put it, lost and the 'questions of meaning' are 'unjustly excluded from the field of sign-theory' ('unregelmäßig aus dem Gebiete der Zeichenlehre ... ausgeschaltet'). 'Semantics' would be left without an object (24).

7.2   Semantic fields

For the British linguist John Lyons, writing in the 1960s, both phonology and grammar were concerned with the expression-plane of language, one with sounds and the other with words and their formal combinations (Lyons, 1968: 54). Semantics was the study of the plane of content and was therefore separate, as in Hockett's scheme of levels (5.2), from both. By then the analysis of words was widely seen as prior to a description of their meanings. But by then too that branch of description had at last substantially progressed, not least through Lyons's own work.

A basic insight was that words are related within what were called 'fields'. The idea was originally from Germany, where it had been central, in the early 1930s, to a famous analysis by Jost Trier of a change in vocabulary in the mediaeval period. The terms involved were in the 'sense area of knowledge' ('Sinnbezirk des Verstandes'); and, around 1200, this was found to be covered in German by the three words *wîsheit*, *kunst* and *list*. A century later it was found to be divided instead into *wîsheit*, *kunst* and *wissen*. But the difference did not lie in a simple replacement of *list* by *wissen*. In the earlier period *wîsheit* had, in brief, been all-embracing: knowledge or understanding in all spheres. But by the later period it was used specifically of 'wisdom' in a spiritual or religious sense. In the earlier period *kunst* applied to the knowledge and manners of a courtly society; *list* to technical skill and knowledge, with no courtly or class connotation. But by the later period *kunst* did not have that connotation either. What was thus affected, in Trier's analysis, was a whole in which each term had a changing place. We have seen how, in a structuralist account of sound change, a system as a whole was said to react to pressure (4.1). But Trier was among the first to turn such arguments against the doctrine in Saussure's *Cours*, by which diachrony was reduced to individual changes. In this Trier was perhaps more truly structuralist. But the division as drawn by Saussure was described at one point at least as 'ein Ausweg der Verzweiflung', or 'counsel of despair' (Trier, 1938).

Trier's theories are expounded lucidly by Ullmann (1957 [1951]: 156ff.), and I confess that I have not gone back in detail to his main work. But in a later article on 'linguistic fields', he referred to structures of this kind as 'living linguistic realities'. The vocabulary of a language as a whole was articulated into partial wholes, which were in turn articulated into the individual words that were their members (compare Trier, 1934: 430, and Ullmann's commentary). The identity of some potential fields will now be obvious. One is that of words for colour, which Hjelmslev was to describe, as we have seen, as an area of 'purport'. Another unites words such as English *drake* and *duck*; *ram*, *sheep* and *ewe*; or *duckling* and *lamb*. Another well-defined field, which became a standard illustration in the 1950s, was of kinship: this is structured in English into *mother*, *father*, *daughter*, and so on.

The structuralists who developed this idea did not need to conceive of fields as quasi-animate entities. But clearly, if the vocabulary as a whole was one big network of relations, there were networks within it that could easily be treated separately. The task for structural semantics was therefore to develop methods for doing so.

For most linguists the comparison with phonology was again seductive. Phonemes were opposed one to another by distinctive features of sound. They formed series in which different phonemes were distinguished in parallel, and the more such parallels there were the more tightly organised the system was. Meanings could also be said to enter, as we have seen, into correlations. As 'drake', once more, was to 'duck' so 'gander' was to 'goose'. As 'ram' or 'ewe' were to 'sheep' so 'stallion' or 'mare' were to 'horse', and so on. Analogously they were opposed by distinctive features of meaning. 'Drake', for example, could be characterised by a set of features of which one is 'specifically male': let us write this, in a notation that has its origin in Jakobson's work on phonology in the 1950s, as '+ Male'. 'Duck' again is 'not specifically male', or '– Male'. 'Mare' may be characterised in part as '+ Female'; 'horse' as both 'not specifically female' ('– Female') and 'not specifically male' ('– Male'); and so on. Not all semantic oppositions would enter into correlations. But for some semantic fields the model did seem promising.

This view was largely to prevail. But the analogy rested on two different assumptions, and it is important to separate them. The first is that we are dealing with a network, again, of relations. That words could be related to other words was a familiar notion, and at least one important relation has a name much older than structuralism. *Nice*, for example, is an 'antonym' of, or is opposite in meaning to, *nasty*. *Good* is similarly an antonym of *bad*. The relation of *drake* to *duck* is in turn like that of *gander* to *goose*, involving, one might say, a different kind of 'oppositeness'. But these are precisely relations 'in meaning' between, as I have represented them in italics, words. The second assumption is that there are entities called meanings that are parallel to sound units. If *nice* is an antonym of *nasty*, it is because a meaning 'nice' is distinguished in just that respect from a meaning 'nasty'. Our task once more was to abstract and define these units, in terms of what they shared and how they differed. This second assumption was long endemic among linguists. But it does not follow from the first. Nor is it obvious that relations among words, if we consider them as such, are like those between sounds.

The study of relations as such was developed in Lyons's remarkable first book, published in 1963. In later work they are described as 'sense relations' (thus Lyons, 1968: 428) and included some that were already traditional, like antonymy or synonymy. But, as he points out, they 'were generally treated in terms of a prior notion of "meaning", independently defined'. For example, two words would be synonyms if their meanings, seen as entities they designate, are the same (Lyons, 1963: 57f.). Likewise, though the example is not his, the relation between *nice* and *nasty* would be reduced to a prior difference between 'niceness' and 'nastiness'. 'Meaning' was in this way seen as 'a more primitive notion' (58), by which semantic relations were in turn defined.

But in 'a structural approach', as Lyons interpreted it, meaning is instead 'a function of these several relations'. Let us take, for example, the relation within the field of colour between *red* and *green*. If something is red in colour it cannot be green, and vice versa. Likewise it cannot be blue, yellow, and so on. In Lyons's terminology this is a relation of 'incompatibility' (59ff.). But to define it we do not need to establish in advance criteria for 'redness', 'greenness' or 'blueness'. All we are saying is that if, in certain sentences, the word *red* is replaced by *green* or *blue*, what will be asserted cannot then, in the same circumstances, be true. *She wore a red dress* will, as Lyons puts it, 'be understood as implicitly denying' *She wore a green dress* and *She wore a blue dress* (61). Another relation within the field of colour is that of *scarlet*, for example, to *red*. Lyons described this as a relation of 'hyponymy', or subordination in meaning. But to establish it we do not first need to establish that a meaning 'scarlet' is included in a meaning 'red'. We are simply saying that the word *scarlet* and the word *red* will replace each other in sentences of which one unilaterally implies the other. Thus, as Lyons puts it, '*X is scarlet* will be understood (generally) to imply *X is red*'; but not the reverse. Forms of antonymy are distinguished similarly (61ff.); also a relation that Lyons calls 'converseness', between words such as *husband* and *wife*. Thus, again, *X is Y's husband* implies *Y is X's wife*; and, in this case at least, vice versa (compare Lyons's definition, 72).

Part II of Lyons's book is a brilliant analysis of the terms for knowledge in the language of Plato's dialogues. Three verbs can be translated 'to know': in the infinitive, which Lyons uses as a citation form, *epístasthai*, *gignóskein*, *eidénai*. Let me refer to these as 'know$_1$', 'know$_2$' and 'know$_3$'. Associated with these are three nouns: *tékhnē*, which I will refer to correspondingly as 'knowledge$_1$', *gnôsis* ('knowledge$_2$') and *epistémē* ('knowledge$_3$'). What someone 'knows$_1$' (*epístasthai*) is thus a 'knowledge$_1$' (*tékhnē*), and so on. At the other extreme there are, for example, terms for particular occupations: *kerameús* 'potter' or *astronómos* 'astronomer'.

Now the evidence from the texts is that such a person had a corresponding 'knowledge$_1$': for example, a potter (*kerameús*) 'knew$_1$' (*epístasthai*) a 'knowledge$_1$' (*tékhnē*) that was specifically the 'knowledge$_1$ pertaining to pottery' (*keramikḗ tékhnē*). Such a person was also a *dēmiourgós*, literally someone 'working' (*(e)rg-*) for a 'community' (*dēm-*). It was thus part of the meaning of this word that its hyponyms included *kerameús* ('potter'), *astronómos* ('astronomer'), and so on. It was again part of the meaning of our 'knowledge$_1$' (*tékhnē*), which was what someone 'knew$_1$' (*epístasthai*), that its hyponyms included that of a potter (*kerameía*) or that of an astronomer (*astronomía*) (compare Lyons, 140ff.).

One 'field', as Lyons describes it, is thus 'dominated by, or structured under' (140), words associated with 'know$_1$' (*epístasthai*). It is again part of the meaning of the subordinate terms, such as the Ancient Greek words that we translate as 'astronomer' and 'astronomy', that they belong to it. What, by contrast, one 'knows$_2$' (*gignō΄skein*) was in general different. For example, one 'knew$_2$' a person: that is, *gignō΄skein* is found in the texts, far more than *epístasthai* ('know$_1$'), with an object such as 'Socrates' (accusative *Sōkrátē(n)*) (199f.). One could also 'know$_2$', for example, a fact or a name. But what one either 'knew$_1$' (*epístasthai*) or 'knew$_2$' (*gignō΄skein*) one could equivalently, on the evidence of other passages, 'know$_3$'. As one could 'know$_2$' facts or names so too one could 'know$_3$' (*eidénai*) them (205ff., 219). 'Pottery' or 'astronomy' was a 'knowledge$_1$' (*tékhnē*), or something that one 'knew$_1$'; but it was also something that one 'knew$_3$' (*eidénai*) and so a 'knowledge$_3$' (*epistḗmē*). Lyons's hypothesis was thus, in its most general form, as follows. Firstly, as 'know$_1$' was to 'knowledge$_1$' (*epístasthai*, *tékhnē*) so 'know$_2$' was to 'knowledge$_2$' (*gignō΄skein*, *gnôsis*) and 'know$_3$' to 'knowledge$_3$' (*eidénai*, *epistḗmē*). That too is argued from the evidence of the texts, though in this summary I have taken the liberty of begging it. 'Know$_1$' is used differently from 'know$_2$'; and, he argues, the two verbs can contrast. But 'know$_3$' (*eidénai*) is 'neutral' (223) between them. In that sense the field of 'knowledge$_3$' (*epistḗmē*) subsumes those of 'knowledge$_1$' and 'knowledge$_2$'.

This is a bare gist, and more could be added. For example, someone who is a *dēmiourgós* ('worker for the community') could be specifically a *kheirotékhnēs*, literally someone with a 'knowledge$_1$' (*tékhnē*) involving 'hands' (*kheir-*); the meaning of this is partly given by its hyponyms, which include *kerameús* 'potter' or *iatrós* 'doctor', and by its incompatibility with, for example, *geourgós* 'farmer' (175f.). But the method is throughout to clarify the meaning of words such as 'know$_1$' or 'knowledge$_3$', for which I have deliberately given no further gloss, by the relations that they contract, in appropriate contexts, with others. A structural analysis is an analysis of sense relations, in the context of specific sets of sentences in which words can be used.

It was on this basis that, at one point in his introductory chapters, Lyons assessed the analysis of meanings into features. Such analyses were by then called 'componential': for example, the meaning of *mother* had a component 'female' or '+ Female', that of *father* a component 'male' or '+ Male'. The question, therefore, was whether it would help to 'factorise' a relation in meaning, between *mother* and *father*, *aunt* and *uncle*, and so on, into parts of that kind. In cases like this it could have advantages, where 'the components to be abstracted', such as sex, can then be 'described in a neutral metalanguage' (80). This could be seen as the metalanguage, though Lyons does not refer to him at this point, of Hjelmslev's 'purport'. But in other cases it did not help. The word *high* is, in the illustration that he uses, to the word *low* as the word *good* is to the word *bad* or the word *big* is to the word *small*. This was as easy to factorise as any other 'proportional equation': 'ax' (*high*) is to 'bx' (*low*) as 'ay' (*good*) is to 'by' (*bad*), and so on (79). But we are still no clearer as to what these words apply to. The component y, for example, would be common to both *good* and *bad*. But as a component of meaning it 'is no more easily described in terms of reference than is the meaning of *good* and *bad* themselves' (80).

Lyons's conclusion was that linguistic units should not be multiplied beyond necessity. But by the time his book was published such analyses were becoming, one might almost say, rife.

The first paper in whose title the term 'componential analysis' appeared was by the American anthropologist Ward H. Goodenough, and belongs with a group of studies that deal mainly, though not exclusively, with words such as *mother* and *father*. 'What', as Goodenough puts it, 'do I have to know about A and B in order to say', for example, 'that A is B's cousin?' 'Clearly', he continues, 'people have certain criteria' by which this judgment is made. 'What the expression *his cousin* signifies is', he says, this set of criteria (Goodenough, 1956: 195).

For Goodenough this illustrated 'very well' the general problem of 'determining what a linguistic form signifies'. But such criteria are analogous, he at once says, to the 'acoustical criteria' that distinguish phonemes. These can be analysed, as he puts it later, 'as combinations of percepts which we conventionally describe with reference to the manner of their production in speech' (197). For example, 'one set of percept values relates to place of articulation'. Similarly, the units signified by forms 'consist of combinations of percepts and/or concepts', such as, in the field of kinship, those of the sex of individuals and the generations to which they belong. In an intervening passage Goodenough proposes even closer parallels. The task of a 'semantic analyst' is 'to find the conceptual units out of which the meanings of linguistic utterances are built' (196). These conceptual units will be what is signified. What we are 'given' are 'the conventional symbols of speech which more or less stand' for these units. Thus we know, from a linguistic analysis as it was seen by Goodenough's American contemporaries, that there are expressions such as *cousin* or *his cousin*. The task of a semantic analyst is accordingly like that of a phonologist who might start from texts in a written language. These would be given, and the problem would be to establish sequences of phonemes to which they relate. The problem in semantics is to establish the conceptual units to which, analogously, expressions like *his cousin* relate.

The analogy makes clear that the 'symbols' and 'conceptual units' are established on distinct planes. To find the latter, we will then begin by noting contexts in which an expression is used. For example, *my cousin* may refer, on some occasions, to a person who is the speaker's father's brother's son: in a notation used by anthropologists, 'FaBrSo'. On other occasions, it might refer instead to, for example, a mother's sister's daughter ('MoSiDa'); and so on. For Goodenough such 'denotative types' were analogous to a phonologist's 'allophones' (3.2). Thus, if phonologists were in fact to start from written forms in English, they would find, as we saw, that written *l* and written *ll* correspond sometimes to clear [l] and sometimes to dark [ɫ]. Their task would then be to determine, by a test of what the Americans called complementary distribution (see again 3.2), whether these were variants of the same or of two different units. Similarly, for Goodenough, the next step for a semantic analyst was to examine 'the mutual arrangements and distributions' of such 'denotative' types, and in that way to arrive at types that are 'significative' (197).

Goodenough's paper dealt in detail with the field of kinship on the island of Truk in Micronesia, and it is in such anthropological studies that componential analysis was first developed seriously. But such accounts were soon proposed by linguists also, both in America and in continental Europe; and, if we may judge by the absence of references, for the most part independently. A field in general would be defined by the component or components that a set of meanings had exclusively in common: for example, words for animals might all have meanings partly characterised by the features 'animate' ('+ Animate') and 'not human' ('– Human'). Within them smaller fields would have additional components: thus the basic meanings of *sheep, ewe, lamb*, and so on might, in addition, include a component '+ Ovine'. Opposite meanings would be distinguished by contrasting features: '+ Male' versus '+ Female', and so on. Eventually the analysis will reach meanings that cannot be factorised.

Thus 'lamb' in a figurative sense might have a meaning characterised in part by '+ Human'; but beyond that it will have to be described, as in a dictionary, as 'person who is meek, endearing, innocent', and so on.

Several versions are discussed in later work by Lyons (1977: 317–35). The most widely cited, however, was that of Jerrold J. Katz and Jerry A. Fodor, which was part of a semantic theory grafted, in the same year as Lyons's first book, onto Chomsky's formulation of a generative grammar.

The problem, as they presented it, was to account for the ability of speakers to 'interpret' sentences in abstraction from the 'settings' in which they might be uttered. Speakers of English 'will agree', for example, that *The bill is large* is 'ambiguous' (Katz and Fodor, 1963: 174). It has 'at least two readings', with *the bill* referring either to a demand for money or to the beak of a bird. One ability, then, that speakers have is 'to detect . . . ambiguities and characterize the content of each reading of a sentence' (175). In *The bill is large but need not be paid* they will understand that the bill must be a demand for money; this 'shows that a speaker can disambiguate' (175) one part of a sentence (*the bill is large*) in terms of another. They will 'at once recognise' that *The paint is silent* is 'anomalous in some way', while *The paint is wet* and *The paint is yellow* are not. Thus 'another facet of the semantic ability of the speaker is that of detecting semantic anomalies'. A 'semantic theory' of English must account for these and other abilities; and part of it, it was 'widely acknowledged and certainly true', was 'a dictionary' (181). Thus, in the dictionary which would form part of a theory of English, *bill* must be assigned at least two different sets of semantic features: perhaps, as in printed dictionaries, by separate 'entries'. The features assigned to *wet* and *yellow* must combine readily with those of *paint*; those assigned to *silent* must not. *Pay* must have features that are not compatible, in the construction of *The bill . . . need not be paid*, with those that would make up the meaning 'beak of a bird'. In addition to the dictionary, a semantic theory then had to include processes of combination. In *The bill was paid*, they will yield a meaning for the sentence as a whole in which the features of *pay* combine with those of *bill* only in the sense of a demand for money. In *The paint is silent*, they will fail to combine those of *paint* and *silent*; and so on.

This 'semantic theory' of a language was presented as additional to a generative grammar that, in the beginning, did not have a 'semantic component'. Its 'lower bound' (175) was fixed accordingly, by the structures that that grammar would itself account for. As soon as grammars did include semantic components, this became instead a boundary within them, initially at a level of deep structure. The upper bound was then the limit of the grammar itself: of the system of rules that, according to

Chomsky, formed, or formed a theory of, a speaker–hearer's 'knowledge' of a language. For Katz and Fodor, a semantic theory was required to account for readings of sentences 'in isolation' (177), not ones determined by 'settings'. Likewise, as one part of a theory of linguistic 'competence', the semantic component of a generative grammar had to assign 'semantic interpretations' to sentences, in implicit abstraction from 'performance'. Katz and Fodor's readings 'in isolation' were equivalent, it would seem, to these 'interpretations'.

The distinction between competence and performance was 'related', as Chomsky put it, to that of 'langue' and 'parole' (see again Chomsky, 1965: 4). But, crucially, a speaker knew not just a 'dictionary'. 'Semantic interpretations' were precisely of sentences; and there a tangle of new problems lay.

7.3   Semantic interpretations

The 'Chomskyan revolution' had begun, and it would have suited no one to relate the ideas of Katz and Fodor to pre-revolutionary antecedents. But there is a parallel, in part, with what Bloomfield had said thirty years earlier.

'Semantics', as Bloomfield defined it, was the second of two 'phases' in the description of a language. The first was phonology, and its task was to establish both the phonemes of the language and the 'phonetic forms', or combinations of phonemes, that 'occur' in it. The task of semantics was then to tell 'what meanings are attached to' phonetic forms (Bloomfield, 1935 [1933]: 138). A 'phonetic form which has a meaning' was a 'linguistic form', and this could be anything from a sentence, as the largest unit that has meaning in the language (2.3), to a morpheme (5.2) as the smallest. For each such form our task, as we have seen, was to establish a 'distinctive' or 'linguistic' meaning, in abstraction from the range of 'situations' in which it is uttered (thus again Bloomfield, 141). Bloomfield did not talk, and for him at least it would not have made sense to talk, of meanings 'in isolation'. But 'linguistic meanings' had to be distinguished from what he called the non-distinctive features of the 'situation'; or, one might equally say, the 'setting'.

In defining 'semantics' Bloomfield said that it is 'ordinarily divided into two parts, *grammar* and *lexicon*' (138). A lexicon was a 'stock of morphemes' (162) and 'the meaning of a morpheme' is called, a few paragraphs earlier, a 'sememe'. In *girls*, for example, the plural ending is a morpheme with the meaning '*more than one* object' (216); *girl* would be another morpheme with the meaning we may once more represent by 'girl'. Grammar, in turn, was constituted by 'the meaningful arrangement of forms' (163). Thus, in *girls*, the plural morpheme is related, in one such arrangement, to *girl*; the meaning of the whole, by implication, would be 'more than one girl'. In *the girls* this word combines, in a larger arrangement, with *the*. This is traditionally 'definite' and, in Bloomfield's account, is one of a class of morphemes used in referring to '*identified specimens*' (203). By implication, the whole phrase would have the meaning 'more than one identified girl'. In *You helped the girls*, this phrase is part of a larger unit *helped the girls*, forming a still larger unit with *you*. The meaning of the sentence is accordingly a function of the meanings of these parts and of the specific syntactic constructions (184) in which they stand. The linguistic meaning of *you* is that of an entity or entities that a speaker addresses, and *you* is related to what follows in what Bloomfield calls an 'actor–action' construction (172 and elsewhere). *Helped the girls* has in turn an 'action–goal' construction. Thus, implicitly, the linguistic meaning is that of 'an actor who is addressed (*you*) having performed in the past (*-ed*) an action of helping (*help*) whose goal was more than one identifiable girl'.

'The statement of meanings' was, for Bloomfield, 'the weak point of language-study' and would remain so, certainly under his physicalist conception of science, 'until human knowledge advances very far beyond its present state' (140). We therefore had first to identify forms, under a fundamental assumption (2.2) which implied that, whether we can state it or not, 'each linguistic form has a constant and specific meaning' (145). The morpheme *girl* is one such form, and in *the girls* there are formally distinguishable ways in which it is 'arranged' in relation to other morphemes. The next and much more difficult step was to identify linguistic meanings, both lexical and grammatical. But it is instructive to recast what Bloomfield said in terms that are more like those of a Saussurean sign theory. Morphemes and their meanings would form simple lexical 'signs'. The smallest 'meaningful arrangements', with their meanings, would form simple grammatical 'signs'. Other units, from a word up to a sentence, would be complex signs, whose forms and meanings could be derived, in parallel, from the smaller signs, lexical and grammatical, that they include.

For Katz and his associates the 'semantic interpretation' of a sentence was arrived at by a similar process of 'amalgamation' (Katz and Fodor, 1963: 197ff.), in which meanings from the 'dictionary' are combined 'in a manner dictated by' a description of its syntax (Katz and Postal, 1964: 12). The main difference, however, is that in Bloomfield's case we can still speak of a sign relation: 'gə:l', for example, was a phonetic form associated directly with a constant meaning 'girl'. But in Chomsky's current theory, the phonetic interpretations were 'determined' by a mediating level of surface structure (5.3). Semantic interpretations were in turn determined by a level of deep structure, and the reason was precisely that the elements and relations which were distinguished on the surface did not bear a one-to-one relation to them.

What distinctions among meanings should a grammar then make? The years immediately before and after 1970 were a period of confusion in the history of generative grammar, in which many new ideas were explored with more enthusiasm than care. It is therefore very difficult to disentangle a specific answer to this question. But let us take for illustration a distinction that has often been drawn by grammarians, between 'effected' and 'affected' objects. The sentence *I painted a picture* will normally mean that, by painting it, the speaker has brought a picture into existence. The object *a picture* will thus refer to something that results from, or is 'effected' by, their actions. But it is also conceivable that the speaker has applied paint to a picture that existed already: compare, for example, *I painted over your picture*. *A picture* would then refer instead to something merely 'affected' by what happens to it. Does the sentence then, 'in isolation', have two readings? If so, the semantic component of Katz and Fodor's grammar had to assign both semantic interpretations to it. Or are these readings merely distinguished by the 'settings' in which it is uttered?

This distinction is one of many discussed in the late 1960s, in an influential study by Charles J. Fillmore. In his terms an 'effected' object was assigned, at the level of deep structure, to a category 'factitive'; an 'affected' object, as we will see in a moment, to a different category 'objective'. But further distinctions could also be drawn between subjects. In an earlier paper Fillmore had begun by comparing, for example, *the janitor* as subject in *The janitor opened the door* with *the door* as subject in the simpler sentence *The door opened*. Though he does not say so, the first sentence would fit perfectly the terms in which its construction would have been described by Bloomfield: *The janitor* (actor) *opened* (action) *the door* (goal). *The janitor*, in particular, refers precisely to someone who performs an act of opening. But *the door*, in the second sentence, did not. The 'semantically relevant condition common' to these sentences was therefore not between their subjects. For Fillmore it was instead shared by *the door*, as subject of the second, and *the door* as object in the first. In both, by implication, *the door* refers to something 'affected' by an opening. He went on to compare the role of *with this key*, in *The janitor opened the door with this key*, with that of *this key* as a subject, in *This key opened the door*. Again 'no constant semantically relevant function' was shared by the subjects: keys do not, like janitors, perform acts of opening. A key was instead an instrument, in the events referred to by both sentences, by which opening of a door is brought about. Therefore the 'semantically relevant function' of *this key* as a subject was said to be shared by the 'instrumental prepositional phrase' *with this key*.

On such evidence, Fillmore did 'not believe that "subject" and "object" are among the syntactic functions to which semantic rules must be sensitive' (1966: 21). The subject *the janitor* would instead derive, in a way that is set out in detail in his later paper, from an underlying phrase whose relation to the verb is 'agentive'. This was the category, as Fillmore defined it, of 'the typically animate perceived instigator of the action identified by the verb' (1968: 24). As subject or object, *the door* would derive from a phrase whose relation was 'objective'. This was for Fillmore 'the semantically most neutral' of his categories; but 'conceivably' should be 'limited to things which are affected by the action or state identified by the verb' (25). Keys in turn are instruments by which doors are opened; therefore, both the subject in *This key opened the door* and the prepositional *with this key* would derive from an underlying 'instrumental'. This was the category of 'the inanimate force or object causally involved' in such an 'action or state' (24).

What was the nature of such categories? In Chomsky's system of grammar, a semantic rule was 'sensitive' to deep structures. Therefore they were identified at that level. But they were also said to form a 'conceptual' system, which was the same for all languages. Thus, in Fillmore's definition, they comprised 'a set of universal, presumably innate, concepts', identifying 'types of judgment human beings are capable of making about the events that are going on around them' (24). He therefore speaks, in his final paragraph, of a 'semantically justified universal semantic theory' or, in inverted commas, 'a "semantic deep structure"', beside which the deep structures that Chomsky described were 'likely' to be 'artificial' (88). But, for many who read this, the conclusion was much simpler. On the one hand there were surface structures, in which all subjects, for example, had the same role. On the other there were representations of the meanings of sentences, or 'semantic representations'. But no valid level of deep syntax lay between them. Therefore 'concepts' underlying surface structures were directly categories of meaning.

The case against deep structures was first made, for quite different reasons, by James D. McCawley: initially in a postscript to a paper that appeared with Fillmore's (McCawley, 1976 [1968]: 92ff.). But for those who agreed with him, the surface structure of a sentence was again not to be specified directly. In Chomsky's account, a grammar had included, first, a series of rules that characterised a set of deep structures; then a series of transformations (5.3) that derived surface structures from them. For adherents of 'generative semantics', as the movement initiated by

McCawley became known, surface structures derived similarly, by a series of transformations that might now be long and drastic, from representations of meanings. Therefore, in proposing a grammar, the first task was to characterise, or 'generate', these. The obvious problem, which many generative semanticists soon came to see as spurious, was how semantic representations generated by a grammar, or what Katz and Fodor had called readings 'in isolation', were to be identified apart from 'meanings' in general. The only constraint was that semantic representations could be related, in some way, to surface structures. Wherever a sentence could mean different things in different settings we could say, in principle, that it was 'ambiguous', and, in these settings, it was 'disambiguated' in one way or another. Wherever a sentence was odd in a specific setting, we could say that this was a 'semantic anomaly' that speakers could detect and that a grammar should explain; and so on.

The polemics surrounding this movement have been surveyed in a book by Randy Harris (1993), and need not concern us. But by the mid-1970s a clear reaction had set in, both in the work of Chomsky, whose main interest, as always, was in syntax, and in that of theorists concerned specifically with sentence meaning. Its terms were also in part different. In particular, ideas from philosophy and logic have since then been at least as influential as those from within linguistics.

The essential point for Chomsky was that grammars had to include some aspects of meaning. Rules of semantic interpretation must indicate, for instance, how much is negated by a word like *not*: for example, *I didn't leave because I was angry* might mean either that the speaker, being angry, did not leave, or that, although they did leave, that was not the reason. Rules must also indicate the antecedent of a pronoun that requires one, or what kind of relation a word like *who* bears to what verb (compare Chomsky, 1976 [1975]: 104). A grammar would in that way distinguish what he called the 'logical forms' of sentences. For example, the logical form of *Who said Mary kissed him?* is illustrated by an expression 'for which person *x*, *x* said Mary kissed him?' (99). But it did not follow that a grammar had to do more. As Chomsky came to see it, it was 'reasonable to say' that, with the characterising of such logical forms, the theory of grammar, which he also called at this stage 'sentence grammar', ends (104). For, beyond that point, it might 'well be impossible', as he put it in an earlier chapter, 'to distinguish sharply between linguistic and nonlinguistic components of knowledge and belief'. An 'actual language' might result instead 'only from the interaction of several mental faculties' (43). The 'sentence grammar' was the domain of one such faculty, which was to become that of an 'internalised language', or 'I-language', in the term that he introduced a decade later (6.2).

Beyond it, logical forms would then be 'subject to further interpretation by other semantic rules . . . , interacting with other cognitive structures, giving fuller representations of meaning' (105).

This formulation was new, and Chomsky's view of grammar was at the time 'quite tentative' (43). But by the 1980s the syntactic component of what was now his 'Universal Grammar' simply mediated between 'representations in phonetic form', assigned by one 'interpretive' component, and 'representations in "logical form"', assigned by another (Chomsky, 1981: 17). The 'properties of L[ogical] F[orm]' were, he said, 'to be determined empirically'. The term was merely 'intended to suggest – no more – that in fact, the representations at this level have some of the properties of what is commonly called "logical form" from other points of view'. But in Chomsky's view the 'representations P[honetic] F[orm] and L[ogical] F[orm]' could reasonably be supposed 'to stand at the interface of grammatical competence, one mentally represented system, and other systems'. These in turn included 'the conceptual system, systems of belief, of pragmatic competence', in a sense that will be clearer in a moment, 'of speech production and analysis, and so on' (18). This part of Chomsky's hypothesis was unchanged in the 1990s. Thus the 'language faculty', in its widest sense, is assumed to have 'at least two components'. One is 'a cognitive system that stores information': this includes again the 'core' assumed to instantiate Universal Grammar. The other consists of 'performance systems that access information and use it in various ways'. The 'cognitive system' is then taken, in particular, to interact with two '"external" systems: the articulatory–perceptual system . . . and the conceptual–intentional system'. Phonetic Form and Logical Form are the 'two *interface levels*' (Chomsky and Lasnik, 1995 [1993]: 2).

If Universal Grammar is delimited in this way, many of the crucial problems of semantics lie outside it. But they are problems nevertheless, and in the last quarter century many have continued to address them. A history of their ideas would take us well beyond the structuralist tradition as I see it. But, from a structuralist viewpoint, the main problem was that 'sentence meaning' has no single definition.

Let us suppose, to take a simple illustration, that a husband and wife are about to have dinner. The husband asks 'What are we drinking?' The wife replies 'I put some wine in the fridge'; the husband fetches a bottle, opens it, and so on. Now what the wife has, 'literally', 'said' is simply that she put some wine in the fridge. This is a statement that could, in principle, be either true or false; and, in one account, the meaning of the sentence that she utters, *I put some wine in the fridge*, would be given by a statement of the conditions under which it would be true. It is also tempting to compare this 'literal' meaning with what Katz and Fodor called a 'reading in isolation', or with Bloomfield's 'linguistic meaning'. But in uttering a sentence with this 'literal' meaning the wife is 'understood', and means to be 'understood', as answering the husband's question. They are going, she suggests, to drink wine; and, since she is perhaps already bringing in the food, he acts as he does. It seems then that we need two different theories. One is a theory of the 'literal meanings' of sentences. This would be a theory of 'linguistic meanings': of the semantics of the language that the couple are speaking. The other would be a theory of how sentences, with such meanings, are 'understood' in 'contexts' in which they are uttered. Since the 1970s, this has in common usage been not part of 'semantics', but a complementary theory of 'pragmatics'.

I have put terms in inverted commas since, although this illustration may seem perfectly straightforward, the distinction between what is 'said' and what must be 'understood' was a crucial difficulty. The sentence that the wife is said to utter is itself an abstraction. What she 'means' or 'intends' by uttering it is already another. In attempting to explain 'her meaning' we are, among other things, ascribing to the sentence itself 'a meaning' which is a still higher abstraction. The problem was whether we had coherent criteria for it.

In the terms inherited from the 1960s, 'meanings' were assigned to sentences by a grammar, and a grammar, as Chomsky had defined it, was an account of a speaker's 'knowledge' of a language (6.2). It was therefore natural to define 'linguistic meaning', or 'meaning in isolation', as a meaning assigned by theories of linguistic 'competence'. Our wife and husband share, among other things, a knowledge of English. The rules that constitute this knowledge will assign an interpretation to the sentence that she utters and, by definition, they belong to a theory of competence. Such a theory is then complemented by a theory of performance, seen by Chomsky as 'the actual use of language in concrete situations' (thus again Chomsky, 1965: 4). By implication, this was concerned with principles that did not reflect a knowledge of particular languages. Semantics, therefore, might be seen as dealing only with linguistic competence; pragmatics only with performance.

A proposal like this was explicit, in the 1970s, in a first book by Ruth Kempson (Kempson, 1975: 207ff.). When it was written Chomsky had yet to publish his doctrine of 'logical forms', or to talk, as he soon did, of 'pragmatic competence' as distinct from 'internalised language'. But it was already unclear whether knowledge of a grammar was the only knowledge of a language that its speakers had to have acquired.

Kempson was also among the first to argue, as a linguist, that the meaning of a statement should be identified with the conditions under which it would be true. That view is now widespread, and semantics generally perceived as 'truth-based' or, in the term that is now standard, 'truth-conditional'. But a speaker's competence, or 'knowledge of a language', is not evidently so narrow. Someone, for example, who knows French knows, among other things, when they should say *tu* and when they should say *vous*. This is a matter, however, of 'context': of the person to whom they are speaking. Were we saying, therefore, that this aspect of their knowledge is a topic of pragmatics? If so, since pragmatics and grammar are complementary, the latter does not cover every aspect of linguistic competence. Or was it too a topic of semantics? If so, sentences with *tu*, like *Tu dois sortir* 'You (familiar singular) must go out', have one semantic interpretation; corresponding sentences with *vous*, like *Vous devez sortir* 'You (non-familiar) must go out', have another. But suppose, say, that a husband, on a particular occasion, uses *vous* to his wife. It is not obvious that the appropriateness or otherwise of what he says reduces to conditions under which it would be either true or false.

This was one of many cases where, as Stephen Levinson was to put it some years later, 'languages encode or grammaticalize features of the *context of utterance* or *speech event*' (Levinson, 1983: 54). 'Pragmatics', as the study of how utterances are understood in contexts, would accordingly include 'both context-dependent aspects of language structure' (like the difference between 'familiar' and 'non-familiar') and 'principles of language usage and understanding that have nothing or little to do with linguistic structure' (9). But let us now return to what we called a 'literal' meaning. In simple cases this could be equated with an account of truth-conditions. Thus, in our example, *I have put some wine in the fridge* is true if the speaker has indeed put some wine in the fridge; and to know its meaning as a sentence is to know that. In other cases it cannot. Thus *Vous devez sortir* would not have the same literal meaning, even when one person is addressed, as *Tu dois sortir*. Can we say, as we at first said, that semantics is a theory of literal meanings?

Suppose, to take another illustration, that I ask a guest 'Would you like a cup of coffee?' This constitutes an offer; and, if my guest says 'Yes, please', I am expected to make good on it. But the sentence I have uttered has a construction like that of a question: *Did you like the wine?* or *Had she enjoyed the concert?* It is therefore tempting to say that, 'literally', it has the meaning of a question. This literal meaning would be a function of the meanings of its individual elements (*would*, *you*, and so on) and of the syntactic constructions, including what grammarians call the interrogative construction, in which they stand. But why have I uttered such a sentence? It cannot be because I simply want this information. Therefore, just as our husband understands, in context, that the wine his wife had put in the fridge was what she was intending they should drink, so my guest understands, again in context, that if coffee is wanted I will supply it.

In the early 1970s utterances like this were called 'indirect speech acts'. Thus, literally or directly, I am asking a question; but, indirectly, the words I utter are an offer. We might then suggest that only the literal meaning would belong to an account of my or my guest's linguistic competence. That account is once again a grammar. The rest remains a matter of pragmatics: of 'understanding' sentences, with prior sentence meanings, in use.

But suppose that, in a similar context, I say 'Would you enjoy a cup of coffee?' This too would have the literal meaning of a question; and, if pragmatics is not concerned with knowledge of a particular language, there seems no reason why my guest should not understand my utterance in the same way. But, of course, I would not dream of saying it. *Would you like . . . ?* is a specific formula, in English, by which offers are made. *Would you enjoy . . . ?*, despite the similar meanings of its parts, is not. If a grammar was a theory of a speaker's knowledge of a language, it should surely distinguish them. If it did not, it was because pragmatics is implicitly not just concerned, in Levinson's words, with 'principles . . . that have nothing or little to do with linguistic structure'.

Indirect speech acts were discussed by Levinson (1983: 263ff.), but not from this angle. For it was soon taken for granted, often without explicit discussion, that a distinction between competence and performance was not simple. As a speaker of English, I know how to phrase an offer; also how, for example, to make requests with varying degrees of diffidence or politeness. I know that some words are used normally by, or in speaking to, children (compare Levinson, 1983: 8); I also know the forms of speech one might use in addressing, for example, a dog. Are these aspects of performance, since they concern use in specific situations? Or are they aspects of competence, since they involve linguistic knowledge that is internalised by specific individuals? The terms and criteria available were obscure and contradictory; and it was natural to restrict semantics to a narrow path that did not stray into this quicksand. In particular, it was natural to borrow from philosophers the apparently clear criterion of truth-conditions.

These were problems of the 1970s, and later theories of meaning have often bypassed them. But to do so is to acknowledge that 'distinctive' or 'linguistic meanings' of sentences, as conceived in Bloomfield's structuralist theory in the 1930s, were abstractions that later theories, of semantic interpretations assigned to syntactic descriptions in abstraction from 'settings', had failed to define univocally.

Is structural linguistics still a living movement, and if not when did it die? The answers will depend on what is meant by 'structuralism'; and, as we found at the outset, that is not straightforward. But for many commentators its creative phase has long been over. Its heyday lasted from the 1930s, when it was named, to the end of the 1950s; and, throughout that period, linguistics was dominated by it. But structuralism in America is said to have been overturned by Chomsky, and by the 1970s his hegemony was world-wide. Other programmes have emerged since, some opposed to and some simply independent of his. But few have reasserted views that he rejected. Therefore structuralism, as an active source of ideas, is indeed dead.

This account should not be seen as an Aunt Sally. Most linguists do not now describe themselves as structuralists, even if they work in fields like phonology, or with units like the morpheme, that the movement defined. When they refer to 'structuralist approaches' to their subject, they will mean ones that have been superseded since the end of the 1950s. To follow these overtly would not, therefore, be a good career move. But if linguistics is no longer officially structuralist, many linguists are still strongly influenced by structuralist ideas. These concern, in particular, the notion of a language as a system and the autonomy of linguistics as defined by it.

The structuralist bible is, by long consent, Saussure's *Cours*. In his classic history of linguistics Robins summarised its contributions under three heads (Robins, 1990 [1967]: 220f.); and, in my own presentation (2.1), I have in essence followed him. Let us therefore recapitulate them, and ask how far beliefs have changed since it was published.

Saussure's first major contribution, following Robins's order, was his separation of synchronic from historical linguistics. A language is once more a system and change in it will involve transition from one 'state' of a system to a new 'state' that results from it. To study the history of a language was to study such transitions; therefore each successive 'state' had to be known. But to study a language as it is at one time was to study it in abstraction from its history. How it arrived in that 'state' did not have to be known and, if known, was irrelevant. Saussure's analysis did not come strictly out of the blue. But it differed from the philosophy of Hermann Paul and many other contemporaries; and 'must be seen', in Robins's words, as 'a major factor in the development of descriptive linguistic studies' in the twentieth century.

Robins was writing in the 1960s, when, if structuralism was moribund, most observers certainly did not know it. But since then this aspect of Saussure's thought has been rarely challenged. For Chomsky in particular, a language is a structure in the minds of individual speakers, and linguistic theory is a theory of such structures. But an individual 'I-language' (6.2) is again a fact of a quite different order from a change between I-languages developed by successive speakers in successive periods. A theory of I-languages explains how individuals develop, in particular, 'core languages'. But a theory of what causes them to develop differently in different periods is separate and subsidiary. In his magisterial *Introduction to Theoretical Linguistics* Lyons integrated Chomsky's early programme with that of Saussure, in a way that formed the thought of many who have since been active in the subject (Lyons, 1968). But 'theoretical linguistics' was tacitly synchronic. In contrast to most of its predecessors, Lyons's introduction did not deal at all with processes of change in language. The logic that then lay behind this seemed impeccable, and its consequences are still generally accepted. Theories of the structure of languages are one thing, and descriptions of individual languages are informed by them. The problems of historical linguistics are another; and, as presented in many recent textbooks, it is just one of a cloud of specialities that surround the centre of the discipline.

The second of Saussure's main contributions was the abstraction of 'langue' from 'parole'. As languages were to be studied in abstraction from their history, so too 'the linguistic competence of the speaker', as Robins puts it, was to be distinguished from 'the actual phenomena or data of linguistics'. Robins's wording may perhaps be thought to savour more of Chomsky than of Saussure; but, in distinguishing 'competence' and 'performance', Chomsky himself remarked on the relatedness of their ideas (again Chomsky, 1965: 4). The main difference in the status of a language is that an individual's competence, as Chomsky defined it, would for Saussure have been an imperfect knowledge of a system whose reality was supra-individual. In Saussure's terms, a language could exist completely only as a 'fait social', or 'social product', in a community. For Chomsky, the reality is precisely the 'I-language', as he later called it, that is developed by each speaker. But the object of investigation is again not speech, but what is claimed to underlie speech.

It is easy to find earlier theorists who did not take that view. 'Language', in the opinion of the Italian philosopher Benedetto Croce, was 'perpetual creation': 'language' here translates 'il linguaggio'. Each new utterance is, precisely, new; and to search for 'the language' which is its model ('la lingua modello') is accordingly to search for 'the immobility of motion' (Croce, 1990 [1902]: 188). These words are from the final chapter of his treatise on aesthetics, in which he argues that the foundations of that subject and of general linguistics are identical. If they appear to be different, it is because we are influenced by grammars in the traditional sense, which encourage the assumption, as Croce put it, that 'the reality of language consists in isolated and combinable words', not in 'living discourses' (190). Croce's ideas were formed at the end of the nineteenth century, more than a decade before Saussure's were published, and through his continuing influence Italy was one country in which structural linguistics did not flourish. But even in English-speaking countries, where it did, the object of investigation was not always as Saussure defined it. For Bloomfield in the 1920s, 'a language' was, once more, 'the totality of utterances that can be made in a speech-community' (2.2). For Zellig Harris, who took this idea to an extreme, the 'structure of a language' was not independent, but a product of the scientific study of the patterns that can be abstracted from the sounds of speech. The definition of a language as 'a set of sentences' was also, under his tutelage, the one first given by Chomsky (6.1).

It does not follow that Bloomfield and his successors were not 'structuralists'. It is perhaps significant that Hockett, among others, did define a language as a system to be inferred from the data of speech: in his terms, which may or may not be thought to betray behaviourist leanings, it was a set or system of 'habits' (Hockett, 1958: 137, 141f.). But still less does it follow that, by the 1960s, Chomsky had turned his back on 'structuralism'. It would be more reasonable to argue, with John E. Joseph in a recent essay, that in defining a speaker–hearer's competence as the primary object of study, Chomsky 'introduced structuralism into American linguistics, more fully than any of his predecessors' (Joseph, 1999: 26).

Robins's third point was that the Saussurean 'langue' must be described as 'a system of interrelated elements', not 'an aggregate of self-sufficient entities'. Its terms 'are to be defined relatively to each other, not absolutely' (1990 [1967]: 221). For Saussure, it was specifically a system of 'values', in which neither what 'means' nor what 'is meant' has an existence independent of a network of oppositions in which they are paired. 'Linguistic signs' were thus established by a symmetrical relation between 'signifiers' and, in a brutal translation that linguists usually avoid, 'signifieds'.

Saussure's definition of a 'sign' has been widely acclaimed, first by linguists and especially, since the 1960s, by literary and other semioticians. For Umberto Eco, it 'anticipated and determined' all those that have followed (Eco, 1975: 25); and in an introduction to Saussure by Jonathan Culler, who is himself a literary theorist, the 'arbitrary nature of the sign' had pride of place (Culler, 1976: 19ff.). Within linguistics, we have seen how Saussure's theory was developed by Hjelmslev in the 1940s (5.1), and by Martinet in his theory of 'monemes' (5.2). It is therefore worth remarking that, in the passage I am citing, Robins did not refer to it. It was in just this period that a general science of 'signs', which Saussure had called 'sémiologie', was beginning to take shape, in France especially. But the development of semiotics was not part of linguistics. By the 1960s many linguists did not think of words, or other units of a language, as 'signs' in Saussure's sense. Nor, in English-speaking countries, had most strictly followed him.

We must be careful, at this point, not to be deceived by terms. In French, the word 'signe' ([siɲ]) is transparently related to the ordinary verb 'to mean' ('[siɲ]ifier'). Therefore, if a language is a system of meanings ('[siɲ]ifications'), it is natural to describe its elements as '[siɲ]es'. But the ordinary verb in English is 'to mean'; and, although 'to signify' (phonetically [sɪɡnɪfʌɪ]) is established as a borrowing from Latin, its relationship to 'sign' ([sʌɪn]) is in etymology and spelling only. When English-speaking linguists use the term 'sign' it is therefore mainly, as in this book, a reflection of French or other continental European usage. But the difference has not only been in terminology. How, for example, does one identify the morphemes in a word like *waiting*? For Bloomfield they were again forms that, according to his 'fundamental assumption', should recur in utterances in parallel with meanings (2.2). But for Zellig Harris, in particular, the description of a language was based simply on the analysis of formal patterns. These could be expected, in the end, to cast light on their meanings. But no light would be cast if meanings were appealed to at the outset. The evidence by which units were to be identified was simply of recurring combinations of sounds, like [ɪŋ], that could replace other combinations of sounds, like the [ɪd] of *waited*, in the context of a set of other combinations of sounds, like [weɪt], whose members could replace one another in turn.

I have explored the history of this idea elsewhere (Matthews, 1993: 111ff.); for Harris's philosophy of linguistics I hope I may also refer to a brief obituary (Matthews, 1999). It was specific to him; for most of Bloomfield's followers, morphemes were still not identifiable by formal patterning alone. But by the 1950s they were no longer anything like Saussure's linguistic signs. They were units at an abstract mediating level, not in itself of either sound or meaning. As such they were related, on the one hand, to the combinations of phonemes by which they were realised. These often varied from one 'allomorph' to another. On the other hand, they were related separately to meanings; and, in principle at least, these too might vary. When Robins was writing, the theory of levels proposed by Hockett and his contemporaries (5.2) was already giving way to Chomsky's scheme of deep and surface structures (5.3), in which forms and meanings were related still more indirectly.

It does not follow, once more, that the American structuralists were not 'structuralist'. For what was common to all schools was the principle, in Robins's words, that units are 'defined relatively to each other, not absolutely'. Phonemes, for example, were identified in opposition to other phonemes. In Bloomfieldian terms, their realisations were in 'contrastive' not in 'complementary distribution' (3.2). Morphemes likewise were to be identified in opposition to other morphemes. We do not approach a language with a check-list of 'sounds', like [l] or [d] or [t], that we expect to find as phonemes in it. Nor do we approach it with a check-list of conceptual categories, such as 'past time' or 'plurality' or 'the person speaking', on which we try to map grammatical units.

In phonology, no competent investigator would describe a language otherwise. That in itself has been one of the triumphs of structuralism. In grammar, however, matters are less clear, and it may help to spell out the principle further.

Let us take, for illustration, the word *we* in English. It is traditionally 'first person plural' and, by ancient definitions, forms are 'first person' if their reference includes "the person speaking" and 'plural' if their referents are "more than one". The words in double inverted commas may be taken to refer to categories that reflect perceptions of the world of which we are part. But it is easy to multiply distinctions. *We* might on occasion refer to a speaker plus a single person who is spoken to ("I" and "thou"). On another occasion it might refer to the speaker plus one other person who is not being spoken to ("I" and "another"); to a speaker plus at least two people who include one who is being spoken to ("I" and "thou" and "another", "I" and "thou" and "others"); and so on. One could therefore imagine an account of English which would treat this one form as a homonym with several different meanings. In Katz and Fodor's terminology (7.2), *We are leaving* would have a set of readings in which the reference of *we* includes a person spoken to, and another set in which it does not. It would then be partly disambiguated in, for example, *We are leaving but you are not*. It would have an intersecting set of readings in which *we* refers to just two people, and another in which it refers to more than two. On that dimension it would be disambiguated in, for example,

We two are leaving. We could easily continue: for example, a difference between sexes would be disambiguated in *We are leaving with our wives.*

But that is not what English grammars do say. In other languages there are indeed distinctions like these, between forms whose reference, for example, 'includes' or 'excludes' the person spoken to, or between a 'plural' and a 'dual'. But *we* in English is again undifferentiatedly 'first person plural'. In a structuralist account this term describes its place in a specific system, formed by oppositions between *we* and *I* ('plural' versus 'singular'), between both *we* and *I* ('first person') and *you* ('second person'), and so on. In other languages the systems may be radically different. Some will have no form that we could call 'first person plural'. They might, for example, have one which will indicate involvement of the speaker: this would appear in a translation of both *I am leaving* and *We are leaving.* The same form might be required in a translation of both *I saw them* or *We saw them* and *They saw me* or *They saw us.* There is therefore no distinction like that, as it is called in English, between forms as 'subjects' (*I*, *we*) and as 'objects' (*me*, *us*). How the speaker is involved, and who else is involved, could then be indicated by distinctions among other categories.

Each different language had, for structuralists, to be 'described in its own terms'. Like other slogans, this can easily be twisted or misunderstood. But it meant above all that we do not look in every language for 'conceptual' categories, such as one of 'we-ness', which in fact reflect distinctions in the languages that we ourselves know. Structuralism in practice was a technique by which errors like that were avoided.

But did it follow that whole languages were systems 'où tout se tient'? Let us grant that *we* must be described specifically in opposition to *I*, *you*, and others. *You*, for example, is then undifferentiatedly 'second person'. But there is already a complication, in that *you* does not always refer to people spoken to. It also has an indefinite sense: for example, in a proverb like 'You can't make a silk purse out of a sow's ear.' In a Saussurean account, these either reduce to just one general meaning (7.1) or have separate meanings entering into separate oppositions. But is it necessary to assume that languages are systems in Saussure's sense, in which every unit has a role defined entirely by the relations that it bears, direct or indirect, to other units?

For Saussure 'la langue' was a system of relations, including those that the *Cours* calls 'syntagmatic'. For Chomsky, in the 1950s, a 'grammar' was instead a system of rules assigning structures to sentences. But it was again a system in which 'everything holds together': alter or delete one rule, and either the whole is incoherent or the language generated will be different. The generative grammar of the 1960s paired determinate semantic interpretations of sentences, via determinate deep structures and surface structures, with determinate phonetic representations (5.3). To know a language was to know the rules of such a system, and this presupposed an independent mental faculty, 'of language', whose development could be investigated separately from that of others. Linguistics 'in the strict sense' had been, in Saussure's terms, an autonomous science of 'la langue'. It was now at heart a science of grammars, whose central aim was to investigate their nature and what made their acquisition possible. 'Generativism' was in these respects in tune with earlier 'structuralism', and, to recall a general judgment of Giulio Lepschy, an 'heir' to it (Ch. 1; Lepschy, 1982 [1970]: 37). But was this conception of a determinate language system, in its Saussurean or Chomskyan version, right?

It is not my business to debate the issue. But what has become clear, since the 1930s and still more since the 1960s, is that, if 'a language' is a system like this, it will have a scope much narrower than that of any lay conception of a language, or of what it means to know one.

The system had always been an abstraction. Thus, for the phonologists of the Prague School, phonemes were defined by features that distinguished them from other phonemes. Other phonetic features were not 'relevant' to the structure of which these units were the elements (3.2). But let us return, for instance, to the difference in English between a clear and a dark 'l'. It is not between phonemes; therefore, in describing the system, we abstract away from it. But the variation is not random; nor is it determined wholly by the structure of our vocal organs. It is a peculiarity of English, or of specific dialects within it. One solution was to ascribe such patterns to a 'norm' established at a lower level of abstraction (4.2). As Coseriu pointed out, a 'language' ('lengua') was, in its ordinary sense, not just the system; but the system plus the ways in which it is normally realised (thus Coseriu, 1962 [1952]: 68). 'Norms' are of their nature not determinate.

There were also disagreements as to what precisely the abstraction should include. A language system was a system of communication through speech, and, as such, was seen as separate from other systems governing the lives of speakers. But what properties of speech were relevant to it? One obvious problem was that of intonation. A sentence like *She's coming* could be uttered, for example, with a fall in pitch (ˋ) centred on the last accented syllable: thus, with that syllable in small capitals, *She's* ˋCOM*ing*. This might perhaps convey a sense of relief, if the fall is emphasised. But the pitch could instead rise: *She's* ˊCOM*ing*. This might on occasion convey a speaker's surprise. Were intonations like these also, in Saussurean terms, the 'signifying' elements of 'signs'? For Martinet, a language was a system of double articulation (5.2), and such processes were then marginal to it ('sur la marge de la double articulation'). In particular, he saw differences in pitch as a continuous scale, without definite units (Martinet, 1970 [1960]: 21f.). But, for Hockett and other contemporaries in America, a language such as English had indeed a definite series of 'pitch phonemes', just as it had definite sets of vowels or consonants. As the latter realised morphemes such as 'she' or 'come', so pitch phonemes entered into the realisation of 'intonational morphemes' (Hockett, 1958: 34f., 125f.).

The criteria of abstraction were to that extent uncertain. But the issue came to a head with Chomsky's shift of focus in the 1960s. A grammar, as he had defined it, was a system of rules that generated a language (6.1); and both could again be justified as abstractions. But the grammar was then said to characterise a 'speaker–hearer's knowledge of his language' (once more Chomsky, 1965: 4). It was therefore natural to ask if 'knowledge' of these rules was all the 'knowledge of the language' that its speakers could be said to have. It seemed easy to think of other aspects of, as Chomsky called it, their linguistic 'competence'. If they 'know' that certain sentences are grammatical in it, they must also 'know' a multitude of norms of usage that are not so readily reduced to rules. If speakers of English 'know' that *Is he coming?* is a question, they must also 'know' that *Would you like a cup of coffee?* is a form of words appropriate to an offer (7.3). They will 'know' that, if they are trying to make an appointment, it would be normal to use a form like *Can I see you tomorrow?* rather than, say, *Can I come to you tomorrow?* To speak the language as others speak it they must certainly have mastered its intonations, whether determinate or indeterminate. They must 'know' which forms of speech, intonations included, are polite and not polite; that certain forms are usual only when one is in conversation with close friends; and so on. I have put the word 'know' in inverted commas, since what was called a 'speaker–hearer's knowledge of his language' was explicitly an idealisation. The implied criterion was that grammars were determinate and existed independently of other mental systems. But this excluded much that, in an ordinary sense, one could say about 'languages'.

Within ten years it was clear, in particular, that it was seen as including only certain aspects of semantics. The 'semantic interpretation' of a sentence was, to be precise, its 'logical form'; and, when Chomsky introduced this term in the 1970s, he made clear that there were other semantic rules, and other representations of meaning in a language, beyond the scope of what he described at that time as a 'sentence grammar' (7.3). The apparent reason was that, if they were included, grammars could no longer be seen as systems operating autonomously. The 'sentence grammar' was the precursor of 'I-language' in the 1980s; and, with the theory of parameters, the system of 'core language' was defined at a yet higher level of abstraction. The scope of the 'periphery' has at best been illustrated; therefore it is not entirely evident what now characterises an I-language, with a core plus a periphery, as a whole. But the core itself is a system that computes relations between 'Logical Forms' and 'Phonetic Forms'. It was an abstraction within an abstraction, and the criterion by which structures are included in it would be simply that of relevance to 'Universal Grammar'.

Chomsky's theory of Universal Grammar was brand new, and addresses problems that his structuralist predecessors had not dreamed of. It might therefore be argued that the ideas of his second 'conceptual shift', as he called it, are beyond my brief. But his is a very structuralist theory of how knowledge of a language is acquired. The basic insight was that our capacity for speech is, in part, genetically determined. When this was first proposed it was a brilliant and exciting idea; and, in the light of what we now know of communication in other species, and of other aspects of behaviour in our own, it is at worst highly plausible. But it does not follow that, within some larger mental structure, which in itself accounts for only part of the way in which a community of people speak, there is a further specific mental structure, supplemented and corrected by the remainder, which is determined solely by a series of choices among genetically determined options. This specific theory did not fully emerge until the 1980s (6.2). But the first step was the reification of a generative grammar, as Chomsky had conceived it in his first phase in the 1950s, as (a theory of) a speaker's 'competence'. The term 'grammar' was defined ambiguously, as we saw, with or without the words in brackets (again Chomsky, 1965: 25). A linguistic theory, as again he had conceived it in the 1950s, was then reified in turn, as a theory of specific mental structures from which grammars develop. Ambiguously again, linguistic theories simply were such structures.

The theory has also raised once more the question of how language systems change. A language, in the formula in French so often said to be Saussure's, was 'a system in which everything holds together'. But, if that was true, why should it not persist in one fixed state? One possible answer was that language systems are like thermostats or other servomechanisms, responding to external changes that affect them (4.1). Some linguists have spoken figuratively as if, in this respect, a system had a will of its own (4.3). Another possible answer was that even systems of this kind had weak links or loose ends, and adjustments at these points could lead to changes whose effects would then be wider. Another answer was that languages were not only systems. Thus, for Coseriu, a shift in 'norms', which were not determinate and changed gradually, could cause a system, in turn, to 'overturn' into a new state (4.2). For 'core languages' to change it seems that only such an explanation will be possible. The core is a system in which 'everything', in the most striking fashion, 'holds together': change the setting of just one parameter, and the repercussions, it is claimed, will be pervasive. How then can one generation come to set parameters differently from earlier generations? The answer must be that the 'language' they hear, in a wider or more ordinary sense of 'language', has changed independently. Explanations for that must again appeal to shifts in norms, or to innovation under the influence of other languages. Hence the diachronic syntax of Lightfoot (6.3) and others.

If languages have properties that change independently of 'grammars' or 'I-languages', it is natural to ask how such abstractions can be justified. The Chomskyan answer is obvious: that a 'Universal Grammar' exists as he says it exists. But what of linguists who are not Chomskyans? When Robins was writing in the 1960s, the summary he gave of 'the structural approach to language' could be seen as underlying 'virtually the whole of modern linguistics'. It was in particular the foundation for its autonomy (2.3), 'as a subject of study in its own right'. 'Few linguists', he added, would 'disclaim structural thinking in their work' (again Robins, 1990 [1967]: 221). As I write, many more might now disclaim it. But for how many is 'a language' not, at some level of reality, a system that defines their objectives?

The most obvious comment is that the discipline is no longer unified. In the 1960s 'modern linguistics' was still centred on what Saussure had called 'la linguistique de la langue' (2.1). The new theory of transformational grammar (5.3) was the latest attempt to clarify the structure of the systems that were its object, and the range of facts that such a grammar could 'capture', in a phrase then very fashionable, was compared directly with the limited success, as it was claimed, of others. This led to intense polemics between schools, whose aims, in developing a theory of a language, were implicitly similar. Other investigations into 'language', in the wider sense of Saussure's 'langage', were peripheral and were obliged to take account of theories of that kind. In Chomsky's terms, there seemed 'little reason to question the traditional view that investigation of performance will proceed only so far as understanding of underlying competence permits' (Chomsky, 1965: 10). It is remarkable how far his contemporaries in fields such as psycholinguistics, both developmental and experimental, have based their research on theories of linguistic structure that they took for granted.

But since the 1970s linguistics has fragmented, less into schools, as in earlier decades, than into virtual subdisciplines, each with its own objectives. Many are indeed concerned directly with 'langage', or with the processes of speech ('parole') as illustrated by a specific language. That is true of much work on semantics and pragmatics since the early 1970s, at least as I read it. Many studies are also truly interdisciplinary. 'The scientific study of language', as some dictionaries define it, does not therefore still rest, in all branches, on the foundation that Saussure or Bloomfield tried to give it. But many investigations do deal with specific languages. How far does that part of the study of language remain structuralist at heart?

We must be careful, once more, to distinguish ideas that were specific to structuralism. One is not a 'structuralist', for example, merely if one uses the word 'structure'. But the structure was 'of a language', and 'a language' was again an object of autonomous study. In a structuralist view, the oppositions between *I* and *you* and *we* and *you* were part of the structure of English, and the 'concepts' that they represent internal to it. The oppositions in French between *je* and *tu* or *nous* and *vous* were part of another structure, which distinguishes its own 'concepts'. We can subsequently compare such structures; we can then define a type of pronoun system of which these are instances; we can also say that many other languages have systems of the same type. We may then seek to explain this by appealing to the world as we perceive it, in which speakers are distinguished from people spoken to, in which "one" is different from "more than one", and so on. But from a structuralist viewpoint categories or concepts of specific languages were one thing. General categories or concepts, which might be established independently or by comparisons between them, were another.

One foundation for this can be found in Hjelmslev's theory of form, substance and 'purport' (5.1). But there has been a reaction against structuralism in that form. One early instance was the assumption, in typologies in the tradition of Joseph Greenberg, that in every language phrases can be identified directly as the 'subjects' and 'objects' of sentences (4.3). But when languages are considered 'in their own terms', categories like these are not always evidently appropriate. Another was Fillmore's proposal, in the 1960s, by which sentences in any language would distinguish, at an underlying level, a 'conceptual system' of 'agentive', 'instrumental', and so on. These were universals that concerned directly 'types of judgment human beings are capable of making' about entities participating in events (7.3). Both suggestions could be taken to deny the structural autonomy of individual languages; Fillmore's, in particular, a distinction between language and other mental capabilities. But these were matters on which structuralism surely had to insist.

Thirty years have passed, in which the basis for proposals like these has emerged more clearly. But one way to judge a discipline is by what is usually taught to students; and, in the textbook introductions that most lecturers recommend, the foundations of linguistics are still presented, in the main, in terms in part structuralist and in part generativist. We have seen already that on many issues, especially that of synchrony and diachrony, these successive movements have been at one. A radical alternative, if indeed it has been truly formulated, has not yet won through.

References

Abercrombie, D. (1949) 'What is a "letter"?'. *Lingua* 2. 54–63.

Anderson, S. R. (1985) *Phonology in the Twentieth Century: Theories of Rules and Theories of Representations* (Chicago: University of Chicago Press).

[Aronoff, M.] (1997) 'The editor's department'. *Language* 73. 465–8.

Barr, K. *et al.*, ed. (1938) *Actes du quatrième Congrès International de Linguistes* (Copenhagen: Munksgaard).

Baudouin de Courtenay, J. (1895) *Versuch einer Theorie phonetischer Alternationen: ein Capitel aus der Psychophonetik* (Strasbourg: Trübner). [Partial translation, omitting formalisms, in Baudouin de Courtenay, 1972: 144–212.]

[Baudouin de Courtenay, J.] (1972) *A Baudouin de Courtenay Anthology: the Beginnings of Structural Linguistics*, trans. and ed. E. Stankiewicz (Bloomington: Indiana University Press).

Bazell, C. E. (1953) *Linguistic Form* (Istanbul: Istanbul Press).

Bloomfield, L. (1914) *An Introduction to the Study of Language* (New York: Holt).

(1926) 'A set of postulates for the science of language'. *Language* 2. 153–64. [Reprinted in Bloomfield, 1970; Joos, 1958.]

(1935 [1933]) *Language* (London: Allen & Unwin). [US edn 1933 (New York: Holt).]

(1946) 'Algonquian'. In H. Hoijer *et al.*, *Linguistic Structures of Native America*, 85–129 (New York: Viking Fund). [Reprinted in Bloomfield, 1970.]

[Bloomfield, L.] (1970) *A Leonard Bloomfield Anthology*, ed. C. F. Hockett (Bloomington: Indiana University Press).

Boas, F. (n.d. [1911]) *Introduction to the Handbook of American Indian Languages* (Washington: Georgetown University Press). [1st edn in *Handbook of American Indian Languages*, Part 1 (Washington: Government Printing Office, 1911).]

Bréal, M. (1911 [1897]) *Essai de sémantique (science des significations)*, 5th edn (Paris: Hachette). [1st edn, 1897. English translation, *Semantics*, by H. Cust (London: Heinemann, 1900).]

Brøndal, V. (1943) *Essais de linguistique générale* (Copenhagen: Munksgaard).

Brown, L., ed. (1993) *The New Shorter Oxford English Dictionary*, 2 vols. (Oxford: Clarendon Press).

Chomsky, N. (1957) *Syntactic Structures* (The Hague: Mouton).

(1959) Review of B. F. Skinner, *Verbal Behavior*. *Language* 35. 26–58.

(1965) *Aspects of the Theory of Syntax* (Cambridge, Mass.: MIT Press).

(1966) *Topics in the Theory of Generative Grammar* (The Hague: Mouton). [Also in T. A. Sebeok, ed. *Current Trends in Linguistic Theory*, vol. I (The Hague: Mouton, 1966).]

(1973) *Language and Mind*, enlarged edn (New York: Harcourt Brace Jovanovich). [First published, without enlargements, 1968.]

(1976 [1975]) *Reflections on Language* (London: Maurice Temple Smith). [First published New York, 1975.]

(1981) *Lectures on Government and Binding* (Dordrecht: Foris).

(1986) *Knowledge of Language: its Nature, Origin, and Use* (New York: Praeger).

(1988) *Language and Problems of Knowledge* (Cambridge, Mass.: MIT Press).

Chomsky, N. and Halle, M. (1968) *The Sound Pattern of English* (New York: Harper & Row).

Chomsky, N. and Lasnik, H. (1995 [1993]) 'The theory of principles and parameters'. In N. Chomsky, *The Minimalist Program* (Cambridge, Mass.: MIT Press), 13–127. [Revised version of paper first published in J. Jacobs *et al.*, eds. *Syntax: ein internationales Handbuch zeitgenössischer Forschung* (Berlin: de Gruyter, 1993).]

Coseriu, E. (1962) *Teoria del lenguaje y lingüística general: cinco estudios* (Madrid: Gredos).

(1967) 'L'arbitraire du signe: zur Spätgeschichte eines aristotelischen Begriffes'. *Archiv für das Studium der neueren Sprachen* 204. 81–112.

(1973 [1958]) *Sincronía, diacronía e historia: el problema del cambio lingüístico*, 2nd edn (Madrid: Gredos). [1st edn Montevideo.]

Cowan, J. M. (1987) 'The whimsical Bloomfield'. *Historiographia Linguistica* 14. 23–37.

Croce, B. (1990 [1902]) *Estetica como scienza dell'espressione e linguistica generale*, ed. G. Galasso (Milan: Adelphi). [1st edn Palermo: Sandron, 1902.]

Crystal, D. (1997 [1987]) *The Cambridge Encyclopaedia of Language*, 2nd edn (Cambridge: Cambridge University Press). [1st edn 1987.]

Culler, J. (1976) *Saussure* (London: Fontana).

Delbrück, B. (1901) *Grundfragen der Sprachforschung, mit Rücksicht auf W. Wundts Sprachpsychologie erörtert* (Strasbourg: Trübner).

Eco, U. (1975) *Trattato di semiotica generale* (Milan: Bompiani).

Fillmore, C. J. (1966) 'A proposal concerning English prepositions'. In F. J. Dinneen, ed. *Report of the Seventeenth Annual Round Table Meeting on Linguistics and Language Studies*, 19–33 (Washington: Georgetown University Press).

(1968) 'The case for case'. In E. Bach and R. T. Harms, eds. *Universals in Linguistic Theory*, 1–88 (New York: Holt, Rinehart and Winston).

Firth, J. R. (1957) *Papers in Linguistics 1934–1951* (London: Oxford University Press).

Gabelentz, G. von der (1901 [1891]) *Die Sprachwissenschaft: ihre Aufgaben, Methoden und bisherigen Ergebnisse*. 2nd edn, ed. A von der Schulenberg (Leipzig: Tauchnitz). [1st edn 1891.]

Gleason, H. A. (1961 [1955]) *An Introduction to Descriptive Linguistics*, 2nd edn (New York: Holt, Rinehart and Winston). [1st edn 1955.]

Goodenough, W. H. (1956) 'Componential analysis and the study of meaning'. *Language* 32. 195–216.

Greenberg, J. H. (1963) 'Some universals of grammar with particular reference to the order of meaningful elements'. In J. H. Greenberg, ed. *Universals of Language*, 73–113 (Cambridge, Mass.: MIT Press).

Hamp, E. P., Householder, F. W. and Austerlitz, R., eds. (1966) *Readings in Linguistics II* (Chicago: University of Chicago Press).

Hanks, P., ed. (1979) *Collins English Dictionary* (Glasgow: Harper Collins).

Harris, R. A. (1993) *The Linguistics Wars* (New York: Oxford University Press).

Harris, Z. S. (1941) Review of Trubetzkoy, 1939. *Language* 17. 345–9.

(1946) 'From morpheme to utterance'. *Language* 22. 161–83. [Reprinted in Joos, 1958; also in Z. S. Harris, *Papers on Syntax* (Dordrecht: Reidel, 1981).]

(1951) *Methods in Structural Linguistics* (Chicago: University of Chicago Press).

(1954) 'Transfer grammar'. *International Journal of American Linguistics* 20. 259–70.

(1991) *A Theory of Language and Information* (Oxford: Clarendon Press).

Hill, A. A. (1936) 'Phonetic and phonemic change'. *Language* 12. 15–22. [Reprinted in Joos, 1958.]

(1980) 'How many revolutions can a linguist live through?' In B. H. Davis and R. O'Cain, eds. *First Person Singular*, 69–76 (Amsterdam: Benjamins).

Hjelmslev, L. (1938) 'Essai d'une théorie des morphèmes'. In Barr *et al.*, 1938: 140–51. [Reprinted in Hjelmslev, 1959.]

(1943). *Omkring Sprogteoriens Grundlæggelse* (Copenhagen: Munksgaard). [English translation, *Prolegomena to a Theory of Language*, by F. J. Whitfield (Baltimore: Waverly Press, 1953; 2nd edn Madison: University of Wisconsin Press, 1961).]

(1959). *Essais linguistiques* (= *Travaux du Cercle Linguistique de Copenhague*, 12) (Copenhagen: Nordisk Sprog- og Kulturforlag).

Hockett, C. F. (1942) 'A system of descriptive phonology'. *Language* 18. 3–21. [Reprinted in Joos, 1958.]

(1947) 'Problems of morphemic analysis'. *Language* 23. 321–43. [Reprinted in Joos, 1958.]

(1954) 'Two models of grammatical description'. *Word* 10. 210–34. [Reprinted in Joos, 1958.]

(1958) *A Course in Modern Linguistics* (New York: Macmillan).

Holtz, L. (1981) *Donat et la tradition de l'enseignement grammatical: étude et édition critique* (Paris: CNRS).

Jakobson, R. (1932) 'Zur Struktur des russischen Verbums'. In *Charisteria Guilelmo Mathesio . . . oblata* 74–84 (Prague: Cercle Linguistique de Prague). [Cited from Jakobson, 1971; also reprinted in Hamp *et al*, 1966.]

(1936) 'Beitrag zur allgemeinen Kasuslehre: Gesamtbedeutungen der russischen Kasus'. *Travaux du Cercle Linguistique de Prague* 6. 240–88. [Cited from Jakobson, 1971; also reprinted in Hamp *et al.*, 1966.]

(1949 [1931]). 'Principes de phonologie historique', trans. J. Cantineau. In Troubetzkoy, 1949: 315–36. [Reprinted in Jakobson, 1962; revised version of 'Prinzipien der historischen Phonologie', *Travaux du Cercle Linguistique de Prague* 4. 247–67.]

(1962) *Selected Writings*, vol. I: *Phonological Studies* (The Hague: Mouton).

(1971) *Selected Writings*, vol. II: *Word and Language* (The Hague: Mouton).

Jakobson, R. and Halle, M. (1956) *Fundamentals of Language* (The Hague: Mouton).

Jespersen, O. (1922) *Language: its Nature, Development and Origin* (London: Allen & Unwin).

Jones, D. (1962 [1950]) *The Phoneme: its Nature and Use*, 2nd edn (Cambridge: Heffer). [1st edn 1950.]

(1975 [1918]) *An Outline of English Phonetics*, 9th edn (Cambridge: Cambridge University Press). [1st edn 1918 (Cambridge: Heffer).]

Joos, M., ed. (1958) *Readings in Linguistics*, 2nd edn (New York: American Council of Learned Societies).

Joseph, J. E. (1999) 'How structuralist was "American structuralism"?' *Henry Sweet Society Bulletin* 33. 23–8.

Katz, J. J. and Fodor, J. A. (1963) 'The structure of a semantic theory'. *Language* 39. 170–210.

Katz, J. J. and Postal, P. M. (1964) *An Integrated Theory of Linguistic Descriptions* (Cambridge, Mass.: MIT Press).

Keil, H. ed. (1855–9) *Prisciani Grammatici Caesariensis Institutionum Grammaticarum Libri XVIII*, 2 vols. (Leipzig: Teubner).

Kempson, R. M. (1975) *Presupposition and the Delimitation of Semantics* (Cambridge: Cambridge University Press).

Koerner, K. (1989 [1987]) 'Meillet, Saussure et la linguistique générale: une question d'"influence"'. In *Practicing Linguistic Historiography*, 401–15 (Amsterdam: Benjamins).

Kuryłowicz, J. (1949) 'La notion de l'isomorphisme'. In *Recherches structurales*, 48–60. [Reprinted in Kuryłowicz, *Esquisses linguistiques* (Wrocław/Kraków: Polska Akademía Nauk, 1960).]

Labov, W. (1966) *The Social Stratification of English in New York City* (Washington: Center for Applied Linguistics).

(1977) *Language in the Inner City: Studies in the Black English Vernacular* (Oxford: Blackwell).

Lees, R. B. (1957) Review of Chomsky, 1957. *Language* 33. 375–408.

Lehmann, W. P., ed. (1978) *Syntactic Typology: Studies in the Phenomenology of Language* (Hassocks: Harvester Press).

Lepschy, G. C. (1982 [1970]) *A Survey of Structural Linguistics* (London: André Deutsch). [First published 1970 (London: Faber and Faber).]

ed. (1994) *Storia della linguistica*, vol. III (Bologna: il Mulino).

Levinson, S. C. (1983) *Pragmatics* (Cambridge: Cambridge University Press).

Lightfoot, D. W. (1979) *Principles of Diachronic Syntax* (Cambridge: Cambridge University Press).

Lightfoot, D. W. (1999) *The Development of Language* (Oxford: Blackwell).

Lyons, J. (1963) *Structural Semantics: an Analysis of Part of the Vocabulary of Plato* (Publications of the Philological Society, 20) (Oxford: Blackwell).

(1968) *Introduction to Theoretical Linguistics* (Cambridge: Cambridge University Press).

(1977) *Semantics*, 2 vols. (Cambridge: Cambridge University Press).

McCawley, J. D. (1976) *Grammar and Meaning: Papers on Syntactic and Semantic Topics* (New York: Academic Press).

Martinet, A. (1949) 'La double articulation linguistique'. In *Recherches structurales*, 30–7.

(1955) *Économie des changements phonétiques: traité de phonologie diachronique* (Berne: Francke).

(1970 [1960]) *Éléments de linguistique générale* (Paris: Colin). [First published 1960. English translation, *Principles of General Linguistics*, by E. Palmer (London: Faber and Faber, 1964).]

Matthews, P. H. (1993) *Grammatical Theory in the United States from Bloomfield to Chomsky* (Cambridge: Cambridge University Press).

(1997) *The Concise Oxford Dictionary of Linguistics* (Oxford: Oxford University Press).

(1999) 'Zellig Sabbettai Harris'. *Language* 75. 112–19.

Meillet, A. (1937 [1912]) *Introduction à l'étude comparative des langues indo-européennes.* 8th edn (Paris: Hachette). [First edn 1912.]

Morpurgo Davies, A. E. (1998 [1994]) *Nineteenth-Century Linguistics. History of Linguistics,* ed. G. C. Lepschy. vol. IV (London: Longman). [Originally 'La linguistica dell'Ottocento'. In Lepschy, 1994: 11–399.]

Murray, J. A. H. *et al.,* ed. (1933 [1884–1928]) *The Oxford English Dictionary* (Oxford: Clarendon Press). [Reissue, originally in fascicles.]

Paul, H. (1920 [1880]) *Prinzipien der Sprachgeschichte.* 5th edn (Halle: Niemeyer). [1st edn 1880. English edn, *Introduction to the Study of the History of Language,* by H. A. Strong *et al.* (London, 1981).]

Percival, W. K. (1981) 'The Saussurean paradigm: fact or fantasy?' *Semiotica* 36. 33–49.

Piaget, J. (1968) *Le structuralisme* (Paris: Presses Universitaires de France).

Pos, H. J. (1939) 'Perspectives du structuralisme'. *Travaux du Cercle Linguistique de Prague* 8. 71–8.

Prague Linguistic Circle (1931) 'Projet de terminologie phonologique standardisée'. *Travaux du Cercle Linguistique de Prague* 4. 309–23.

Recherches structurales = Recherches structurales 1949: interventions dans le débat glossématique (= *Travaux du Cercle Linguistique de Copenhague,* 5) (Copenhagen: Nordisk Sprog- og Kulturforlag).

Robins, R. H. (1990 [1967]) *A Short History of Linguistics,* 3rd edn (London: Longman). [1st edn 1967.]

Sapir, E. (n. d. [1921]) *Language: an Introduction to the Study of Speech* (London: Rupert Hart-Davis). [First published 1921 (New York: Harcourt Brace).]

[Sapir, E.] (1949) *Selected Writings of Edward Sapir in Language, Culture, and Personality,* ed. D. G. Mandelbaum (Berkeley: University of California Press).

Saussure, F. de (1879) *Mémoire sur le système primitif des voyelles dans les langues indo-européennes* (Leipzig: Teubner).

(1972 [1916]) *Cours de linguistique générale,* published by C. Bally and A. Sechehaye, with the assistance of A. Riedlinger. Edition with introduction and notes by T. de Mauro (Paris: Payot). [1st edn 1916. English translation, *Course in General Linguistics,* by R. Harris (London: Duckworth, 1983).]

Siertsema, B. (1965 [1955]) *A Study of Glossematics,* 2nd edn (The Hague: Nijhoff). [1st edn 1955.]

[Sweet, H.] (1971) *The Indispensable Foundation: a Selection from the Writings of Henry Sweet,* ed. E. J. A. Henderson (London: Oxford University Press).

Thibault, P. J. (1997) *Re-reading Saussure* (London: Routledge).

Trager, G. L. (1949) *The Field of Linguistics* (Norman, Okla.: *Studies in Linguistics,* Occasional Papers 1).

Trier, J. (1934) 'Das sprachliche Feld. Eine Auseinandersetzung'. *Neue Jahrbücher für Wissenschaft und Jugendbildung* 10. 428–49.

(1938) 'Über die Erforschung des menschenkundlichen Wortschatzes'. In Barr *et al.*, 1938: 92–7. [Reprinted in Hamp *et al.*, 1966.]

Troubetzkoy, N. S. (1949) *Principes de phonologie*, trans. J. Cantineau (Paris: Klincksieck).

Trubetzkoy, N. S. (1929) 'Zur allgemeinen Theorie der phonologischen Vokalsysteme'. *Travaux du Cercle Linguistique de Prague* 1. 39–67. [Cited from Vachek, 1964.]

(1931) 'Gedanken über Morphonologie'. *Travaux du Cercle Linguistique de Prague* 4. 160–3.

(1933) 'La phonologie actuelle'. In *Psychologie du langage*, 227–46 (= *Journal de Psychologie* 30. 1–4) (Paris: Félix Alcan).

(1936) 'Die Aufhebung der phonologischen Gegensätze'. *Travaux du Cercle Linguistique de Prague* 6. 29–45. [Cited from Vachek, 1964.]

(1939) *Grundzüge der Phonologie.* (= *Travaux du Cercle Linguistique de Prague* 7). [French translation Troubetzkoy, 1949. English translation, *Principles of Phonology*, by C. A. M. Baltaxe (Berkeley/Los Angeles: University of California Press, 1969).]

(1958 [1935]) *Anleitung zu phonologischen Beschreibungen.* 2nd edn (Göttingen: Vandenhoeck & Ruprecht). [1st edn 1935 (Brno: Association Internationale pour les Études Phonologiques).]

Ullmann, S. (1957 [1951]) *The Principles of Semantics*, 2nd edn (Glasgow: Jackson, and Oxford: Blackwell). [1st edn 1951.]

Vachek, J., ed. (1964) *A Prague School Reader in Linguistics* (Bloomington: Indiana University Press).

van Wijk, N. (1939) *Phonologie: een Hoofdstuk uit de Structurele Taalwetenschap* (The Hague: Nijhoff).

Vendryes, J. (1968 [1923]) *Le langage: introduction linguistique à l'histoire* (Paris: Albin Michel). [First published 1923 (Paris: La Renaissance du Livre).]

Vennemann, T. (1975) 'An explanation of drift'. In C. N. Li, ed. *Word Order and Word Order Change*, 269–305 ([Austin]: University of Texas Press).

Wartburg, W. von (1969 [1943]) *Problèmes et méthodes de la linguistique*, trans. P. Maillard. 2nd edn, rev. S. Ullmann (Paris: Presses Universitaires de France). [Originally *Einführung in Problematik und Methodik der Sprachwissenschaft* (Halle: Niemeyer, 1943).]

Weinreich, U. (1963 [1953]) *Languages in Contact: Findings and Problems* (The Hague: Mouton). [First published New York, 1953.]

Weinreich, U., Labov, W. and Herzog, M. I. (1968) 'Empirical foundations for a theory of language change'. In W. P. Lehmann and Y. Malkiel, eds. *Directions for Historical Linguistics*, 95–195 (Austin: University of Texas Press).

Weiss, A. P. (1925) 'One set of postulates for a behavioristic psychology'. *Psychological Review* 32. 83–7.

Whitney, W. D. (1867) *Language and the Study of Language* (New York: Scribner).

[Whitney, W. D.] (1971) *Whitney on Language: Selected Writings of William Dwight Whitney*, ed. M. Silverstein (Cambridge, Mass.: MIT Press).

Wundt, W. (1911–12 [1900]) *Völkerpsychologie*, vol. I: *Die Sprache.* 2 parts. 2nd edn (Leipzig: Engelmann). [1st edn 1900.]

Index

Abercrombie, 34
acoustic images, 11f., 75, 93
affixes, 82
allomorphs, 86
allophones, 47
alternations, 32, 36–7, 39, 43
ambiguity
  grammatical, 92, 99
  semantic, 132, 137, 146f.
Anderson, 32
antonymy, 127–8
arbitrariness, 17, 119–20
articulation of language, 81, 83–4
associative relations, 50f.

'balance', 57ff., 65, 114
Baudouin de Courtenay, 36–8, 40–3, 46
Bazell, 88f.
Bloomfield, 4, 11, 21–32, 52–3, 82, 84–6,
    96–8, 103, 124, 133–45 *passim*, 152
  on the autonomy of linguistics, 26ff.
  his 'fundamental assumption', 23
  on historical linguistics, 25f., 53
  on linguistic meaning, 121, 133–4
  on morphemes, 82, 84, 133f.
  as 'physicalist', 21f., 134
  on the sentence, 28f.
Boas, 35–6, 39
Bréal, 118
Brøndal, 48
Brugmann, 8

change in language
  compared to chess, 15, 53f., 61f.
  in norms, 65f., 150–1
  phonological, 55ff.
  as self-regulation, 58, 69
  in syntax, 62, 70–3, 114ff.
  as therapeutic, 55, 57, 73, 114
  and universals, 70ff., 113–17
  and variation, 62–9

Chomsky, 3, 25, 68, 89–117, 132–50
    passim
  on competence and performance, 103,
    151
  his 'conceptual shifts', 96f., 103, 111
  on deep and surface structure, 94f.
  on evaluation procedures, 101f.
  on generative grammars, 98–9, 104–6
  on I-languages, 109, 111–12
  on languages as sets of sentences,
    98–9
  on logical forms, 137–8
  on semantic interpretations, 92–5,
    137f.
  on transformations, 91–5, 99
  on Universal Grammar, 106ff.
Chomskyan revolution, 25, 96, 133
commutation, 76ff., 81
competence, 103–4, 149–50
  grammatical *v.* pragmatic, 138
  v. performance, 103, 151
  in semantics, 133, 139–40
complementary distribution, 47, 85–6
componential analysis, 130ff.
components
  of language system, *see* levels
  of meaning, 131f.
concepts
  in signs, 11f., 75
  as universal, 136, 146, 152
constructional homonymy, 99
content *v.* expression, 75–81
converseness, 128
core language, 111–12, 116, 150–1
Coseriu, 17, 63–6, 114–15, 148, 150f.
Croce, 144
Crystal, 3
Culler, 145

deep structures, 94–5, 135–6
  'semantic', 136

160

Index

162   Index

Levinson, 140–1
Lightfoot, 113–17, 151
linguistic meaning, 121, 133–4
linguistic signs, 17–19, 74ff., 83–6, 118ff.,
    134, 144–5
linguistic universals, 70; see also Universal
    Grammar
linguistics
    as autonomous, 25ff.
    descriptive, 52
    historical, see diachrony
    as science of languages, 5, 11ff., 103
logical forms, 137–8
logical positivism, 21
Lyons, 126, 128–30, 143

McCawley, 136f.
marked v. unmarked, 123f.
Martinet, 58–62, 67, 73, 83–6, 88, 96,
    148f.
meanings
    as concepts, 11f.
    of grammatical categories, 122–5
    as invariants, 95, 119f.
    linguistic, in isolation, 93, 121, 133–4,
        139, 141
    literal, 138–41
    of morphemes, 86–7, 133–4
    of sentences, see semantic interpretations
    and transformations, 92
Meillet, 6f., 28
methods of analysis, 44–5, 49–51, 85
models of description, 100–1
monemes, 83; see also morphemes
morphemes
    v. syllables, 82f.
    as units of grammar, 82–91
    as units with meaning, 83, 86–7, 133–4
morphophonemic system, 87, 92
morpho(pho)nology, 43
morphs, 86
Morpurgo Davies, 7f.

natural serialisation, 72f.
neogrammarians, 52
norm(s), 64ff., 114, 148, 150

operational definitions
    of morpheme, 86
    of phoneme, 47
Osthoff, 8

paradigmatic relations, 50f.
parameters, 110–11, 115–17, 151
'parole', 11f., 103, 143

Paul, 26, 27, 52f., 143
Percival, 31
performance v. competence, 103, 133, 138,
    143, 151
periphery v. core, 112f.
phonemes, Chs. 3–4 passim
    change in, 55ff.
    definitions of, 37, 43, 45–7, 93
    as invariants, 44
    v. morphemes, 82ff.
phones, 47
phonetic forms, representations, 93–5,
    138
phonetics
    anthropo- v. psycho-, 37
    as peripheral system, 87
    v. phonology, 40–2, 46
    as study of speech sounds, 33
phonology
    diachronic, 55ff., 114
    v. grammar, 81–7
    its influence in linguistics, 47–8
    methods in, 44ff.
    v. phonetics, 40–2, 46
phrase structure grammar, 90
physicalism, 21, 121, 134
Piaget, 69
pitch phonemes, 149
planes, see levels
Pos, 49
Postal, 134
'poverty of stimulus', 106
pragmatics, 139–41
Prague School, 40; see also Jakobson,
    Trubetzkoy
'primary linguistic data', 104
'Principles and Parameters', 112f.
Priscian, 27, 82
psychophonetics, 37, 41, 46
purport, 80, 119–20, 152

realisation
    of morphemes, 85f.
    as norm, 64–6
    of phonemes, 44
'relevance', 42f.
Robins, 142–6, 151

Sapir, 26, 35–6, 38–40, 43f., 46, 71
Saussure, 2, 4, Chs. 2–3 passim, 53, 74–6,
    80, 93, 96, 103, 113, 118–20, 126,
    Ch. 8 passim
    on associative relations, 50f.
    on form v. substance, 78–9
    and Indo-European, 8–9